Jesus Son of Man

A Fresh Examination of the Son of Man Sayings
in the Gospels
in the Light of Recent Research

Barnabas Lindars SSF

WILLIAM B. EERDMANS PUBLISHING COMPANY
GRAND RAPIDS, MICHIGAN

Copyright © Barnabas Lindars 1983
First published 1983 by
SPCK, London

This American edition published 1984 through
special arrangement with SPCK by
Wm. B. Eerdmans Publishing Company
255 Jefferson Ave. S.E., Grand Rapids, Mich. 49503

Library of Congress Cataloging in Publication Data

Lindars, Barnabas.
Jesus, Son of Man.

Bibliography: p. 223
Includes indexes.
1. Son of Man.   2. Bible. N.T.   Gospels — Criticism,
interpretation, etc.   I. Title.
BT232.L56   1984   232   84-4050

ISBN 0-8028-0022-X

Contents

Preface   vii

Abbreviations   x

1   The Myth of the Son of Man   1

2   The Son of Man in the Sayings of Jesus   17

3   Six Son of Man Sayings in Mark and Q   29

4   The Passion Predictions   60

5   The Future Son of Man in Q   85

6   The Son of Man in the Christology of Mark   101

7   Matthew and the Parousia of the Son of Man   115

8   The Son of Man in Luke and Acts   132

9   The Son of Man in the Theology of John   145

10   The Son of Man and Christology   158

Notes   190

Bibliography   223

Index of Ancient Sources   236

Index of Modern Authors   243

Preface

This book is an attempt to break the deadlock in the debate concerning the Son of Man in the New Testament. This seemingly innocent expression has been the cause of endless controversy during the present century. A new direction was given in 1965, when Geza Vermes gave his celebrated lecture on 'The Use of *barnash/bar nasha* in Jewish Aramaic' at the international New Testament Congress in Oxford.[1] He denied that there ever was a Son of Man title in Judaism. Thus in using this expression, and applying it to himself, Jesus did not identify himself with a current messianic designation. But Vermes did not leave only a negative result. He showed in detail the actual usage of the expression in the language spoken by Jesus. As a result, a complete reappraisal of the meaning and use of the Son of Man in the New Testament has become necessary. That is what is undertaken here.

Reactions to Vermes' work have been varied. He has published a brief review of them in his article, 'The Present State of the "Son of Man" Debate', which takes the story down to 1978.[2] Since then the important book of Maurice Casey, *Son of Man: the Interpretation and Influence of Daniel 7* (London 1979), has given strong support to his views. Even this work, however, does little more than clear the ground for the re-examination of the New Testament which is needed.

The Son of Man (Greek, *ho huios tou anthropou*) is confined to the sayings of Jesus, or allusions to them, in the four gospels, except for Acts 7.56. So study of the Son of Man is primarily study of the sayings tradition. It is customary to classify the relevant sayings in three groups: *present* sayings, in which Jesus refers to himself as the Son of Man in connection with his present activity; *passion* sayings, in which Jesus uses the same expression in speaking of his approaching death; and *future* sayings, in which the expression operates as a messianic title in connection with his future glory. It has been shown, however, that the idiomatic usage of Aramaic *bar nasha* fits only the first and second of these groups, but not the third, which therefore cannot be considered authentic.

In the present work the Aramaic idiom is reviewed in order to reach a more accurate understanding of Jesus' meaning and intention when he referred to himself in this way. Neither Vermes nor Casey has quite succeeded in seizing the precise nuance. But once it is grasped, Jesus' references to his ministry and to his passion appear in a fresh light. The authentic sayings are characterized by irony and reticence on the part of Jesus in speaking about himself, but they also reveal deeply held convictions concerning his vocation from God. They thus provide important evidence for his understanding of his mission, which must be taken into account in any attempt to trace the origins of Christology back to Jesus himself.

To isolate the authentic sayings is not enough. The rest must also be accounted for. Seeing that the Son of Man was not a current title in New Testament times, the explanation cannot be found in influences outside the sayings tradition. It will be shown that the future sayings, and others which cannot be traced back to Jesus himself, have their origin within the literary activity involved in collecting and editing the sayings of Jesus and in the use of these collections by the evangelists themselves. Each evangelist has his own way of making use of this feature of the sayings tradition, corresponding with the special emphasis of his Christology. Thus the further history of the Son of Man sayings reflects contemporary developments in Christology. On the other hand the Son of Man was never used as a christological title in early Christianity. It was always understood to be a feature of Jesus' personal style of speech, even though its precise meaning was quickly lost, once the sayings of Jesus were translated into Greek.

If the Son of Man is removed from the centre of the stage as a christological title, it gains fresh importance as a remarkable commentary upon the larger process of the transition from the Jesus of history to the Christ of faith. Here we have a phrase which brings us to Jesus' awareness of his own mission from God with peculiar vividness. It was, and it remained, a phrase which he used in order to refer to himself. But in the later developments it is invested with the results of the early church's assessment of Jesus as the exalted Lord.

This book began as a lecture entitled 'The New Look on the Son of Man', delivered at the New Testament Conference at Glasgow in September 1980, and subsequently at the John Rylands University Library of Manchester.[3] The comments of those who heard the lecture have encouraged me to work out more fully the ideas which were then sketched out. It will be apparent to those who are familiar with articles which I have written previously on the Son of Man problem that I have changed my views. The process has not been easy. But I believe that views based upon the supposed currency of the Son of Man as an apocalyptic title, which have held the field, particularly in German scholarship, for the greater part of this century, can no longer be sustained, and that the view advanced in this book (which is in many ways a common-sense view) provides the way forward for the future.

Several of my colleagues in the Faculty of Theology and the Department of Near Eastern Studies in the University of Manchester have helped me by their advice, for which I am very grateful. In particular I owe a great debt of thanks to Miss Margaret Hogg, who typed the manuscript.

Manchester, 2 July 1981   *Barnabas Lindars* SSF

Abbreviations

ASTI	*Annual of the Swedish Theological Institute*, Jerusalem
BDF	Blass, J. & Debrunner, A., *A Greek Grammar of the New Testament and Other Early Christian Literature*, ET and ed. by R.W. Funk, Chicago and London 1961
Bib	*Biblica*, Rome
BJRL	*Bulletin of the John Rylands Library*, Manchester
BSNTS	*Bulletin of the Studiorum Novi Testamenti Societas* I–III, reissued in one volume, Cambridge 1963
BZ (N.F.)	*Biblische Zeitschrift* (Neue Folge), Paderborn
BZNW	Beihefte zur *Zeitschrift für die neutestamentliche Wissenschaft*, Berlin
CBQ	*Catholic Biblical Quarterly*, Washington, D.C.
EQ	*Evangelical Quarterly*, Exeter
ET	English Translation
ExpT	*Expository Times*, Edinburgh
HTR	*Harvard Theological Review*, Cambridge, Mass.
ICC	International Critical Commentaries
JBL	*Journal of Biblical Literature*, Philadelphia
JJS	*Journal of Jewish Studies*, Oxford
JQR	*Jewish Quarterly Review*, Philadelphia
JSJ	*Journal for the Study of Judaism*, Leiden
JSNT	*Journal for the Study of the New Testament*, Sheffield
JTS (N.S.)	*Journal of Theological Studies* (new series), Oxford
LXX	Septuagint
MT	Massoretic text
N.T.	*Novum Testamentum*, Leiden
NT	New Testament
NTS	*New Testament Studies*, Cambridge
OS	*Oudtestamentische Studien*, Leiden
OT	Old Testament

SBT	Studies in Biblical Theology, London
SJT	*Scottish Journal of Theology*, Edinburgh
SNTSMS	Society for New Testament Studies Monograph Series, Cambridge
TDNT	*Theological Dictionary of the New Testament*, ET, G.W. Bromiley, 10 vols., Grand Rapids, 1964–76.
ThZ	*Theologische Zeitschrift*, Basel
TU	Texte und Untersuchungen zur Geschichte der altchristlichen Literatur, Berlin
WMANT	Wissenschaftliche Monographien zum Alten und Neuen Testament, Neukirchen-Vluyn
ZNW	*Zeitschrift für die neutestamentliche Wissenschaft und die Kunde der älteren Kirche*, Berlin
ZThK	*Zeitschrift für Theologie und Kirche*, Tübingen

1

The Myth of the Son of Man

1 *Introduction*

The Son of Man problem has been the great centre of debate in New Testament studies in the twentieth century. The century opened with a strong sense among critical scholars that the gulf between the Jesus of history and the Christ of New Testament faith could not be bridged.[1] Jesus was a man of his time, a Jew preaching to Jews, who possibly never claimed to be the Messiah, and certainly never thought of himself as the Son of God. Such claims were made about him by his followers after his death in the light of the faith of the resurrection. It was held by many scholars at this time that the decisive influence making for this assessment of Jesus were the religious ideas of the Graeco-Oriental world.[2] Thus the problem was not to relate the historical Jesus to the faith of the primitive church, but to reconstruct the beliefs of the original Jewish church, before it expanded into the Hellenistic world and became transformed in the process.

In order to do this, it was necessary to find criteria for separating out the primitive strata of the New Testament from the overlay of more developed Christian expressions. The chief tool was the discernment of Aramaic elements in the gospel traditions. Study of the sayings of Jesus from this point of view has been a central concern of New Testament scholarship ever since.[3]

On this basis it was not difficult to show that Jesus rarely, if ever, made messianic claims concerning himself. But this observation only served to highlight the fact that Jesus does frequently refer to himself as the Son of Man. The Son of Man is one who will be seen 'coming in clouds with great power and glory' (Mark 13.26). The phrase, then, appears to be a title of honour. In this instance there is a clear allusion to the vision of Daniel (7.13f):

> I saw in the night visions,
> and behold, with the clouds of heaven

1

> there came one like a son of man,
>   and he came to the Ancient of Days
>   and was presented before him.
> And to him was given dominion
>   and glory and kingdom,
> that all peoples, nations and languages
>   should serve him;
> his dominion is an everlasting dominion,
>   which shall not pass away,
> and his kingdom one
>   that shall not be destroyed.

There was a natural wish to deny that Jesus could have identified himself with this personality. It runs counter to the non-messianic character of the sayings tradition as a whole. But the remarkable fact is that the Son of Man phrase is never used as a title of Jesus outside the sayings of Jesus himself, with the one exception of Acts 7.56.

Consequently the Son of Man has been crucial to the discussion of Christology in this century. It is a phrase which is confined to the sayings tradition, and this raises the presumption that it has an authentic basis in Jesus' own words. As such, it is an unusual form of self-reference, and the way in which it is used by Jesus often suggests that it is more than just a way of referring to himself. In fact some, at least, of the Son of Man sayings imply that Jesus identified himself with the man-like figure of Dan. 7.13. This has seemed to many to be the best evidence that Jesus did, after all, regard himself as the Messiah.

Those who wished to deny this conclusion have generally resorted to one of two alternatives. On the one hand there have been those who have denied that any of the Son of Man sayings is authentic.[4] All of them are to be regarded as developments of the sayings tradition which grew up at a time when Hellenistic influence had laid the foundations of Christology. This drastic solution fails to convince, however, because it cannot explain why the title is found only in the sayings tradition, and is never used by Paul, the chief promoter of such a Christology. On the other hand there have been those who have held that Jesus did use the title on occasions, but that in doing so he referred to a messianic figure other than himself.[5] This view also has to face formidable

2

difficulties. It is inconceivable that the evangelists thought that Jesus was referring to anyone but himself when they incorporated these sayings into their gospels. It is equally unlikely that they survived in the underlying oral tradition with this interpretation, because there is no hint of a distinction between the risen Jesus and the future agent of God elsewhere in the New Testament. Moreover such a view cannot meet the difficulty, pointed out by Vielhauer,[6] that Jesus never speaks of the coming of God's kingdom and the coming of the Son of Man together, so that these two facets of eschatological expectation are not brought into relation with one another. Finally, it presupposes that the phrase was sufficient in itself to be understood universally by Jesus' audience to denote the Danielic figure as a conventional feature of popular apocalyptic eschatology. But this, as we shall see, was not the case.

2 *The Rise of a Modern Myth*

The common factor behind all these interpretations has been the assumption that 'the Son of Man' (*ho huios tou anthropou*) was a title for a distinct personality in Jewish thought of New Testament times. Two reasons lie behind this assumption. First, it was possible to point to Dan. 7.13–14 as the *origin* of the whole conception. For here 'one like a Son of Man' (*hos huios anthropou* in the Greek versions) receives royal power and state at the hands of God. As he receives no other designation, it could be inferred that he would normally be referred to as 'the Son of Man'. Although it was recognized that, in the vision of Dan. 7 as it actually stands, he functions as a symbol of the victorious people of God, and so was never intended to be an historical person, there was the evidence of the gospels themselves to show that in New Testament times he was identified with the Messiah as the agent of God's future kingdom. It could thus be assumed that this was a current idea in Judaism at this period.

Secondly, there was never any doubt that the Greek phrase corresponds with an Aramaic expression (*bar enash* in Dan. 7.13; *bar enash(a)* in the Aramaic of the time of Jesus) which simply means 'a man'. The corresponding Hebrew expression (*ben adam*) occurs a number of times in the Old Testament to denote mankind collectively, and is used frequently in Ezekiel to refer to the prophet as the representative of the people to whom he was sent. From this

3

point of view the Son of Man is the representative man. This fits very neatly with the actual function of the Danielic figure as representative of the victorious Jews. It also suggests a wider reference, inasmuch as the Hebrew form relates the title to the first man, Adam. That this reference was intended by the author of Dan. 7 was reinforced by the setting of the vision in the creation mythology which lies behind Gen. 1–2, and by the contrast between the primeval monsters which represent the hostile kingdoms and the man-like figure who represents the Jews.

These views were supported by evidence from outside the Bible. For the Son of Man concept in Judaism, the most important source was the Similitudes (or Parables) of Enoch (1 Enoch 37–71).[7] This Jewish work is a distinct element in the composite book of Enoch, and has survived only in the Ethiopic version of the book. In it the patriarch Enoch sees in a series of visions the eschatological judgement and the vindication of the righteous Jews. For this purpose God (usually referred to as the Lord of Spirits) has prepared the Messiah as his agent in performing the judgement and as the leader of the righteous in the everlasting kingdom. He is often referred to as the Chosen One or the Righteous One. These titles correspond with the designation of the people of God as his Chosen or his Righteous Ones. Most of the book is concerned with the preparations for the judgement, which comes at the end. This is not the real climax of the book, however, because the crucial issue is the identity of the Messiah. In the end it is revealed to Enoch that the Messiah is none other than Enoch himself. Now at one point in the visions Enoch is shown a preview of the future act of judgement, and sees the Messiah ready for action. The description is directly modelled on the setting of Dan. 7.9–14, and the Messiah is identified with the 'one like a son of man' of Dan. 7.13 (1 Enoch 46.1–3):

And there I saw one who had a head of days, and his head [was] white like wool; and with him [there was] another whose face had the appearance of a man, and his face [was] full of grace, like one of the holy angels. And I asked one of the holy angels who went with me, and showed me all the secrets, about that Son of Man, who he was, and whence he was, [and] why he went with the Head of Days. And he answered me and said to me: 'This is the Son of Man who has righteousness, and with whom righteousness dwells; he will reveal all the treasures of that which is secret, for the Lord of Spirits has chosen him, and through righteousness his lot has surpassed all before the Lord of Spirits for ever.'[8]

From this point in the Similitudes onwards the Messiah is occasionally referred to as 'that Son of Man', as an alternative to the other titles that are used for him. Here, then, was the proof of the existence of the Son of Man title in Judaism of the time of Christ.

R.H. Charles dated the Similitudes in the first half of the first century BC on the grounds that the work reflects the opposition of the Pharisees against the Hasmonean rulers, and especially against their usurpation of the throne of David.[9] But allusions to the political situation at this time cannot be identified with certainty. Later dates have been proposed, keeping within the period of Christian origins, by E. Sjöberg (after 38 BC, but before AD 70)[10] and by C.L. Mearns (about AD 40).[11] It now has to be recognized, however, that a date after the Jewish War is required, because no fragments of the Similitudes have been found in the Qumran literature (deposited in caves in the year AD 70, or thereabouts), in spite of the fact that Aramaic portions of no less than eleven different copies of Enoch have been identified, embracing all parts of the book except the Similitudes. Accordingly a date towards the end of the first century AD is now proposed by Knibb,[12] and even later dates have been suggested.[13] It may be pointed out, further, that the only certain literary allusions to Enoch in the New Testament are confined to the older strands, if the Son of Man title itself is excluded from consideration.[14]

Thus a date later than the time of Jesus has had to be conceded for the Similitudes of Enoch. This does not altogether deprive it of evidential value for the time of Christ. For, though it has now become clear that the Son of Man in the teaching of Jesus cannot be traced to literary dependence on the Similitudes, they support each other as independent witnesses, seeing that they have this feature in common.[15]

Another pointer in the same direction was the vision, directly based on Dan. 7, described in 2 Esd. (4 Ezra) 13. This book is also dated to the end of the first century AD, and there has never been any suggestion of influence from it upon the New Testament. The original text, which was probably in Hebrew,[16] is lost, as also is the Greek translation of it. It is thus known only from secondary translations taken from the Greek. In this vision, one 'like the figure of a man' (RSV, on basis of the Syriac version) comes up out of the heart of the sea, eventually revealed to be the Messiah ('My Son', verses 32, 37). The Latin text first refers to him as 'that man' (*ille homo*), but later uses the term *vir*. This corresponds exactly with the Syriac, which has *bar nasha* and *gabra* respectively. It has thus been widely held that the lost original contained the term 'the son of man' or 'that son of man', where the Latin has *homo*.

On these grounds it was supposed that the Son of Man was a concept familiar to Jews in the time of Jesus. The clear connection between the use of the expression in the Similitudes of Enoch and the figure in Dan. 7 was taken to imply that the expression *alone* would be sufficient to establish the reference to Dan. 7 in the minds of Jesus' audience. By referring to himself as the Son of Man he automatically cast himself in the role of the Danielic figure. He thereby gave a hint of his future messianic status and at the same time indicated his universal role on account of the representative character of the Son of Man both in Daniel and in the Similitudes of Enoch.

Further ramifications of the Son of Man concept were deduced from supposed affinities between the expression and the figure of Adam. The name Adam is, of course, the Hebrew word for man as a species (Latin *homo*), so that there is no necessary connection between *ben adam* (literally 'the son of man', but capable of being taken as 'the son of Adam') and the first man. A 'son of man' is really just a member of the human species. But when it has the definite article, it may well be taken to mean 'the man' in a special sense. The fact that Paul contrasts Adam and Christ in Rom. 5, and speaks of them as 'the first man Adam' and 'the last Adam' in 1 Cor. 15.45, suggested that the Son of Man concept could be related to speculations about the first man in the ancient world. A further contribution from Paul was found in Phil. 2.5–11, where the fashioning of Jesus as a man reflects the creation of Adam in the image and likeness of God in Gen. 1.27. Outside the New Testament it was possible to adduce Philo's treatment of Adam as a representative figure. He took Gen. 1.27 to refer to God's making of the pattern for the whole of humanity.[17] The same passage of Genesis also lies behind the Anthropos myth in the Hermetic tractate *Poimandres* (second century AD), in which Anthropos (Man) is a product of the divine *nous* (mind), and so is the origin of the spiritual part of mankind in the material creation. A similar idea of a pre-mundane Primal Man is also found in early Christian Gnosticism (Valentinus),[18] in Manicheism,[19] and in the Mandaean religion.[20] It has a pre-Christian counterpart in the Zoroastrian Primal Man (Gayomart), which has been held by some to lie behind the figure of Dan. 7.13.[21]

These speculations seem totally foreign to the Son of Man sayings in the gospels, but the influence of such ideas was felt to be feasible by those scholars who denied that Jesus ever spoke of himself as the Son of Man. Gayomart was not only the Primal Man, but also the first to die, and was destined to be the first to rise at the judgement. The application of the Son of Man title to Jesus as the first to rise from the dead and the one who is to come to perform the judgement could then be derived from this, if the resurrection and apocalyptic functions of Jesus were attributed to him before the title became current. The advantage of this view is that it explains features of the Son of Man concept which are *not* found in Dan. 7, where the Son of Man figure does not rise from the dead and does not perform the judgement. But this also implies that it is very unlikely that the Danielic figure is derived from this Zoroastrian concept in the first place. It must then be regarded as a later influence on Jewish ideas of the Son of Man between Daniel and the gospels.

However, such influence cannot be documented. The only Jewish writing which would be relevant is the Similitudes of Enoch. But this, as we have seen, is probably later than the gospels. It must also be questioned whether the figure of Gayomart has had any influence upon the Messianic concepts in the Similitudes. The Messiah is not presented in terms of the Primal Man. The essential features which need to be explained, i.e., the resurrection and the judgement, may indeed owe something to Zoroastrian religion in a more general way. But in Zoroastrianism the relevant figure is Sōšyant rather than Gayomart, for it is Sōšyant (a descendant of Zoroaster) who is the saviour-figure, destined to perform the eschatological functions.[22] That the cosmology and eschatology of Judaism in New Testament times was elaborated under the influence of Zoroastrian ideas need not be seriously doubted. The point at issue, however, is the adoption of a particular feature of Zoroastrianism in such a way as to suggest detailed knowledge of the system and direct and deliberate borrowing. The parallels between the messianic Son of Man in the Similitudes of Enoch and the Zoroastrian Primal Man are not close enough to prove a connection of this kind.

Moreover it is a mistake to put together the diverse references to man, or a man-like figure, from such widely differing sources, as if there were a single, identifiable concept in Judaism of the time of Christ, and then to make this the origin of the Son of Man ideas in the gospels. Such a single concept can never be other than a hypothetical reconstruction. We have to deal with the actual texts, recognizing that the influences behind any given passage may be multiple, but without assuming that a unitary concept is a common factor behind all of them.

In this case the hypothesis is extremely insecure, because it depends upon the assumption that the Son of Man could be recognized as a title of an eschatological figure in Jewish thought. That assumption has now been demolished, and with it the whole theory that there was a commonly accepted concept of the Son of Man along these lines in the intertestamental period collapses.

The irony of this is that the idea that there was a myth of the Son of Man in the time of Christ itself turns out to be a myth, created, not by the thinkers of New Testament times, but by modern critical scholarship. A fresh look at the Son of Man problem in the gospels has to take as its starting-point the fact that no such myth existed in the setting in which the gospels were composed.

3 *The linguistic background*

The modern myth of the Son of Man has been exploded on linguistic grounds.

a. In the New Testament the Greek phrase *ho huios tou anthropou* occurs only in the Gospels and Acts 7.56. In these passages it frequently functions as a title. This differentiates it from the four places (dependent upon the LXX) where the anarthrous form[23] is used: (i) Heb. 2.6, quoting Ps. 8.4, where *huios anthropou* is parallel to *anthropos*, applies the quotation to the exalted Jesus. But the Son of Man is not a title for him in this position. The writer appears to be completely unaware of a titular usage. (ii) Rev. 1.13 has a description of the risen Jesus based directly on Dan. 7.13. He is *homoion huion anthropou*, i.e. a man-like figure, as in the Danielic vision. This is especially notable, because the usage is again not

8

titular, in spite of the wealth of mythological imagery employed by the writer and the specific allusion to Daniel. (iii) Rev. 14.14 depicts one like a son of man (*homoion huion anthropou*) sitting on a cloud with a sickle in his hand, ready to reap the harvest of the redeemed. This certainly presupposes the application of the Danielic figure to the glorified Jesus, and includes the apocalyptic developments which appear in connection with the Son of Man in Matt. 13.37–43. But again the remarkable thing is that the phrase is descriptive only. It is not used as a title, but depends upon the identification of Jesus with the Danielic figure, of which it is one element only in a composite description.

b. It has already been mentioned that *bar enash(a)* may be translated 'a (the) man'. It is necessary to suppose, if it is a title outside the gospels, that it was possible to speak of 'the Man' in a titular way, and on this assumption Paul's Adam typology has been brought into relation with it. But this fails, because Paul does not use *ho anthropos* as a title.

c. In the Apostolic Fathers the anarthrous form is used as correlative to 'son of God'. Thus Ignatius to the Ephesians 20.2 has *huios anthropou* and *huios theou* in a context which appears to reflect Rom. 1.3–4. It refers to the humanity of Jesus, and does not carry with it the Danielic overtones implied by the titular usage. Similarly Barnabas 12.10 is concerned to show that Jesus is not merely an ordinary person, by contrast with his namesake Joshua, and in spite of the possible implications of the descent from David. So the writer says *ouchi huios anthropou alla huios tou theou*, i.e., not a son of man but [the] Son of God. The phrase here accords with normal Jewish usage of *bar enash* or *ben adam*.

d. In the Similitudes of Enoch 'that Son of Man' does not occur before the opening description in 46.1, which is directly based on Dan. 7.13–14. The phrase is derived from Daniel, and the connection is maintained by the use of the demonstrative 'that' in almost all the other places in the Similitudes where the Son of Man is mentioned. On the other hand the other messianic designations (the Messiah, the Chosen One, the Righteous and Chosen One) do not have the demonstrative. This is because they can stand as messianic titles in their own right. But this is not true of 'the Son of Man' (or, more idiomatically,'the Man'). When the writer of the

Similitudes wishes to refer to the Messiah as the Danielic figure, he has to say 'that Son of Man' (i.e., 'that man'), unless the context is clear enough without the demonstrative. The phrase simply means 'the man of the Danielic vision', and does not give evidence for it as a current messianic title.[24]

e. Dan. 7 also lies behind 2 Esd. 13. Here the man from the sea is identified with the Messiah, but 'the man' is not used as a title. Casey has argued that the lost Hebrew original had *ha-adam* where the Latin has *homo*, and *ish* where it has *vir*. On the less likely supposition that the original was in Aramaic, the phrase *bar enash(a)* might have been used. But if so, it would not have functioned as a title, any more than in the underlying passage in Daniel. Casey holds, however, that the Greek translation, on which the Latin is based, must have had *anthropos* where the Latin has *homo*. If the original had been in Aramaic, the word would have been translated *huios anthropou* in the Greek and *filius hominis* in the Latin. Of course the person referred to is the Danielic Son of Man. But the writer does not take this designation to be a title, but as a way of denoting a man, or the figure of a man, seeing that the reference is to a personality seen in vision.[25]

f. In Dan. 7.13 itself the phrase *ke-bar enash* (=like a son of man) means a human figure seen in vision, not, as is often supposed, a heavenly figure with human characteristics.[26] It is thus not clear whether he is intended to be a human being, in which case he would most likely be a symbolic representative figure for the loyal Jews, or an angel, in which case he might be the guardian angel of their interests, i.e., Michael.[27] This much debated question need not concern us, because it has no effect upon the meaning of the phrase, and it has no consequences for the interpretation of the Son of Man in the New Testament.

The above facts show that, outside the gospels and Acts 7.56, the Son of Man does not function as a title in the relevant literature, both Jewish and Christian. The phrase *bar enash* (and its usual Greek equivalent *huios anthropou*) means a man or human being. It carries with it no further implications, except when these are supplied by the context. It is the context as a whole in 1 Enoch 46; 2 Esd. 13; Rev. 1.13; 14.14 which provides the reference to the figure of Dan 7.13–14, using descriptive features which make the allusion unmistakable. As a number of the Son of Man sayings in the gospels include similar features, it is reasonable to conclude that the titular use of the phrase is intended to identify Jesus with the Danielic Son of Man in these instances.[28] No other possible identifications are suggested by the sayings.[29] It may thus be concluded that, in so far as the Son of Man is used as a title in the sayings tradition, it carries with it the identification with the Danielic figure. But it is important to realize that this is not due to any supposed currency of the phrase as a title in Jewish thought of the time of Christ. The identification of Jesus with the Danielic Son of Man, taken to be the Messiah in his eschatological role, has been achieved first, and the titular use of the phrase depends upon this prior activity. In this way the Son of Man can and does function in a number of the sayings in much the same way as 'that Son of Man' functions in the Similitudes of Enoch. From this point of view the definite article in the Greek form used in the gospel sayings (*ho huios tou anthropou*) has the force of a demonstrative. But it is important to remember that this applies only when there are Danielic allusions in the context. It cannot be taken for granted that the articles have this demonstrative force in sayings where such allusions are absent. For the moment the meaning in these cases must be left open for fuller consideration later. It should also be considered by no means a foregone conclusion that the consistent use of the definite article in the gospel sayings correctly represents the meaning of the underlying Aramaic in those sayings which may be traced back to Jesus himself.

4 *The rise of an ancient myth*

The myth of the apocalyptic Son of Man depended upon the assumption that the phrase was sufficient by itself alone to indicate a figure of eschatological expectation in intertestamental Judaism, derived mainly from Dan. 7.13–14, but developed under the influence of more widespread mythological ideas in the Graeco-Oriental world. The linguistic evidence shows that there was no Son of Man title to form a focus for such ideas. The apparently titular use of the phrase in the gospel sayings is unique, and its explanation is not to be found in literature outside the New Testament.

At the same time the figure of one like a Son of Man in Dan.

7.13–14 was clearly an important factor in New Testament times. The Similitudes of Enoch show a development of messianic thought which has been influenced by the Danielic vision. In this work the name of the Messiah/Son of Man has been decided before the creation (1 Enoch 48.2). This is typical of the determinist view of history which is presupposed by all apocalyptic literature, which claims to have advance information concerning the future. Eventually it transpires that Enoch is himself the Son of Man whom he has seen in the vision (1 Enoch 71.14). Thus it is the thesis of the writer of the Similitudes that Enoch, the righteous[30] man who 'walked with God; and he was not, for God took him' (Gen. 5.24), has been reserved in heaven in order to fulfil the role determined for him from the very beginning . This role is to be God's agent in the coming judgement. The idea is not derived from Dan. 7, though as Daniel's vision is a court scene, it provides the scenario for the Enoch presentation.

The Man from the sea in 2 Esd. 13 is a parallel development, in which the Danielic figure is identified with the Messiah and performs the judgement at the inauguration of the everlasting kingdom. Here, however, there is no identification of the Messiah with a character of history. His appearance from the sea suggests that his origins are inscrutable.[31] This agrees with the rather similar vision of 2 Esd. 11–12, which is also based on the imagery of Dan. 7, but does not include the Son of Man. Instead the Messiah is represented as a lion who 'was roused out of the forest, roaring' (11.37), though he speaks with 'a man's voice'. He is later identified as 'the Messiah whom the Most High has kept until the end of days, who will arise from the posterity of David' (12.32).

Both of these are post-Christian developments, but they are in no way dependent upon Christian thought, and they are independent of each other. They take up the long-standing court-room imagery of Jewish eschatology, and use the Danielic vision to identify the Messiah as God's agent in performing the judgement. This identification does not happen suddenly and without precedent in Jewish literature. The basic picture of Jewish eschatology is the coming of God himself to perform judgement. This is attached to the ancient picture of the Day of the Lord in Zech. 14.1–5, a passage which must be dated some time before the Maccabean revolt.[32] It ends with the words, 'Then the Lord your God will come, and all the holy ones with him.'[33] These words are quoted in the oldest strand of Enoch in a passage which is partially preserved in the fragments of the original Aramaic recovered from Qumran (1 Enoch 1.9):[34]

> And behold! He comes with ten thousand holy ones to execute judgement upon them, and to destroy the impious, and to contend with all flesh concerning everything which the sinners and the impious have done and wrought against him.

This passage reappears, in direct quotation attributed to Enoch, in Jude 14f. Here the coming of the Lord has been identified with the parousia of Jesus, according to a tendency which we shall find again in the development of the Son of Man sayings in the gospels.

For our present purpose, however, it is necessary to observe the development within the older strands of Enoch itself. Two passages are relevant. First, although there is no suggestion of identifying Enoch with the Messiah, he is represented as playing a part in the judgement process, inasmuch as he takes the petition of the fallen angels to God and brings back to them God's verdict of eternal punishment (1 Enoch 12–16). Secondly, in an entirely different literary stratum, there is a dream vision given to Enoch, which takes the form of a long allegory of Israel's history in the form of animals (1 Enoch 85–90). This also can be assigned to a pre-Christian date because of the internal evidence of the historical references, and also the survival of passages of it in the Aramaic fragments. In this allegory God himself performs the judgement. The temple is then renewed for the sake of the blessed. At this point the Messiah is born, to be the leader of all the redeemed. Thus the Messiah has nothing to do with the judgement. On the other hand God is not without assistance for this purpose. For at intervals in the long catalogue of history we hear of a person who records the wickedness of men in a book for use at the judgement.[35] This function corresponds with that of Enoch in the other passage. The recorder is probably intended to be an angel, though his identity is not clear. Meanwhile Enoch has been snatched away to heaven at the point in the story to which he properly belongs (i.e., after the birth of Noah; cf. Gen. 5.21–28),[36] and has remained there, watching all the events of history. He finally returns to join the company of the redeemed just before the final judgement (1 Enoch 90.31), and so is present at the time of the birth of the Messiah. Enoch's last comment is 'and I was asleep in the middle of them' (1 Enoch

90.39). It is thus possible that the writer intends to imply that Enoch is himself the Messiah, occupying the focal point in the midst of the redeemed.[37]

From these two passages, we can see that Jewish apocalyptic in New Testament times is capable of thinking of celestial assistants in the process of the divine judgement, who may include persons like Enoch who are reserved in heaven. We can also see what the figure of the Messiah is like in an apocalyptic setting. He is not a political deliverer, but the leader of the redeemed in the new and everlasting kingdom which follows the final judgement. The idea of a heavenly agent for the judgement is attested independently in the fragmentary Melchizedek document from Qumran.[38] He actually performs judgement on behalf of God. It is not clear, however, whether he is intended to be the historical Melchizedek of Gen. 14, reserved in heaven for this purpose, or whether he is an angel with the same name.[39]

The messianic interpretation of Dan. 7 was bound to bring about a correlation of these ideas in due course. It is surprising that we have to wait until after the rise of Christianity for clear evidence of this in Jewish literature. 2 Esd. 13 stands in the line of messianism which we have seen in the dream vision of 1 Enoch 85–90, in which the Messiah appears at the end of the present order of history. The picture is drawn from Dan. 7, but the only new features in the apocalyptic programme are that the Messiah acts as God's spokesman to judge the nations and that he gathers up the redeemed for the everlasting kingdom. Neither of these are found in Dan. 7, but they accord well with the precedents which we have seen in 1 Enoch 85–90 and the Melchizedek scroll. The Similitudes of Enoch break new ground, perhaps following up the hint in 1 Enoch 90.39 mentioned above, by identifying Enoch with the Messiah. As before the use of Dan. 7 is purely pictorial, and the messianic characteristics attributed to the Son of Man in the Similitudes are derived from such precedents as the dream-vision of 1 Enoch 85–90.

These developments run parallel to the growth of Christology and the formation of the New Testament. The dream-vision of 1 Enoch is older than the rise of Christianity. 11QMelchizedek is roughly contemporary with the beginning of the Christian era. 2 Esdras and the Similitudes of Enoch must be dated to the period of the close of the New Testament. Early Christian messianism identified Jesus with the Messiah who is kept in reserve by God for the time of the judgement. Thus Jesus joined the company of those righteous individuals like Enoch and Elijah who were exalted to heaven and destined to perform eschatological functions. The function of Jesus is to be the focus of the company of the redeemed (1 Cor. 15.23–28). He will gather in the elect (1 Thess. 4.16f; Mark 13.26f). At some stage in the early history of Christology Jesus was identified with the Son of Man figure of Dan. 7.13–14. This had certainly happened by the time that Mark compiled his Little Apocalypse (Mark 13), as the literary allusion is unmistakable. It is not so clear in Paul, as he does not make direct allusion to Dan. 7.13–14.[40] But the identification may well have happened before Paul, as it is also implied by some of the sayings of Jesus in the Q tradition (cf. Luke 17.22–30).

It should now be clear that the use of Dan. 7 in the growth of Jewish apocalyptic messianism and in the development of Christology outside the gospels in the early church has nothing to do with the phrase Son of Man as such. In the Similitudes of Enoch and 2 Esd. 13 the vision of Dan. 7 is used in order to express apocalyptic messianic ideas which were already taking shape in Jewish thought. In making use of Daniel, the authors of these works not unnaturally employ Daniel's expression, which simply means a man. In early Christian thought there is very little sign of the use of Dan. 7, and the absence of it from both Paul and Hebrews is remarkable. But Jesus is certainly presented as the apocalyptic Messiah, the one who is held in reserve for the inauguration of the everlasting kingdom. This idea has been achieved without the aid of the Danielic Son of Man. The most significant factor of all from this point of view is the failure of Revelation to use the Son of Man as a title. For here we have not only the same christological development of apocalyptic messianism, but also the employment of words and images from Daniel, including the actual phrase *huios anthropou*, in order to express it. But this phrase is not used as a title of Jesus. It merely forms part of the description.

It is only in the gospels and Acts 7.56 that we have to reckon with a development based on the titular use of *ho huios tou anthropou*. Seeing that *ke-bar enash* in Dan. 7.13 was not recognized as a title even in such works as refer to the passage (Rev., 2 Esd., Similitudes of Enoch), and seeing that identification of Jesus with the apocalyptic Messiah was effected in the first instance without reference to Daniel's vision, it is altogether improbable that the Son of Man always carried an allusion to this passage. The phrase by itself could not do this. Only when other features of a saying connect it with Dan. 7.13–14 does the phrase necessarily presuppose identification with the Danielic figure. Such features are lacking in the majority of Son of Man sayings, particularly in those which are found to have the best claim to authenticity when examined critically. It is thus most likely that the phrase did not refer to the Daniel passage to begin with. The original meaning of the Son of Man on the lips of Jesus must be found elsewhere.

2

The Son of Man in the Sayings of Jesus

---

1 *The Meaning of the Phrase*

The Son of Man is an unusual phrase in English. It is also unusual in Greek. As Greek requires repetition of the definite article,[1] the phrase *ho huios tou anthropou* can either represent 'the son-of-man' as a compound expression, or refer to 'the son of the man', 'the man's son', where a particular man is under discussion. It is obvious that the second alternative does not apply to the sayings of Jesus where this phrase is used. Consequently it has generally been assumed that the Greek translates the Aramaic compound expression, *bar enash*, but using the emphatic state, which replaces the definite article with nouns in Aramaic. This gives the form *bar enasha*.[2]

This is a compound expression, and causes difficulties precisely for this reason. The use of *bar*, son, is idiomatic, and has a wide range of meanings in compound expressions. One of these is to denote a member of a group. Thus a son of man is a member of the human species, therefore simply a man. There is an almost exact parallel to the usage of Dan. 7.13 in an earlier passage, Dan. 3.25: *dameh le-bar alahin* = like a son of gods, i.e., like a god.

The basic nuance is therefore a human being, corresponding with Greek *anthropos* and Latin *homo*, rather than an individual person. It is thus not surprising to find that the expression is much more common in Aramaic in the plural, 'the sons of men'.[3] In the singular it would normally be anarthrous, as in Dan. 7.13 itself. But instances of this kind are rather rare, because when the required meaning is man in general (e.g., mankind, anyone, or each and every person) the idiomatic *bar* is not felt to be needed, and the simple *enash* is used.[4] On the other hand the usual word for a particular man is *gebar*, corresponding with Greek *aner* and Latin *vir*.

It was recognized as long ago as 1896 by H. Lietzmann that in Aramaic literature this expression is not used at all in the same way as the Son of Man in the gospels.[5] He therefore suggested that *ho huios tou anthropou* was not a rendering of *bar enasha*, but had its origin in Hellenistic speculations. This was the beginning of the modern myth of the Son of Man, which has been shown above to be untenable.

Lietzmann correctly observed that in the few places where the singular *bar nasha* occurs in Galilean Aramaic, it is used generically. This is found in certain tractates in the Jerusalem Talmud. Dalman replied that the generic usage (which we shall consider below) is not relevant to the Son of Man problem in the gospels, because the Talmud comes from a much later date.[6] He pointed out that *enash* is the usual singular form, and claimed that in the time of Jesus *bar enash(a)* was used only when translating Hebrew *ben adam*. It was therefore possible to argue that the special usage in the gospels, in which *bar enasha* is to be accepted as the underlying Aramaic expression, was a coinage on the part of Jesus himself. This was not open to misunderstanding, because in any case the expression was not in common use in the singular, except for the purpose of translation.

Dalman's argument is scarcely convincing, but it raises an important point. The chronological factor has to be taken into account.[7] It is true that *bar enash* in the earlier period appears to be exactly equivalent to Hebrew *ben adam*, as far as its semantic range may be ascertained. But this does not mean that it was never used except as a translation of the Hebrew. In fact this is most unlikely, because, as already indicated above, Aramaic shares with Hebrew the idiomatic use of 'son of', and indeed tends to extend it. On the other hand the later Aramaic, and especially the form of Aramaic known as Syriac, used the compound expression much more widely still, so that it takes over many of the uses of *enash* and can even interchange with *gebar*. For this reason, when the Syriac version of the gospels was made in the early part of the second century, the translators had to coin a new expression to represent *ho huios tou anthropou*, in order to preserve the distinctiveness of it over against the common use of *bar nasha* for a man. The Old Syriac version thus has either *bereh de-nasha* or *bereh de-gabra* instead. The later Syriac Peshitta adopted *bereh de-nasha* as the only form, for the sake of consistency. This is an idiomatic way of saying 'the son of the man', which is precisely what the Greek *ho huios tou anthropou* is *not* intended to mean (see above). But it illustrates the difficulty involved in the changing use of language. Similarly the Christian Palestinian version of the gospels, which is West Syrian and which may be as late as the fifth century AD, but is entirely independent of the Syriac versions, sometimes uses *bereh de-gabra*, but more frequently it has the grotesque form *bereh de-bar nasha* (literally 'the son of the son-of-man'). Here the sense that the common expression for 'a man' is really 'a son of man' has disappeared altogether.

It seems that there is not enough evidence to support Dalman's rejection of the generic use of *bar enasha* in the time of Jesus. It cannot be proved that this expression was used only as a translation of Hebrew *ben adam*, and indeed it is intrinsically improbable that this was so. On the other hand the Aramaic of the Jerusalem Talmud is remarkable, in that it does not show the tendency to broaden the use of *bar (e)nash(a)* which we can see in Syriac and the late Palestinian (West Syrian) Aramaic. Seeing that this development has been resisted in the Jerusalem Talmud, there is no reason to suppose that the generic use which it contains is a linguistic development which is necessarily later than the time of Christ. In fact, as we shall see, the generic use, as found in the Jerusalem Talmud, is the only possible explanation of some of the sayings attributed to Jesus in which the Son of Man occurs.[8]

It is the merit of Vermes' work on the Aramaic background of the Son of Man that he has taken the generic use of *bar enasha* seriously.[9] His work has, indeed, opened up an entirely new perspective on the Son of Man problem, which it is the aim of this book to take through to its proper conclusion. It is obvious to those reading the gospels that the Son of Man in the sayings of Jesus is a self-reference on Jesus' part. Vermes has shown that *bar enash(a)*, when used generically, may be a self-reference in this way. This, then, makes the proper starting point for understanding the gospel sayings.

The generic use would normally be expected to be anarthrous (*bar enash*, referring to any man). Hebrew and Aramaic, however, frequently use the generic article, where it is not suitable in English (e.g., Judg. 4.21: 'Jael . . . took the hammer in her hand', i.e., the one required for the job). This usage also occurs in Greek (e.g., Luke 6.45: 'the good man'=any good man). Thus the definite form *bar enasha* is used in contexts where the indefinite form might be expected.

Unfortunately Vermes spoilt his own case by asserting that the idiomatic use of *bar enash(a)* to represent a self-reference is not truly generic. He illustrated the idiom with the aid of another similar expression, 'that man' (*hahu gabra*), which can be used as a self-reference, but refers exclusively to the speaker. J. Jeremias at once pointed out that the two expressions are not equivalent.[10] Casey has re-examined the discussion, and concludes that Jeremias' objections hold good.[11] But Casey's own idea of what is involved in a generic expression also is faulty. As the matter is crucial for the interpretation of the Son of Man sayings, it is necessary to set out the facts in a little more detail.

a. For the idiomatic use of *hahu gabra*, Vermes cites among other examples Gen. R. 100.5:[12]

> Jacob asked Esau: Do you want money or a burial place? Esau replied: Does *that man* (=Do I) want a burial place? Give me the money and keep the burial place for yourself.

Here Esau uses the third person to dissociate himself from the thought of his own death. But the reference is exclusively to himself.

b. Next Vermes gives an example with anarthrous *bar nash*. The speaker is Rab Kahana (y Ber.5c):

> If *bar nash* is despised by his mother but honoured by another of his father's wives, where should he go? Yohanan replied: He should go where he is honoured. Thereupon Kahana left. Then Rabbi Yohanan was told: Kahana has gone to Babylon. He exclaimed: What! Has he gone without asking leave? They said to him: The story he told you was his request for leave.

The point is that Kahana feels that his master R. Yohanan does not appreciate him, and wishes to return to Babylon, where he has previously received more credit. The third-person form, and indeed the use of a parable in which a man's wives stand for the rabbis, indicate the delicacy which Kahana feels is required in broaching such a request. Here it is clear, as Vermes admits in this instance, that *bar nash* is generic (a man), because it is the subject of the parable, which is put forward as a case which can receive a general ruling. That is indeed how Yohanan understands it. He has no idea that it is *also* a self-reference, until reminded of the incident after Kahana's departure. He takes it, quite naturally, to refer to *any* man in such circumstances. It is obvious that *hahu gabra* could not have been used in this instance.

c. The third example has both *bar nasha* and *bar nash* together in almost identical sentences (y Ket. 35a):

> It is related that Rabbi (Judah) was buried wrapped in a single sheet, for he said: It is not as *bar nasha* goes that he will come again. But the rabbis say: As *bar nash* goes, so will he come again.

Here Rabbi's unusual wish to be buried very simply is said to have been carried out. The usual procedure for a rich man would be to be buried in rich coverings, suitable to his expected status at the resurrection. This is expressed in the opinion of the rabbis at the end: *every man* passes to the next world in the same condition as he leaves the present world, so that the rich will be rich and the poor will be poor. Rabbi, apparently, objected to this principle, and suggested a reversal of conditions, which can be compared with the story of the rich man and Lazarus in Luke 16.19–31. Vermes insists that, when Rabbi gave his burial instructions with these words, he can have intended the reference to be only to himself, because of the definite form. But this would not have occurred to anyone, except for the following sentence, where the indefinite form is used. As the first sentence stands, the definite form gives the impression of being a case where the generic article is used, i.e., any man in these circumstances. The fact is that the generic use is equally possible with or without the article.[13] There may, however, be a slight difference of nuance in this case between the two statements. Rabbi's statement is a proverb, explaining why he wishes to be buried in this way. The following sentence is not a proverb, but the approved teaching, or ruling, of the rabbinate in general. The use of the generic article is appropriate to a proverbial type of sentence. The indefinite form better suits a general ruling.

d. For the fourth example only the relevant part need be quoted (y Ber. 3b):

> Rabbi Simeon ben Yohai said: 'If I had stood on Mount Sinai when the Torah was given to Israel, I would have asked the Merciful One to create two mouths for *bar nasha*, one for the study of the Torah and one for the provision of all his needs.'

21

Vermes rightly sees that this is a self-reference, as Simeon's wish is for himself. Of course the saying is a vivid way of expressing the supreme bounty of the Torah, which can be matched only by continuous recitation, unimpeded by the necessity of eating. The request is, then, that God should not only give the Torah but also provide the means of appreciating it properly. It is not a prayer for people in general, nor for the Israelites as a whole who were assembled on that occasion. But it is a prayer that *anyone* would make *for himself* who was as deeply conscious of the divine generosity as Simeon himself. From this point of view *bar nasha* is a self-reference, because Simeon is the only member of this class. But it is still a generic usage, because it does not exclude any other person who might have been in the same class and made the same request. The precise nuance is a matter of emphasis, which can be appreciated if the request is put into direct speech, 'Create for a man two mouths!' The self-reference permits a rendering with the first person, but the generic *bar nasha* makes it unemphatic: 'Create for me *two mouths*!', not 'Create *for me* two mouths!' To gain the latter sense *haden bar nasha* (this son of man), or a similar expression, would have been required.

Now the interesting thing is that, when the story is retold in another place in the Talmud (y Shab. 3a) *haden bar nasha* actually occurs. To Vermes this clinches the argument that *bar nasha* here is used in an exclusive sense, no different in meaning from *hahu gabra*. It may be said in reply that this version has emphasized the self-reference at the expense of the generic idiom, and thereby subtly alters the sense. We shall see the same tendency at work when we come to consider *ho huios tou anthropou* in the gospels.[14]

e. This tendency to make the self-reference explicit occurs again in the last example which Vermes adduces. It is another saying of R. Simeon (y Sheb. 38d):

> At the end of those thirteen years, he said: 'I will go forward and see what is happening in the world . . .' He sat down at the entrance to the cave. There he saw a fowler trying to catch birds by spreading his net. He heard a heavenly voice saying [in Latin!], *Dimissio!* [release] and the bird escaped. He then said: 'Not even a bird perishes without the will of heaven. How much less *bar nasha.*'

Simeon has been in hiding since the Jewish War, and he is wondering whether it is now safe to leave his cave. He concludes that the divine protection afforded to a bird must surely apply even more to himself as a man (cf. Matt. 6.26; 10.29). Vermes argues against the generic use by appealing to the contrast between anarthrous *ṣippor* (a bird) and the definite *bar nasha*.

But this difference cannot be pressed. Casey has compared the parallels to this pericope found in Genesis Rabbah 79.6; Ecclesiastes Rabbah 10.8; and Esther Rabbah 3.7.[15] These are slightly more elaborate versions. In each case it is stated at the outset that Simeon has his son R. Eleazar with him in the cave, so that what is said applies to them both. Moreover there is a second saying of the heavenly voice, again in Latin: *Spiculum!* (judgement),[16] and then the bird is caught. This shows more clearly that the escape and death of the bird depends in each case on the divine will, expressed by the heavenly voice. Finally there are variations to the concluding *bar nasha*. In Gen. R. 79.6 (*nephash de-bar nash*) and Eccles. R. 10.8 (*nephash bar nash*) the generic sense is confirmed, because the words ('how much less the soul, i.e. life, of a man') refer to both Simeon and Eleazar. It is no accident that the text in these two versions reads *bar nash* and not *bar nasha*. But in Est. R. 3.7 it has disappeared altogether, and the text reads, 'How much less our souls' (*naphshathana*; some texts have singular, 'our soul', *naphshana*). Here the possessive pronoun 'our' turns the generic statement into an exclusive reference to Simeon and Eleazar. There are in fact other variants, and *naphshi* ('my soul') occurs in some texts of Gen. R. 79.6 in place of *nephash de-bar nash*. In this case the reference is to Simeon alone, in spite of the presence of Eleazar with him in the cave.

All these variations show the ambiguity of the original text. It is not at all likely that the oldest form has an expression denoting an exclusive reference to Simeon, which has been turned into a general statement in some texts of Gen. R. 79.6 and Eccles. R. 10.8. The tendency is certainly to move in the opposite direction. The form which best explains the variants is *bar nasha*, as in y Sheb. 38d, because it is an ambiguous expression. It does not mean 'How much less mankind' (general statement), nor does it mean 'How much less I' (exclusive self-reference), but 'How much less a man in my position' (idiomatic use of generic article).

There are thus three ways of referring to oneself by means of the third person. There is the general statement, in which the speaker includes himself. It is the mistake of Casey to suppose that this is the clue to the meaning of the Son of Man sayings in the gospels.[17] Secondly there is the exclusive self-reference in which the speaker refers to himself alone. Vermes seems to be mistaken in thinking that this is the proper meaning of *bar nasha* in this type of speech. Thirdly there is the idiomatic use of the generic article, in which the speaker refers to a class of persons, with whom he identifies himself. This is well illustrated by the version in y Sheb. 38d of the final example (e). It is this idiom, properly requiring *bar (e)nasha* rather than *bar (e)nash*, which provides the best guidance to the use of the Son of Man in the sayings of Jesus.

2 *From Aramaic into Greek*

Jesus spoke in Aramaic. If he used *bar enasha* as a self-reference, it is to be expected that he did so according to the idiom just described. It follows that those sayings in which the Son of Man functions in this way have the highest claim to be considered authentic.[18]

In these sayings Jesus must certainly have used the definite form (*bar enasha*), because the Greek translation has the definite article in every case which may be claimed as authentic.[19]

It thus appears that, in the Greek *ho huios tou anthropou*, we have a much too literal translation of the Aramaic, and a remarkable consistency in the rendering. At the same time the difference from the equally consistent usage of the Septuagint, which *never* has the definite article, needs to be taken into account. These facts have been variously explained.

a. The consistency has been attributed by Martin Hengel, probably rightly, to the circumstance that the earliest collection of the sayings of Jesus was translated into Greek at a particular time and place.[20] He connects this with the conversion of Hellenistic Jews in Jerusalem, who were Greek-speaking and had their own synagogues (cf. Acts 6). It is thus not accidental that the only Son of Man saying outside the Gospels occurs in connection with Stephen, who was a prominent member of this new element in primitive Christianity (Acts 7.56).[21]

b. The difference from the Septuagint has been explained by C.F.D. Moule as an indication that the underlying Aramaic was neither the indefinite form *bar enash*, nor the same form with generic article.[22] He suggests that the definite articles have demonstrative force ('that son of man', referring to Dan. 7.13), and proposes *bereh de-gabra* as the underlying Aramaic, or another form similar to the Syriac versions (*bereh d-enasha* or *bera d-enasha*).[23] This would have been a fresh coinage on the part of Jesus himself, as nothing like it is known in Aramaic literature to express this meaning. It cannot be proved that the demonstrative in the Ethiopic Similitudes of Enoch represents the definite article in the underlying Greek, itself derived from an Aramaic form such as Moule postulates for Jesus. The suggestion fails, partly because it gives the wrong meaning, as already noted (i.e., 'the man's son'), and partly because it depends on the currency of the Son of Man as a phrase which could directly recall the figure of Dan. 7.13. But this has already been shown to be wrong.

c. The simplest view is that of Casey.[24] He suggests that the Greek is the natural and literal translation of the definite form *bar enasha* by people who are already familiar with *huios anthropou* for the indefinite form, which is the *only* form used in the Septuagint. This suits the Hellenistic Jewish converts, who were accustomed to the language of the Septuagint. The phrase in the gospels, however, has the definite article, representing the generic use, because that was so in the underlying Aramaic. But because the context alone shows the usage, it was inevitable that isolated Son of Man sayings should be taken to imply an exclusive self-reference on the part of Jesus. In this way the phrase began to function as a title, and in due course the identification was made with the man-like figure of Dan. 7.13, interpreted as the Messiah. On this view *ho huios tou anthropou* is 'translationese' derived from the Septuagint, though it differs from the Septuagint form on account of the generic article.

d. Casey may well be right, but his position is not without difficulties.[25] In the first place, it is doubtful if *ho huios tou anthropou* would be recognized as generic in Greek, so that *all* the gospel sayings do in fact treat it as an exclusive self-reference, and therefore virtually as a circumlocution for the first person. Secondly, it cannot be assumed without question that Aramaic *bar enasha* was *always* translated in this way. Not all the sayings of Jesus have come through the same channel of tradition. There is, of course, no way of detecting other cases where *bar enasha* stood in the underlying text, but whenever the generic use of *ho anthropos* occurs this must be considered at least possible.[26] Mark 2.27, 'the sabbath was made for man (*dia ton anthropon*) and not man (*ho anthropos*) for the sabbath,' is a very likely case.[27] There is no example, however, of *ho anthropos* to represent the idiomatic self-reference.[28] This means that *ho anthropos* was not considered a suitable rendering for the idiom. But, thirdly, the tendency to make the self-reference explicit at the expense of the generic meaning, which we have observed in the rabbinic examples, was certainly a factor in the interpretation of the Son of Man sayings, and may be true also of the translation in some cases. This would take the form of substituting the first person for the third person. There are, in fact, several cases where a Son of Man saying has a parallel in first person form, and in one of them at least (Matt. 10.32f = Luke 12.8f and Matt. 16.27 = Mark 8.38 = Luke 9.26) a case can be made out that this difference depends on two independent Greek translations of the same Aramaic saying.[29] If this is correct, we must reckon with the possibility that the existing Son of Man sayings do not exhaust the deposit of sayings in which Jesus referred to himself idiomatically with *bar nasha*, though they cannot be recovered, because they have been preserved only in first person form.

A further point is that, if the translators of the Aramaic sayings were guided by the practice of the Septuagint in their choice of expressions, we should not exclude the possibility of attention to the context on their part. This at once fastens attention on Dan. 7.13, because it is the *only* place where *bar enash* occurs. All other occurrences of *huios anthropou* represent Hebrew *ben adam*. If Jesus had already been identified with the Danielic figure, because of the obvious relation which it bears to the proclamation of his exaltation, before the sayings were translated into Greek, then it may well be that *ho huios tou anthropou* is a deliberate, interpretative translation rather than mere 'translationese'. If so, the tendency to create Son of Man sayings which definitely allude to Daniel has its origin in the translation adopted for the authentic sayings, which was aimed at incorporating the identification into the sayings tradition. In any case the translation of the sayings in Greek had a catalytic effect on the development of Christology.[30]

It may be said further in favour of this suggestion that the growth of Danielic Son of Man sayings appears in both Mark and Q, which embody traditions older than Paul's letters. There is thus no compelling reason to assign this development to a later date, in spite of Paul's failure to make use of Daniel. Moreover the doubly attested saying mentioned above, which tells of Jesus' future activity at the time of the judgement (e.g., Luke 12.8: '. . . the Son of Man also will acknowledge before the angels of God'), belongs to the original deposit of Son of Man sayings, and might easily have suggested the connection.

However this question is decided, the essential point is that the Aramaic *bar enasha*, as used by Jesus, cannot have been a title which would have been familiar to his audience. No other reconstruction of the Aramaic behind *ho huios tou anthropou* is convincing. Jesus used it as an oblique way of referring to himself. According to the Jewish evidence for this usage, he must have spoken generically, so that there must have been a sense in which his words need not refer to himself exclusively. On the other hand the self-reference was intentional, and the point of the saying would be lost without it. This does not mean, however, that he identified himself with the Danielic Son of Man. Such an identification cannot be secured by the Aramaic phrase alone. This is a development which belongs either to the process of translation of the sayings into Greek, or to a slightly later time when Dan. 7 has been brought into the range of Christology.

A developmental history[31] of the Son of Man title in the New Testament must start with those sayings which preserve the Aramaic idiom. It will be shown below that nine sayings retain the idiom, including three which belong to the passion predictions. These are found in Q and Mark. This may seem to be a small number to claim for Jesus out of the total of Son of Man sayings in the gospels. But it is enough to establish the idiom as a characteristic of Jesus' style. This must have been all the more striking, because the idiom appears to have been rather rare. The fact that we have here a stylistic feature can help us to understand the later development. It accounts for the almost complete absence of the Son of Man title *outside* the sayings tradition. It also explains the proliferation of Son of Man sayings *within* the tradition. This was not an arbitrary process. It arose out of the implications of the authentic sayings. But it tended to make the identification of Jesus with the Danielic Son of Man explicit. This can be seen in Q and Mark and the editorial work of Matthew. In Luke, on the other hand, we shall see that the determining factor is the evangelist's recognition of the phrase as a stylistic feature. John has his own special development, presupposing the process which can be observed in Mark and Q, and dependent upon it. But here also the *reason* why John has constructed Son of Man sayings in his highly individual presentation of the gospel traditions is that they are a feature of Jesus' style, which enhances the impression of authenticity.

3

Six Son of Man Sayings in Mark and Q

In this chapter we shall examine those sayings in Mark and Q which may fairly be claimed to be authentic, excluding the passion predictions. In each case the Aramaic idiom can be detected. The Son of Man phrase is not necessarily used as a title, and there is no overt allusion to Dan. 7.13.

1 *Matthew 8.20 = Luke 9.58*
Foxes have holes, and birds of the air have nests, but bar enasha *has nowhere to lay his head.*

Although the editorial setting differs, the saying is identical in Matthew and Luke. It also occurs in almost identical form in the Gospel of Thomas, logion 86, where it has the distinction of being the only Son of Man saying in the whole collection:

> Jesus said: [Foxes have their holes] and birds of the air have [their] nests, but the Son of Man has nowhere to lay his head (and) to rest.[1]

Although the Gospel of Thomas is a Gnostic work, compiled in its present form after the canonical gospels were written, it often appears to preserve more ancient versions of the sayings of Jesus, especially the parables. Thus it may well be dependent upon Q or a comparable early collection, rather than on the canonical gospels themselves.[2] On the other hand, it is most unlikely that it is based on an Aramaic collection, because when Greek words occur in the Coptic text they usually correspond with the Greek of the gospels. It is thus most probable that Son of Man here is derived from the Greek, and is not a direct translation of Aramaic *bar enasha*. On the other hand, the compiler of Thomas shows no awareness of christological overtones in the title.[3] Moreover the absence of a narrative context deprives the saying of the key to understanding it. It appears to be a statement concerning Jesus himself, assuming that Thomas takes it as a self-reference, but the application to discipleship is not expressed. Alternatively, if there is no self-reference, it may refer to the true disciple. In so far as the sequence of the sayings in Thomas can be accepted as a guide to interpretation, it would seem that it relates to the 'other worldliness' which Thomas seeks to inculcate. From this point of view Jesus (or the true disciple) does not belong to this world and will not remain in the conditions of this life.

In Q, however, the saying is spoken by Jesus in response to a prospective disciple. It forms part of a longer unit, in which similarly proverbial sayings are given in reply to possible recruits (one more in Matthew, but two more in Luke). The setting is essential in order to appreciate the characteristic irony of Jesus' answer. Jesus wishes to make a severe demand upon this disciple, in line with teaching elsewhere on the cost of discipleship. But he does so gently by means of the irony of this proverbial sentence. The point is that, just as Jesus himself has given up the security of a permanent home and the comfort of his own bed, so the disciple must be prepared to accept similar deprivations.

It is thus clear that the Son of Man here is a self-reference. There is a difficulty, however, in seeing it as a generic usage. At first sight it seems either to be an exclusive reference to Jesus himself, equivalent to *hahu gabra*, or to be a description of mankind in general, by contrast with foxes and birds. The first is excluded *ex hypothesi*, as it is not true to the Son of Man idiom. The second, however, is manifestly untrue of people in general, who usually do have houses and beds.[4] But we have seen from the rabbinic examples collected by Vermes that there are other ways of understanding the generic usage. The nearest example to the present case is Rabbi Simeon's prayer for two mouths (example *d* on p. 21). As a generic usage, *bar nasha* refers to anyone who might have been in the same class as Simeon himself and made the same prayer. So here Jesus means anyone who shares in the conditions of his own missionary vocation. This is precisely what the prospective recruit wishes to do. Thus the generic usage is *essential* to the purpose of the saying. By means of it Jesus associates the disciple, not only this one but any others who may also desire to follow him, with his own life-style, and thereby turns it into a searching demand. But because the demand is a hard one, he softens the impact by associating what he requires of the disciple with what he requires of himself. This is the irony of the saying. It can be achieved only by the *bar enasha* idiom actually used. It would not be achieved by an exclusive self-reference, nor by a universal statement which does not fit the facts. Thus the best translation of the phrase in this saying is 'a man such as I'.[5] The contrast is not between men and animals, but between Jesus with his group of disciples and all other men, and indeed *even* the animals.

This interpretation excludes all ideas of a contrast between present humiliation and future glory.[6] This can be read out of the text only if the Son of Man is taken to be a title for the exalted Messiah. This may well be the way in which the saying was understood by the evangelists, or even the interpretation intended by the Greek translator, if the argument for interpretative translation is accepted. But if the saying is authentic—and there are no good grounds to dispute it—the consequences of recognizing the Aramaic idiom must be accepted.

This does not deprive the saying of christological significance altogether. The context is discipleship, and the saying is most naturally understood in relation to Jesus' itinerant mission. Jesus refers to the conditions in which his mission is undertaken. It is implied that such conditions are unavoidable. Jesus has accepted for himself the vocation to work which requires some measure of hardship. Obedience to a divine call is an indispensable feature of Christology. It is echoed in passages where Jesus speaks of being 'sent',[7] a theme which is much exploited in the Fourth Gospel.[8] All the Son of Man sayings considered in this chapter refer to Jesus' personal vocation in this way. The generic *bar enasha* is a device whereby Jesus can refer ironically to his position as one called by God without making exaggerated claims about himself.

2 *Matthew 11.16–19 = Luke 7.31–35*

To what then shall I compare the men of this generation, and what are they like? They are like children sitting in the market place and calling to one another,
  'We piped to you, and you did not dance;
  we wailed, and you did not weep.'
For John the Baptist has come eating no bread and drinking no wine; and you say, 'He has a demon'. Bar enasha *has come eating*

31

and drinking; and you say, 'Behold, a glutton and a drunkard, a friend of tax collectors and sinners!' Yet wisdom is justified by all her children.

As before, the Greek text is almost identical in the two gospels, Luke's (which is followed here) being generally accepted as closer to the original. But none of the differences is substantial. The pericope forms the conclusion to a longer sequence (Matt. 11.2–19=Luke 7.18–35), which brings together items relevant to the question of the relationship between Jesus and John the Baptist. Some of these items have partial parallels in the Gospel of Thomas, but not the present passage. The dependence of the two evangelists upon a common source is particularly clear, because Matthew characteristically inserts a related, but not strictly relevant, saying from elsewhere in Q (Matt. 11.12f=Luke 16.16), and adduces the evidence of Mark, which he uses again himself in its proper context (Matt. 11.14=Matt. 17.12=Mark 9.13), whereas Luke adds details which he feels to be required from a narrative point of view (Luke 7.20f, 29f). The final proverbial comment, where a different word for 'children' is used,[9] may be a separate unit, with which the whole sequence was rounded off in the source.[10]

The Semitic character of this pericope has often been stressed.[11] It is therefore pertinent to point out that the words for 'man' accord with Aramaic idiom. 'Men' (*anthropous*) at the beginning corresponds with the plural of *enash*, 'the son of man' with *bar enasha*, and 'a glutton and a drunkard' includes the idiomatic *anthropos*, representing the indefinite use of *enash*. Though it may seem at first sight that *bar enasha* here is an exclusive reference to Jesus, which is no doubt how Matthew and Luke understood it, recognition of the generic usage once more proves to be both possible and illuminating.

The point at issue is the response to Jesus' preaching. Jesus complains that 'the men of this generation' refuse to heed his words. Obviously this is not true of all his hearers. But there are some among them who excuse themselves from accepting the challenge of his message on the grounds that his behaviour disqualifies him from any claim to be a spokesman for God. Jesus shows up the shallowness of this criticism by comparing the reaction to John the Baptist. In his case also the people, presumably the same people, refused to accept his message, but this was on the grounds that his ascetical behaviour was proof that he was possessed. So they rejected the Baptist because he was an ascetic, and now they reject Jesus because he in *not* an ascetic! The comparison with the unresponsive children in the market is very apt.[12]

Evidently there is an element in Jesus' audience which is opposed both to the Baptist (now no longer active) and to Jesus. The same situation is found in the question of authority, Mark 11.27–33, where 'the chief priests and scribes and elders' refuse to accept the authority of both, whereas 'the crowd' regards John as a prophet and (by implication) Jesus too. The use of the term prophet shows that the point at issue is whether Jesus preaches by divine inspiration or not. It appears that this cannot be reasonably denied, so that those who wilfully refuse to accept his teaching are forced to resort to unfair criticisms. In the question on authority Jesus refuses to give an answer, so that it seems that the question is a trap to lure him into saying something incriminating. In the present case the issue of authority is not brought out into the open. But it is clearly what is at stake. Thus in both cases Jesus is wary about making an open claim regarding his divine inspiration.

In the present case Jesus avoids making an open claim by means of the *bar enasha* idiom. Whereas John the Baptist was called a madman when he came as an ascetic, when *someone else* comes to do similar evangelistic work, but carefully avoids the rigorous asceticism which was held against John, he is dismissed as a self-indulgent person. It is implied that a true assessment would recognize that *both* John and Jesus could justly claim divine inspiration for their teaching. The challenge which this entails cannot be evaded by resorting to the tactics of a smear-campaign. The personal reference to Jesus is obvious. But the generic *bar enasha* raises the matter to the level of a principle. If the criticism of the Baptist is false, then comparable criticism of anyone who may be classed with him is equally false. Thus Jesus indicates his personal position indirectly, by classing himself with the Baptist as another of the same group. It is not necessarily implied that there could be no others in this group. The use of the illustration from children's games places all the emphasis on the illogicality of the response of Jesus' detractors. It also combines with the *bar enasha* idiom to produce a disarming irony. Jesus is appealing to his opponents to think, and does not wish to be drawn into open hostilities. Consequently Jesus does not refer to himself directly, but sets the issue in a wider context. It is easy to see why 'the great throng heard him gladly' (Mark 12.37), and the saying stuck in people's minds.

Finally, the saying has christological significance, because the point at issue is divine authority. Jesus may or may not have claimed to be the Messiah. But he certainly made *some* claims with regard to himself. So here he refuses to allow any denial of his commission from God.

3 *Matthew 12.32 = Luke 12.10*

Whoever says a word against bar enasha *will be forgiven; but whoever speaks against the Holy Spirit will not be forgiven.*

The text followed this time is that of Matthew, omitting the final words 'either in this age or in the age to come', which are clearly a Matthean elaboration based on Mark, and do not appear in Luke. As very often happens, the two versions are so closely similar that dependence on a common written source seems certain, but the differences between them show characteristic divergences on the part of the two evangelists. Thus Luke retains the Semitic 'everyone who' (*pas hos* and indicative representing Aramaic *kol* and participle) against Matthew's more idiomatic *hos ean*.[13] On the other hand Luke changes the relative clause into a participle in the second member of the saying out of a liking for stylistic variation,[14] whereas Matthew retains the formal identity between the two halves.[15]

It has long been recognized that the Son of Man in this verse gives a false impression of Jesus' meaning, if it is taken to be the apocalyptic title of the glorified Christ. This is a clear case where the generic use of *bar enasha* is required, for the contrast is between slandering men and blaspheming the Spirit of God. Moreover there is an independent version of this saying in Mark 3.28–9, which does not include the Son of Man, though 'the sons of men' are mentioned, suggesting a bifurcation of the tradition before the Greek translations were made. Luke omits the Marcan version, but Matthew has brought the two versions together in typical style.[16] The relationship between the two versions can be seen when they are set out in parallel in literal translation (see table below).

Matt. 12.31f	*Mark 3.28f*	*Luke 12.10*
Therefore I say to you, every sin and blasphemy will be forgiven to men,	Amen I say to you that all things will be forgiven to the sons of men, the sins and the blasphemies, whatever they blaspheme;	
but the blasphemy against the Spirit will not be forgiven.		
And whoever speaks a word		And everyone who will speak a word
against (*kata*) the son of man, it will be forgiven to him;		against (*eis*) the son of man, it will be forgiven to him;
but whoever speaks against (*kata*) the Holy Spirit it will not be forgiven to him,	but whoever blasphemes against (*eis*) the Holy Spirit does not have forgiveness	but to him who blasphemes against (*eis*) the Holy Spirit it will not be forgiven.
neither in this world (*aiōn*)	for ever (*aiōn*), but is guilty of an	
nor in that which is to come.	eternal (*aiōnios*) sin.	

The comparison shows that Matthew has conflated the two versions of the saying in such a way as to leave both of them virtually intact.[17] On the other hand Luke, preferring to give the Q version only, has been influenced by Mark, from whom he has derived the verb 'blasphemes'. This represents a more idiomatic Greek translation of the underlying Aramaic, which in Q is rendered more literally by 'speaks a word against'. It thus seems probable that the Q version (beginning 'everyone who', as in Luke, but in *both* members of the saying, which otherwise is most closely rendered in Matthew) is nearer to the original than Mark's more elegant Greek. This is confirmed by the *casus pendens* construction in both Matthew and Luke ('everyone who' picked up by 'to him' at the end of the sentence), which is another Semitism.

Further examination of the two versions resolves the remaining differences between them in favour of Q. If 'blasphemes' is an idiomatic translation of 'speaks a word against', it is clear that it *must* have an object, for to 'speak a word' does not mean to 'blaspheme' unless it includes 'against'. Hence in Mark 3.28 'the sons of men' is required as the object of 'blasphemes', though as it now stands it does duty for 'to him' in the Q version. This is because the indeclinable word 'all' (rendered 'everyone' in Q) has been

35

taken to mean 'all things', and so regarded as in apposition to 'word' (understood as 'things'), and the sentence has been wrongly divided, thus:

	we-	kol	di	yomar		millah	le-bar enasha
Q	And	everyone	who	says		a word	against a man,
Mk	—	every	which	one blasphemes		thing,	to mankind

	yishtebeq	leh
Q	there will be forgiveness	to him.
Mk	there will be forgiveness	for it.

The form in Mark is possible, because *millah*=a word can also mean 'affair', 'thing', like Hebrew *dabar*. It is in any case used collectively. This accounts for the plural in Mark. Similarly the generic *bar enasha*[18] can be a collective (hence the translation 'mankind'), so that Mark's plural does not require a different underlying form. At the end of the sentence 'to him' in Q resumes the logical subject of the sentence (everyone who says). But in Mark the logical subject is 'mankind', so that *leh* refers back to 'every . . . thing'.[19] The translation 'blasphemes' for *yomar* is not strictly correct, as already explained, but depends upon the following parallel ('speaks against the Holy Spirit'), in which 'a word' has been omitted by ellipsis (*we-kol di yomar le-rucha de-qudsha, la yishtebeq leh*). Consequently Mark's form has the explanatory addition of 'the sins and the blasphemies' in apposition to *kol . . . millah*. Finally, in this second member of the saying, Mark's 'never' represents a strengthening of the negative at the end of the sentence, which might have been made already in one tradition of the underlying Aramaic (*la . . . le-'alema*). Matthew has strengthened it still further.

The general meaning of the saying is the same in both Mark and Q: slander against a man can be forgiven by God,[20] but not slander against the Holy Spirit. This might be taken to be an entirely general statement. But it is unlikely that it was spoken without relation to particular circumstances, and Mark may well be right in bringing it into the context of the Beelzebul controversy. The opponents of Jesus attempt to discredit Jesus by attributing his spiritual powers to collusion with the evil spirits themselves. But since Jesus' exercise of spiritual power is wholly for good, the suggestion is obviously false. More than that, spiritual powers not derived from evil spirits must be derived from the Spirit of the Lord himself,[21] so that the suggestion amounts to blasphemy.

With this setting in mind, we can see that the saying is both a general statement and a particular defence of Jesus himself. As in the preceding example, Jesus refuses to allow any suggestion that his commission does not come from God himself. To slander him as a man would be pardonable, but to slander the Spirit who inspires him and works through him is far more serious. Jesus uses the generic *bar enasha* to categorize one of two classes of slander, which have been confused in the attack upon his integrity. But because he is himself the person who is under attack, *bar enasha* also has a self-reference. Thus the saying can be paraphrased as follows: You can slander me as a man, because anyone who slanders a man can be forgiven; but you may not slander me as one who is inspired by the Spirit, because anyone who slanders the Spirit cannot be forgiven. More briefly: Anyone who slanders me as a man can be forgiven; but anyone who slanders the Spirit who works in me cannot be forgiven.

The Greek translation preserved in Mark has lost the self-reference involved in Jesus' use of the idiomatic use of generic *bar enasha*. The Q form on the other hand has lost the general application, because in this form of sentence the article with Son of Man cannot be generic in Greek.[22] Hence it is bound to be a specific self-reference, and therefore a quasi-title, whether the identification with the Danielic Son of Man is intended or not. Naturally it was very soon interpreted as the apocalyptic title, and thus has caused difficulties to commentators both ancient and modern.[23] The Fathers applied the first part of the saying to sins done in ignorance before the baptismal confession of Jesus as Lord, which are done away by repentance and faith, and the second part to post-baptismal sin. This is obviously wrong, as there is no difference of time implicit in the two parts of the saying. But it probably explains the form in which the saying has been preserved in Thomas, logion 44, where the distinction seems to be made between the ignorant common believer and the true gnostic who possesses the Spirit:

> Jesus said: he who blasphemes against the Father will be forgiven, and he who blasphemes against the Son will be forgiven; but he who blasphemes against the Holy Spirit will not be forgiven, either on earth or in heaven.

In this form, the saying appears to be a warning against apostasy on the part of the gnostic who claims to have been illumined by the Spirit.

So long as modern scholarship held that the Son of Man was an apocalyptic title, it was customary to avoid the difficulty, either by taking Mark to preserve the original better, or by accepting Q but denying that any self-reference on Jesus' part was intended. Thus on the latter view the general meaning of *bar enasha* was regarded as the original intention, and the translation 'the Son of Man', and with it any reference to Jesus personally, was taken to be a mistake. But we have seen that Q does indeed preserve the original form of the saying better than Mark. We have also seen that the generic idiom allows *both* the general meaning *and* the specific reference to Jesus. The saying thus joins that which we have just studied in Matt. 11.19=Luke 7.34 in giving valuable insight into the way in which Jesus defended his position against those who accused him of being a charlatan. As before, there is in this saying an irony which carries with it a hint of a christological claim.

4 *Luke 11.30*

For as Jonah became a sign to the men of Nineveh, so will **bar enasha** *be to this generation.*

Once more we have to reckon with the relationship between Mark and the Q tradition, but this time it is complicated by important divergences between Matthew and Luke in their handling of the material. The feature that is common to Mark and Q is the request for a sign and its refusal. The use of a Son of Man saying in connection with the refusal is confined to Q. This in its turn is differently represented in Matthew and Luke.

Mark has the request for a sign, with curt refusal by Jesus, in Mark 8.11–12, and it is clear that the latter overlaps the refusal in Q:

Mark 8.12	*Luke 11.29*
Why does this generation seek a sign? Truly, I say to you, no sign shall be given to this generation.	This generation is an evil generation; it seeks a sign, but no sign shall be given to it except the sign of Jonah.

Mark breaks off abruptly, and proceeds to report a conversation in the boat on the significance of the feeding miracles (Mark 8.14–21). It is thus not clear whether his source included mention of 'the sign of Jonah', as in Q, and he omitted it deliberately, or whether this belongs only to the Q version.

Luke omits the whole Marcan sequence of which this forms a part, and it is not at all certain that he has been influenced by Mark in the course of reproducing Q.[24] He has this Q material in the context of the Beelzebul controversy, to which it very likely belonged in Q. This is indicated by Matthew, who, as we should expect, has the material in both places, the Q material in the Beelzebul controversy (Matt. 12.38–42), and the Marcan material in his version of Mark's sequence (Matt. 16.1–4). Where the two overlap he has assimilated the text, so that both passages read, 'An evil and adulterous generation seeks for a sign, but no sign shall be given to it except the sign of Jonah (+the prophet, 12.39) . . . '.

The Son of Man saying which we now have to consider provides the explanation of the sign of Jonah,[25] which has just been referred to. Matthew's version appears at first sight to be totally different from Luke's:

Matt. 12.40	*Luke 11.30*
For as (hosper) *Jonah was* (en) in the belly of the whale three days and three nights, *so shall the son of man be* in the heart of the earth three days and three nights.	*For as* (kathos) *Jonah was* (egeneto) a sign to the men of Nineveh, *so shall the son of man be* to this generation.

The italicized lines show, however, that both stem from the same original. Luke's version is clearly to be preferred, because it keeps wholly within the terms of reference set by the preceding verse. The manner in which Jonah was a sign to the Ninevites is described in the accompanying double saying (Matt. 12.41f=Luke 11.31f):

The men of Nineveh will arise at the judgement with this generation and condemn it; for they repented at the preaching of Jonah, and behold, something greater than Jonah is here.

The queen of the South will arise at the judgement with this generation and condemn it; for she came from the ends of the earth to hear the wisdom of Solomon, and behold, something greater than Solomon is here.[26]

Jesus pictures the Ninevites and the Queen of Sheba taking part in judgement upon the present generation.[27] They are entitled to join in condemnation of it, because they themselves responded in a proper manner when faced with a similar claim upon their attention. Moreover their own response appears more creditable, because the claim upon them was not so compelling. This is because 'something greater' is offered to the present generation. The Greek does not say 'someone greater'. The reference is to the preaching (wisdom) of Jesus rather than to Jesus himself. It is the context of his message that is greater than that of Jonah or than the wisdom of Solomon. Jesus is not really concerned with the personalities who will be present at the future judgement. He is concerned with the people's response *now*.

This gives the clue to the meaning of the Son of Man saying in Luke. Interpretation becomes impossibly difficult and complex if *bar enasha* is assumed to refer to Jesus as the apocalyptic Messiah, rather than to Jesus in his present capacity as a preacher of the kingdom of God. For it raises the question how 'this' generation can receive the assurance which is here promised. Even if Jesus expected to be revealed as Son of Man in this sense in the very near future, it would still be too late from this point of view, for the time of judgement would have already arrived.[28] Another difficulty is that Jonah and Jesus are not comparable, if Jesus is represented as the apocalyptic Son of Man, so that the whole point of the analogy is lost. The only way to get round this is to suppose that the comparison consists in two displays of divine power, the resurrection of Jonah from the whale's belly and the appearance of the Son of Man in glory.[29] This still fails to overcome the problem of relating present assurance to the future decisive act. So it then becomes necessary to suppose that Jesus is referring to his own death and resurrection. Of course the resurrection of Jesus can certainly be thought of as a sign to the present generation of the display of divine power that is yet to come. It will prove that Jesus was indeed the spokesman for God in this generation. In this way it can be argued that the reference is to a future event (as the future verb in Luke 11.30 requires), which will be available to the present generation, quite apart from what is said in the double saying which follows. The advantage of this interpretation is that it takes as the point of comparison the most notable thing in the book of Jonah, and it receives confirmation from the parallel in Matthew, in which this has become explicit.

A moment's thought will show that this line of interpretation cannot possibly be right. Even if the sign of Jonah could be understood by the audience to be his resurrection from the whale, they have no means of telling what Jesus is expecting concerning himself. They can scarcely be regarded as in a position to make out the analogy correctly, and reach the conclusion that Jesus is about to experience something comparable to being swallowed by a whale and spewed out onto the shore. In any case the Son of Man phrase is incapable of suggesting Jesus' future position, because it could not be recognized as a title of the apocalyptic Messiah without further definition. The most that can be said on the basis of the actual words in Luke 11.30 is that—in spite of refusing to give a sign as requested—Jesus will himself be a sign to the people in some way which is comparable to Jonah in his generation.

The double saying which follows has already suggested that the point of comparison between Jonah and Jesus is the preaching of repentance.[30] The *bar enasha* idiom at once overcomes all the difficulties of interpretation. It is another case of the generic usage, comparable to those which we have already studied. Just as Jonah was a sign to the Ninevites, i.e., bore witness to God through his preaching to them, so there is a man who will be a sign to the present generation. Those who seek for a sign must look around them and see where they can find anything comparable to the situation of Jonah and the Ninevites. Of course it is implied that they should be able to see it in Jesus himself. Like Jonah, he is preaching and men are repenting. The point of naming Jonah rather than any other prophet is the exceptional fact that his hearers actually did respond to his preaching, contrary to the usual experience of the Old Testament prophets. It is no accident that Jesus has chosen to refer to Jonah. No other prophet would make the point. Thus people who demand a sign are invited to look at the response which Jesus is actually receiving, and they will no longer need to have a dramatic sign from heaven.

Objection has been made to interpretation along these lines on the grounds that it fails to account for the future tense. The double saying, asserting that 'something greater . . . is here',[31] raises no problem, but this only serves to increase the difficulty of the present passage. In what sense does Jesus mean that 'a man *will be* a sign to this generation'? Two explanations are possible. It can be taken as a logical future, not signifying any particular time in relation to the present, but only the relationship to the past example of Jonah. From this point of view the present time is intended, because it is seen in terms of the divine ordering of events. Jonah was, in God's plan, a sign to the Ninevites, and God's plan also includes a sign for the present generation. The use of the future in this way follows naturally upon the use of the future in the preceding verse ('no sign *shall be* given'). An alternative explanation, which would remain valid if the saying were detached from its introduction in verse 29, is that the future here represents the idiomatic use of the Aramaic imperfect (future) tense to express modal tenses where there is an implication of indefiniteness.[32] This implication is provided by the generic *bar enasha*. It thus allows for the Aramaic original the translation, 'so a man *may be* to this generation'. This translation would not be possible if *bar enasha* referred exclusively to Jesus.

Before we leave this saying, two further points demand attention. In the first place the *composition* of Luke 11.29–32 is peculiar. There are three elements: request for a sign, with conditional refusal; the Son of Man saying, elucidating the mysterious 'sign of Jonah'; and the perfectly balanced double saying, of which only one member refers to Jonah. Precisely the symmetry of this saying causes the trouble, because it suggests that it was originally a complete unit in itself. We have already seen that the refusal of a sign has no exception in Mark, which casts doubt on the integrity of the first of the three elements. It is thus possible to argue that the sequence has been evolved in the Q collection of traditions by bringing together the request for a sign which originally made no mention of Jonah, with the double saying which was originally a separate unit. In this saying the presence of Jesus can be taken to constitute a sign, and so the refusal of a sign in the other material has to be modified in the light of it and the exception is added. Then the Son of Man saying is composed to provide a bridge between the first and third elements.[33]

It may be said in reply that the Son of Man saying does not necessarily depend upon close connection with the double saying, although on our exposition it is making the same point. It need not be regarded merely as a bridge saying, because the interpretation given above makes it fully comprehensible and extremely effective in itself. From this point of view we can accept the objection that 'the sign of Jonah' in verse 29 is an improbable phrase for Jesus to use. It is *this* which is the bridge, forming the link between the refusal of a sign (also attested in Mark 8.12) and the fact that this saying actually offers a sign. Hence 'the sign of Jonah' is a catchphrase formed on the basis of the use of 'sign' in the saying, thus linking the Q version of the refusal of a sign to the saying about Jonah. Finally, the relationship between verse 30, the Son of Man saying, and the double saying in verses 31–2, whatever their original form and ordering, is sufficiently explained in terms of catchword connection.

The second matter outstanding is the formation of the Son of Man saying in Matt. 12.40. Matthew presupposes the complete Q sequence of request for sign, promise of sign of Jonah, and the double saying, just as in Luke. It has already been shown that the basic structure of Matt. 12.40 is the same as that of Luke 11.30. It thus looks very likely that Matthew's version is a secondary alteration of the Q form preserved in Luke. Further examination confirms this impression. In Matt. 12.40 the Son of Man does not function as the generic *bar enasha*. It must refer to a particular person, who is to have the unusual experience of being in the heart of the earth for three days and three nights. The reference can only be to the death and resurrection of Jesus, which in the teaching of the early church was the sign of the coming fulfilment of the gospel message. The alteration of the saying in order to make this point has been undertaken simply to elucidate the lack of specification in the original. In spite of the double saying which follows, the original fails to explain in what way Jonah and Jesus can be said to be *signs*. In the original, with its idiomatic use of *bar enasha*, the emphasis falls on the *person*: so shall *a man* be to this generation. But when *ho huios tou anthropou* is taken to be an exclusive self-reference on the part of Jesus—which is certainly the way in which the evangelists understood it—so that it becomes merely a periphrasis for the first person (but carrying with it an overtone of future glory), the emphasis falls on the *sign*: something about Jesus will be so significant as to remove the necessity to seek any other sign. From this angle, exposition of the original saying will look for something comparable in the life of Jonah and the life of Jesus. The fact that this is 'death' and 'resurrection' need cause no surprise, because Jonah was a standing symbol of resurrection.[34]

It is most probable that Matthew himself is responsible for the change.[35] Matthew has a special interest in Old Testament prophecies of the life of Jesus, and frequently makes his own exegetical additions to his sources.[36] The use of the Son of Man in this saying is in line with his own understanding of the phrase. The forecast of resurrection has a precedent in the passion predictions, which Matthew will take over from Mark later in the gospel. It is true that the three nights suits better the Marcan form of the predictions ('after three days he will rise again', Mark 8.31) than Matthew's version of them ('on the third day he will be raised up', Matt. 16.22). This is because Matthew has adapted the wording of the predictions to the kerygmatic formulation in terms of Hos. 6.2.[37] But the 'three days and three nights' belongs to the Old Testament type (Jonah 1.17), and no doubt Matthew understood it correctly as a Semitic expression for 'three days'. There was no need to worry about the exact details of the calculation.[38]

5 *Matthew 9.6 = Mark 2.10f = Luke 5.24*

'*But that you may know that* bar enasha *has authority on earth to forgive sins'—he said to the paralytic—'I say to you, rise, take up your pallet and go home.*'

The three versions are identical as far as 'forgive sins', apart from slight variations in the order of words. Thereafter the differences between them are merely stylistic. The saying comes at the climax of the story of the paralysed man, who was let down through the roof of the house where Jesus was teaching, because the crowd around the door made it impossible to gain entry any other way. The saying is prepared for by the immediate response of Jesus to the situation.[39] Instead of healing the man, as is obviously expected and desired, he announces the forgiveness of his sins. The passive form, 'your sins are forgiven', suggests that he does so in the name of God.[40] This raises the question of his right to speak in God's name. The healing which follows then provides incontrovertible proof that he does have this right, for this is a divine act where, in contrast with forgiveness of sins, the result can actually be seen.

It is clear that the Son of Man saying cannot be detached from its context as an isolated unit of the Jesus tradition which circulated separately. In fact the only reason why critics have sought to remove it is the difficulty caused by the Son of Man phrase itself.[41] But this disappears when it is put back into Aramaic. Once again, the saying gains its most convincing interpretation when full value is given to the generic usage of *bar enasha*. This does not necessarily imply a universal statement, that *any man* has authority on earth to forgive sins.[42] For, quite apart from the question whether Jesus is likely to have held this opinion, it is most improbable that he would refute the scribes by blandly denying their objection. His reply is much more cautious, 'But that you may know that *a man may have authority* . . . '. The indefinite quality of the generic *bar enasha* applies to the verb (unexpressed in Aramaic in such a sentence as this),[43] just as in Luke 11.30. The generic article limits the application to those to whom such authority is given. The authority to forgive sins may belong to God alone as of right, but this does not prevent him from delegating it to those whom he chooses.

Vermes has drawn attention to the relevance of the fragmentary Prayer of Nabonidus found at Qumran to this passage.[44] In this document Nabonidus, the last of the Babylonian kings, tells how he was cured of an ulcer by a Jewish exorcist.[45] The situation is reminiscent of the story of Nebuchadnezzar in Dan. 4, though the connection between them (if any) remains unclear. The part of the document which concerns us is rendered by Vermes as follows:

> The words of the prayer uttered by Nabunai king of Babylon, [the great] king, [when he was afflicted] with an evil ulcer in Teiman by decree of the [Most High God]. I was afflicted [with an evil ulcer] for seven years . . . and an exorcist pardoned my sins. He was a Jew from among the [children of the Exile of Judah, and he said], 'Recount this in writing to [glorify and exalt] the Name of the [Most High God].'

Two features have a bearing on our present passage. Firstly, the Jew is the agent of the forgiveness of Nabonidus' sins, which Nabonidus himself assumes to be the cause of his ulcer. He suffered this affliction by divine decree. Hence it is the forgiveness of God which the Jew has mediated. Secondly, the healing is not described, but the implication is that healing and forgiveness are one and the same thing. The cure (not necessarily an exorcism) performed by the Jew is itself the act of divine forgiveness, releasing Nabonidus from the consequences of his sins.

The text justifies us in seeing a very close connection in the thought of the times, not only between sin and sickness, but also between healing and forgiveness. One who has power to heal also has power to forgive in God's name. It is quite wrong, however, to suppose that this applies to everyone. In a culture where medical remedies had little effect, charismatics possessing healing powers

45

were in much demand. We have already seen in connection with the Beelzebul controversy that Jesus insisted that his healing powers came from the Spirit of God, and regarded it as blasphemy to deny it. Here again the scribes are attempting to discredit his claim to act on behalf of God. Whereas in the other case they suggested that his powers come from a compact with the demons themselves, here they counter Jesus' claim to forgive in the name of God by denying that *anyone* has the authority to do so. Jesus replies by drawing attention to the close connection between forgiveness and healing. It cannot be said that healing does not come from God. So the scribes must allow that there are *some* people who have God's mandate to heal, and if so they also have his mandate to forgive sins in his name. To such people Jesus himself belongs.

It has often been remarked that the account in Mark 2.1–12 fails to capitalize this controversial point. Instead, the story finishes with the astonishment of the crowd at what has happened. But Mark does say that they 'glorified God', and this surely implies that they acknowledge that the powers which Jesus has displayed come from God. Interestingly, Matthew expands this by saying that 'they glorified God, who had given such authority to men (*tois anthropois*)'. It might almost seem as if he has correctly understood the *bar enasha* idiom here. But this is not really likely to be the case, because he normally understands the Son of Man as an exclusive self-reference on Jesus' part. The plural 'men' may well be a reference to the authority of the church to forgive sins, which is derived from him (cf. Matt. 18.18).

The above interpretation places the *bar enasha* saying in the same category as several which we have already considered. Jesus uses the idiom in order to defend himself against his detractors. The idiom is often ironical. It avoids any suspicion of egotism. It suggests a strong sense of commission from God without putting this in the form of aggressively open claims. The present passage differs, however, from preceding examples, because this time it is not merely a matter of a saying of Jesus, which might well be remembered with a fair degree of accuracy, but a well-articulated miracle story. Can it be accepted as historical? If not, does the Son of Man saying lose its claim to authenticity?

The story as a whole stands at the head of a series of controversy stories (Mark 2.1—3.6), which may have existed as a collection before Mark incorporated them into his gospel.[46] These episodes have been brought together because of their representative character. They are typical illustrations of a distinctive feature of the ministry of Jesus, as it was remembered by his followers. It would be a mistake to press the details historically, for such memories are concretizations of the general impression given by an outstanding personality rather than verbatim reports of precise occasions. They thus share many of the characteristics of hagiography in general and conform to the well known laws of folk-lore. The question of authenticity should be attached, not to the details of the story, but to the personality which emerges from it. Does the story ring true as an expression of the kind of man Jesus was and the sort of things which he did and said? The answer must be yes, though the story is artificially contrived, and the most colourful motif of it, the lowering of the man through the roof (which may preserve a factual memory), is not typical.[47] Other features, however, recur frequently: the success of Jesus in his approach to the common people, the declaration, or display, of the graciousness of God, the hostility of the scribes, and the skill with which Jesus refutes their objections. Our study of the Son of Man sayings in this chapter has shown his very effective use of the *bar enasha* idiom to fend off such criticisms in four out of the five examples which we have considered, the only exception being the first. This is enough to establish it as a style-feature of Jesus. So this last of the four examples of this usage can be regarded as authentic, inasmuch as it does conform to the pattern of one facet of the personality of Jesus which is strongly attested.

It may well be the case that the Son of Man saying which we have just considered, so far from being an intrusive element in the story of the paralyzed man, is the most authentic item in the whole pericope. Interpretation of it in the light of the *bar enasha* idiom places it in a fresh category. Instead of being the means of a personal claim on the part of Jesus, it is seen to belong to his vital concern for the integrity of his message from God. It is because he recognizes that the personal attack upon him is an attempt to discredit the gospel itself that he defends his position with such skill and circumspection.

6 *Matthew 10.32f = Luke 12.8f.*

Everyone whoever will make
  confession
of me before man,
I also will make
confession of him before
my Father who is in the
  heavens;
but whoever may deny
me before men,
I also will deny him
before my Father who is in
the heavens.
	Everyone who may make
	  confession
	of me before men,
	bar enasha *also will make*
	confession of him before
	the angels of God;
	
	but he who denies
	me in the presence of men
	will be denied
	in the presence of the angels
	of God.

This is a specially interesting saying, because there are versions of it in both Mark and Q, and it can be shown that the differences between them arise from independent translations from a single Aramaic original, which has bifurcated in the oral stage of transmission. I have given above a very literal translation of the Q form of the saying, and the differences between Matthew and Luke's versions of it are represented exactly (e.g., will make/may make; before=*emprosthen*/in the presence of=*enopion*, etc.). I have also attempted to indicate the Semitism, common to both Matthew and Luke, which appears in the phrase *homologesei en*, by using 'make confession of' intead of 'confess'. Before we look at the version in Mark, some of the salient features in the Q form may be pointed out.

In the first place, the saying is an antithetic couplet, and the symmetry of the two parts is better preserved in Matthew. Each part can be subdivided further into a synthetic couplet, in which the first half ('everyone . . . before man') balances the second half, although grammatically and syntactically it forms a *casus pendens*, in apposition to 'of him' (*en auto*) in the second clause. The structure of each part is thus:

> everyone . . . me . . . men
> I . . .   him . . . the Father.

A more idiomatic translation in English would bring the first half into the main clause, i.e., 'I will confess before the Father everyone who confesses me before men'. It need hardly be said that the structure and parallelism of the saying are typical of Semitic proverbial sentences.

Both Matthew and Luke have retained 'everyone' (*pas*) in the first part. As we saw in connection with Matt. 12.32=Luke 12.10, this is another Semitic feature, which might well be dropped in an idiomatic translation. It is thus probable that it also stood in the underlying Aramaic at the beginning of the second half too, but the absence of it there from both Matthew and Luke suggests that it was already omitted in Q. The Semitic construction requires that 'everyone' should be followed by a participle, but this is correctly represented by the 'whoever' clause with either future indicative (Matthew, first half), or more idiomatically *an* with subjunctive (Matthew, second half; Luke, first half). Luke's use of the aorist participle in the second half (='he who denies'), however, is not to be taken as closer to the original, which would certainly have produced the present participle if the participial construction had been retained, but is simply due to Luke's stylistic preference. He dislikes symmetry, and uses the aorist participle for the sake of variation (cf. 12.10, p. 34 above). This would also be regarded as more elegant Greek.

On the other hand Luke is closer to the original in his expression 'before the angels of God', varied only to 'in the presence of the angels of God'.[48] This is a typical Semitic circumlocution for God, in which the attendant angels 'are introduced as agents in place of God, to dissociate feelings and decisions from God'.[49] Matthew has changed this to his customary formula, presumably regarding it as more consonant with Jesus' style.

The chief and most obvious difference is that only Luke uses the Son of Man with third person verb in the main sentence, whereas Matthew has the pronoun *ego* and first person verb. Astonishingly, in view of the important overtones of the Son of Man title in the gospels, Luke has removed it from the second part of the saying. The verb is changed to passive,[50] and so the subject does not need to be expressed. This again spoils the symmetry of the saying. It also affects the interpretation, as it reduces the strongly marked correlation between the one who denies Jesus and Jesus himself, and indeed virtually cuts out the activity of Jesus altogether. Whereas in the first half Jesus himself (for, of course, Luke does not mean anybody else when he mentions the Son of Man)[51] acknowledges the one who confesses him, in the second half the part played by Jesus has to be deduced by inference. All the emphasis goes on the verb (which Luke uses here in a strengthened form),[52] and so concentrates attention upon the divine verdict. It may be that, while Luke was content to represent Jesus as advocate in the coming judgement, he wished to avoid representing him as accuser.

It does not need to be argued that Matthew's *ego* form and Luke's *bar enasha* form virtually mean the same thing, and go back to one original. But it is not so easy to decide what that was. Matthew tends to add the Son of Man to his sources, and the one occasion when he removes it is only an apparent exception.[53] On the other side, it is often claimed that Luke does not create Son of Man sayings. This claim may be doubted, as we shall see, but the possibility that the original did make use of the *bar enasha* idiom cannot be lightly dismissed. For we have further evidence in the Marcan form, to which we now turn:

Matt. 16.27	*Mark 8.38*	*Luke 9.26*
For	For whoever may be ashamed of me	For whoever may be ashamed of me
	and of my words in this adulterous and sinful generation,	and of my words,
bar enasha	of him will *bar enasha* also be	of this one will *bar enasha* be
is about to come in the glory of his Father	ashamed, when he comes in the glory of his Father	ashamed, when he comes in the glory of him(self) and the Father
with his angels, and then he will repay everyman according to his work.	with the holy angels.	and the holy angels.

At first sight the differences from the Q saying are greater than the similarities. Mark 8.38 corresponds only with the second half of the complete saying. On the other hand it has undergone expansion in ways which affect the interpretation. Instead of the picture of Jesus as the prosecuting witness at the heavenly tribunal, the latter part of the saying has been turned into a more conventional representation of the parousia of the Son of Man alluding to Dan. 7.13, in which the Son of Man is both prosecutor and judge. There is no difficulty about this combination of functions, because it is normal in apocalyptic judgement scenes.[54] Matthew has seized on this feature as the real point of the saying. He has cut out the first part, no doubt because he has already used this motif in its Q form in 10.32–3, and has added a description of the Son of Man's judicial activity in words drawn entirely from the Old Testament.[55] Luke slightly enhances the impression given by Mark. Significantly, neither Matthew nor Luke has changed the Son of Man into the *ego* form.

The fact that we really do have here an independent version of the same saying as we have been considering, and not a separate saying with a similar motif, receives striking confirmation when the underlying Aramaic is reconstructed. The Q saying has the verb 'deny' and Mark has the verb 'be ashamed of'. This appears to be a substantial difference in English. But it has been shown that the difference has arisen out of confusion between two Aramaic words which are very similar in sound, *haphar* = be ashamed of, and *kephar* = deny.[56] This at once suggests that a common original has bifurcated at the oral stage, resulting in two different Greek translations. Moreover this must have happened after the second half of the complete saying had been detached from the first half. For the ideas of confession (acknowledgement) and denial are correlative, and so long as the integrity of the saying was maintained it would be less likely that *kephar* would be misheard as *haphar*. The separation of the second half can be explained by its value as a moral warning. This has been emphasized by the addition of 'and my words', which spoils the correlation of subjects (whoever/*bar enasha*) and objects (me/him).[57] It is the teaching, rather than personal allegiance to Jesus, which may be the object of shame. This alters the implied setting from the witness which disciples may have to give in the synagogue or court-house to their example in the world at large. Hence there is another change, as 'before men' becomes 'in this adulterous and sinful generation'. This phrase (more characteristic of Q than of Mark and therefore probably added in the pre-Marcan stage) stems from a natural tendency to use stereotyped phrases, when the saying is exploited in the course of moral teaching. It is implied that there is a danger that the disciples will fall away from the standards of Jesus' teaching and be ensnared by the wicked ways of the world. So yet another correlation of the underlying saying is lost, as the contrast between the tribunal of men and the tribunal of God disappears.

All the features which differentiate the Q form from the Marcan form have now been accounted for with one exception. It remains to decide whether the original Aramaic, which lies behind both forms, employed the *bar enasha* idiom or not.

The experience which we have so far gained in handling these sayings suggests that the evangelists thought of *ho huios tou anthropou* primarily as a circumlocutory self-reference on the part of Jesus. Although they were aware of the connection with Dan. 7.13, they did not make the modern mistake of regarding it as a recognized title for the Danielic figure, and therefore were not bound to use it only in apocalyptic contexts. When Luke, in 22.48, makes Jesus say, 'Judas, would you betray the Son of Man with a kiss?' he is continuing the style of the passion sayings, and introduces no apocalyptic allusions. If, then, our saying had had the *ego* form, as in Matthew, in the original Aramaic, it would be necessary to suppose a deliberate change to the *bar enasha* form at a later stage to account for the forms in Mark and Luke. This could scarcely have taken place before translation into Greek, because the natural way of changing from first person to third person is to adopt an expression such as *hahu gabra* which makes the self-reference exclusive. But if the change were made at the Greek stage, and *ho huios tou anthropou* were substituted for *ego*, we then have to explain why this was done in the second part of each half of the saying only, and not from the very beginning. What would be wrong with, 'Whoever confesses the Son of Man before men, him will the Son of Man also confess . . . '? But neither Mark nor Luke has done this.

It is necessary to give a satisfactory account of both forms. This can be done if *bar enasha* stood in the original saying. Seeing that we have to postulate bifurcation of the saying before the Greek translation was made, it follows that we are dealing with two independent Greek translations. In one of them, employed by Mark, the usual literal translation of *bar enasha* was used. This makes sense, for the saying lends itself to interpretation in the light of Dan. 7.13, and this is precisely what has happened in Mark's version of it. In the other, however, which found its way into Q, the *ego* form was adopted as an idiomatic rendering of the Aramaic which better expressed the identity between Jesus' references to himself, and so sharpened the point of the saying. This is the form given in Matthew. Luke, however, has already reproduced the Marcan form, with some abbreviation but very little change, at

Luke 9.26. Moreover his interpretation of the saying is guided by another Son of Man saying which we have already considered, and which he now incorporates as the very next verse in his compilation, i.e., Luke 12.10. He thus has every encouragement to insert *ho huios tou anthropou* into the Q saying, so as to bring it into line with the Marcan form which he has already used.[58] Thus the *ego* form belongs to the Q version and the Son of Man form to the Marcan version, but both go back to a common original using *bar enasha*.

It is, of course, impossible to be sure of this reconstruction of the inter-relationships between the various forms of the saying, because it is necessarily a matter of guesswork to some extent. But there can be some confidence that all these forms go back to one Aramaic original which was not identical with any one of them, and read as follows:

> Every one who confesses me before men,
> him will *bar enasha* confess before the angels of God;
> every one who denies me before men,
> him will *bar enasha* deny before the angels of God.

We must now turn to the interpretation of the saying, and first we must try to decide the kind of situation to which it is addressed. The contrast of confession and denial places it in the context of the warnings of persecution, which Mark has in the Little Apocalypse (Mark 13.9–13) and Matthew has in the mission charge to the twelve apostles (Matt. 10.16–23). This indeed is the reason why Matthew has included it in the same chapter. This setting suits very well the situation in the post-resurrection period, when the young church had to face hostile reactions to its missionary work. But it is not impossible for the teaching of Jesus himself, because he certainly encountered opposition, and was well aware that the disciples whom he sent on mission (Mark 6. 7–13) would be likely to have the same experience.

But we may well ask whether confessing or denying *Jesus* can be taken behind the interests of the primitive church to the teaching of Jesus himself. It is precisely because this is a saying in which Jesus makes the attitude to himself the central issue that it seems to belong better to the post-resurrection situation, when confession of Jesus as Lord became the distinguishing feature of the Christian movement. In the light of this confessional position the saying makes a logical and satisfying sense. For one who confesses Jesus as Lord before an earthly tribunal can certainly hope that the exalted Lord himself will speak on his behalf before the tribunal of God.

The *bar enasha* idiom, however, forbids this simple interpretation. The generic usage does not permit an exclusive identification of Jesus with *bar enasha*, even though he has used the necessarily exclusive first person pronoun in the first clause. Thus it is not sufficient to explain the change from first person to *bar enasha* as motivated merely by the delicacy required in speaking of one's personal position.[59] This would still leave it as an exclusive self-reference, just as it is in the Greek, whether in the *ego* form of Q or in the form with *ho huios tou anthropou* in Mark.

If, then we take the idiom seriously, we shall have to paraphrase the saying something like this: 'All those who confess me before men will have a man to speak for them (i.e., an advocate) before the judgement seat of God; but all those who deny me before men will find that they have an accuser before the judgement seat of God.' The irony of the *bar enasha* idiom in the sayings of Jesus suggests that he intends to identify himself with this advocate or accuser in some way, but this is not the primary meaning of what he is saying.

To grasp the real meaning, we have to move away from the literal interpretation, which has inevitably been imposed upon it in the course of transmission in the early church, and which explains why it found its way into the mission charge in Matt. 10. Jesus is not really speaking about actual tribunals. He is using the idea as a metaphor. The matter is complex, because the heavenly tribunal is, in a sense, meant literally. For the apocalyptic tradition constantly uses the metaphor of a court-room to describe God in terms of royal state, and the coming judgement is, in Jesus' eyes, a real event. But this is analogical language, and the subtle ironies of Jesus' teaching do not support the idea that he conceived the judgement in crudely literal ways. For the earthly level, however, the implied court-room setting is required only for the parallelism between the earthly and the heavenly situations. Metaphorically, Jesus depicts his hearers as either publicly confessing him or publicly denying him. If a situation outside forensic procedures is intended, then it must be seen in a more general way, in terms of personal allegiance to Jesus and practical response to his message. From this point of view the pre-Marcan addition of 'and my words' in Mark 8.38 is a correct gloss.

It is thus not essential to assume that Jesus is referring to actual tribunals, and the persons to whom the saying is addressed need not be confined to the group of twelve who were sent out on mission. Jesus is speaking to all and sundry. The context in Q gives a correct impression of the kind of general exhortation to which the saying belongs. Jesus warns his hearers that things spoken in secret will ultimately be revealed (Luke 12.2f).[60] They are not to be afraid of men, but of him who has power over life and death, i.e., God himself (Luke 12.4f). They are to trust in God's providential protection (Luke 12.6f). Our saying immediately follows this, and by its antithetical construction takes up both sides of what has just been said. Those who respond to Jesus positively, and accept his message, and throw in their lot with him, will find themselves on the right side on the day of judgement. But those who are afraid to do so will ultimately regret it.

The purpose of the saying is to give ultimate significance to the response of the audience. Jesus' message is from God, and it is so important that to respond to him as God's messenger has ultimate consequences. The decision which confronts his hearers is crucial.

Jesus makes this assertion by means of a close correlation between response to him in the present and the judgement which is to come in the future. The point is that, at that dire moment, their response to him will be quoted back at them. Thus it is their own response which is the advocate or the accuser, whichever is appropriate. What Jesus is saying has a splendid parallel in a saying ascribed to Rabbi Eliezer ben Jacob (a pupil of Akiba in the early second century AD):

> He that performs one precept gets for himself one advocate; but he that commits one transgression gets for himself one accuser. Repentance and good works are a shield against retribution.[61]

This is a typically rabbinic spiritualizing of the judgement, carefully removed from the eschatological setting which characterizes Jesus' preaching of the kingdom of God, and gave to it its sense of urgency. The need for an immediate decision, affecting the whole of one's life, is here replaced by a timeless situation, in which it is possible to count up one's successes or failures in keeping the precepts of the law. They will all be weighed up at the final judgement, and the verdict will be given according to merit. There is thus a fundamental difference between this rabbinic saying and the essential stance of Jesus. Nevertheless the motif of the two sayings is strikingly similar.

It now becomes possible to see that *bar enasha* in Jesus' saying is simply one element in a larger metaphorical construction. The real point is the positive or negative attitude of the audience themselves. Their own words will be quoted back at them when they come face to face with God. This could be the witness of their own hearts, for it is a time when secrets are exposed. But that might suggest the possibility of covering up the truth, if it depends upon themselves to unlock the secrets. But God knows already, and can confront them with the truth about themselves. Following a well known pictorial concept of the divine judgement, Jesus presupposes that God has his own source of information, which makes it impossible for men to hide anything from him. This idea is often expressed in apocalyptic descriptions by the idea of the book of life.[62] But in the Enoch literature, which flourished in New Testament times, the patriarch Enoch has the duty of recording the wickedness of mankind and bringing it to God's notice at the proper time.[63] Thus *bar enasha* in our saying could be pictured as a sort of recorder in this way, an Enoch figure, though it is important to remember that here we are concerned with a recorder of good as well as evil, whereas Enoch is specially concerned with men's sins.

In the light of these considerations, it might almost seem as if there is no need to identify the advocate or accuser with Jesus himself. But the irony of the idiom with *bar enasha* requires this too. Metaphorically speaking, Jesus will be there at the judgement to give the appropriate testimony. But this side of the matter must not be overemphasized. The object of the second part in each half of the saying is to reinforce the first half. It is to impress upon the hearers the importance of their reaction to him, whether it takes the form of confession, as he hopes, or it takes the form of denial. It is now, in this moment of crisis, that the response to Jesus matters so much. But this is not because Jesus holds a formal eschatological position, but because it is his own teaching from God which is at stake. Because of his certainty that his message is derived from God, he can assert that acceptance of his message is bound to procure a favourable verdict from God. And the opposite is equally true.

The use of the *bar enasha* idiom positively reduces the emphasis on the person of Jesus himself. The stress falls on the relationship between the two situations in which confession and denial take place respectively, i.e., before men and before the tribunal of God. There is certainly a self-reference on Jesus' part, but it is not his purpose to make any personal claim. Paraphrasing the saying briefly, we can put it like this, 'If you confess me before men, I will confess you *before God*'. That is the tremendous implication of the decision which Jesus requires, and gives it its ultimate quality. An exclusive self-reference, on the other hand, would alter the emphasis, 'If you confess me before men, *I myself* will confess you before God'. This draws attention to the personal position of Jesus. Naturally, insofar as he thought of the divine judgement in realistic terms, he would expect to be there, and, as God's spokesman, to have an important position in the proceedings. But his ironical and allusive references to this situation suggest that he wishes to turn attention away from such details to the essential matter of people's personal relationship with God.

The Greek translations, both the *ego* form in Q and the Son of Man form in Mark, have failed to preserve the subtlety of the *bar enasha* idiom. They have made it into an exclusive self-reference, and thereby placed the emphasis on the eschatological position of Jesus himself. This need cause no surprise, for such an understanding of the saying was inevitable in the light of the primitive confession of Jesus as Lord. The saying thus holds a very important position in the development of the Son of Man sayings. Here is an example which has the marks of authenticity, and which requires an understanding of the *bar enasha* idiom for its proper elucidation. But it is easily interpreted in terms of the apocalyptic Son of Man, and is capable of being conformed to the picture presented by Dan. 7.13–14. It thus provides a bridge from the authentic sayings to sayings of the future coming of the Son of Man, which appear to be creations of the Church on the basis of identification of Jesus with the Danielic figure. We can now see that this was not an arbitrary development, but follows the lead already given by a saying which has every claim to be considered authentic, even if it was to some extent misunderstood.[64]

Finally, it is characteristic of Jesus to give first place to the element of grace. The saying is not intended as a dire warning, but as an exhortation to fearless confession, and the reference to the future judgement is a promise of reward. The negative aspect in the second half of the saying is thus intended to press home this point by drawing attention to its opposite, and not meant to strike terror in the breasts of the audience.[65] But the judgement metaphor inevitably tends to raise the spectre of condemnation. It is thus not surprising that the second half of the saying circulated apart from the first half as a moral warning. In this reduced state the verb was heard as 'to be ashamed of' rather than 'to deny', and although the difference of meaning is slight it is a verb which more naturally has an impersonal object. This explains the addition of 'and my words' in the form found in Mark 8.38, and justifies the suggestion that, when Paul says, 'I am not ashamed of the gospel', in Rom. 1.16, he is alluding to this same version of the saying.[66]

The six Son of Man sayings considered in this chapter are all amenable to interpretation according to the idiomatic use of generic *bar enasha* with a self-reference on the part of the speaker. In each case the meaning of the saying is illuminated when understood in this way. They thus have a high claim to be considered authentic. Several of them belong to the context of the opposition which Jesus encountered in the course of his ministry. They are concerned with his authority as a preacher on behalf of God. In these sayings Jesus defends himself in a subtle and ironical manner, which avoids making an open messianic or similar claim. As an unauthorized itinerant preacher, Jesus was bound to attract the attention of the religious establishment, and to be subjected to scrutiny. We are told that the scribes tried to trap him into incriminating himself, so that he had to be very careful about what he said. If they attempt to defame him on the grounds of keeping bad company, he can point to their equally hypocritical response to John the Baptist, who was an ascetic. If they object to his declaration of divine forgiveness, he can reply that it is within God's power to delegate this function to whomsoever he will. If they ascribe his healing ministry to a secret compact with demonic power, he can show that such an idea is a perversion of the truth. If they require a sign of authority, he can point to his success in conveying the message of God to the people as an indication of his commission from God, comparable to the success of Jonah with the Ninevites. But such controversies are not the only occasions when Jesus employs the *bar enasha* idiom. He uses it, too, in order to suggest to a prospective disciple the difficulties which he would have to share. He also uses it as a dramatic and telling way of pressing home the crucial importance of the people's response to him, because of the ultimate quality of the decision with which he confronts them.

These sayings differ sufficiently to make it most improbable that we are dealing with a stereotyped tradition. On the contrary, the idiomatic *bar enasha* is a genuine feature of Jesus' style. Imitations of it betray their secondary character by the fact that they do not properly represent the idiom, but require to be understood as exclusive self-references on the part of Jesus. They thereby lose the peculiar genius of his authentic voice, which has come across so strongly in the sayings which we have considered.

4

The Passion Predictions

The designation Son of Man is a special feature of the passion predictions in Mark. The relevant sayings have been taken over by Matthew and Luke. They have also probably influenced the Fourth Gospel to some extent. Just how important they were for Mark can be appreciated from the fact that the Son of Man is mentioned by Mark no less then nine times in connection with the passion of Jesus, but only five times elsewhere. Our enquiry will thus be chiefly concerned with the three formal predictions of the passion in Mark 8.31; 9.31; 10.33–4. But it will also take into account the references to the Son of Man which occur in Mark 9.9 and 12, and which are directly dependent upon 8.31. We shall also consider the very important 'ransom' saying of Mark 10.45. Finally, the Son of Man is mentioned three times in connection with the betrayal of Jesus by Judas Iscariot (Mark 14.21, 41). It will be shown that these sayings depend on three underlying Aramaic sayings, which can be reasonably regarded as authentic, and which have profoundly influenced the understanding of the death of Jesus in the primitive church.

1 'Bar enasha *may be delivered up*'

It is widely held that the three passion predictions in Mark go back to one underlying form, which Mark has expanded and varied for the purpose of his presentation of the gospel. The reason for this is the importance which Mark attaches to the passion of Jesus in relation to the confession of faith. The so-called 'messianic secret' is fundamental to the structure of Mark's Gospel.[1] The fact that Jesus is the Christ, and therefore the exalted Lord to whom Christians owe allegiance, is the message of the whole book. The gospel materials available to Mark, however, contained very little evidence that Jesus openly claimed to be Christ. Mark therefore presents it as a hidden truth, which is perceived gradually. It is known to the demons, who have access to the world of spirit, but these have to be silenced, to prevent the truth from being declared prematurely (1.24f, 34; cf. 5.7). Jesus speaks in parables, to hide the truth from all but the discerning (4.11f, 34). In spite of this the disciples are slow to grasp the truth (6.52; 8.14–21). But at Caesarea Philippi he challenges them on the subject, and Peter confesses that he is the Christ (8.27–9). Jesus at once orders the disciples to keep this secret, and then makes his first prediction of the passion (8.30f). Peter refuses to accept this, and earns a stern rebuke (8.32f). The juxtaposition of these two references to Peter is deliberate. Peter's confession is inadequate, if it does not include the fact that Jesus must suffer as Messiah. Jesus is the Christ, but only as the Christ who must be crucified before he rises and is glorified. In the narrative which follows, describing the journey of Jesus through Galilee and Peraea to Jericho and Jerusalem, this thought is kept before the reader's mind by the repetitions of the passion prediction and by the 'ransom' saying (10.45). Thereafter the narrative moves inevitably towards the arrest and trial and crucifixion, in which the predictions are fulfilled.

This brief survey is sufficient to show that the passion predictions have kergymatic significance for Mark. They perform an important role in the structure of the Gospel. This, as we shall see, is enhanced by the fact that they bear a close relationship with Mark's description of the passion itself. Moreover, each one ends with a prediction of the resurrection. This obviously carries further the kerygmatic character of the predictions in accordance with the confession of faith. But from the point of view of the purpose of Mark's Gospel, this feature has an importance all its own. For the resurrection is the climax to which the whole narrative leads. But it is not described! Mark finishes his Gospel with the story of the empty tomb, in which the angel announces that Jesus is risen and gives the message for the women to take to to the disciples that they must return to Galilee, where they will see him. But no description of this event is given.[2] We need not go into the question why this should be so. But it seems clear that Mark did not intend to include a resurrection appearance, and compensated for this by means of the resurrection predictions. Besides the three predictions with which we are now concerned, he added the story of the transfiguration immediately after the teaching on the cross (9.2–8), and made Jesus refer to the resurrection directly at the conclusion of it, so that its significance as a preview of post-resurrection glory should not be missed (9.9f). He also inserted Jesus' promise, 'After I am raised up, I will go before you into Galilee', into the forecast of Peter's denials (14.27–31), and inserted the angel's reference to this same saying in the empty tomb narrative (16.1–8).[3] Thus the reader has had ample preparation, and need be in no doubt, once the tomb has been found to be empty, that Jesus did appear to the disciples in Galilee in the end, even though this is not described. The connection of the resurrection predictions with the passion predictions is thus a matter of the greatest importance for Mark, because the accuracy with which the latter can be seen to be fulfilled in the story of the passion carries with it the presumption that the resurrection predictions were also fulfilled. It will be observed that Mark is careful to refrain from any elaboration in the resurrection predictions. For the only circumstantial detail which he gives in connection with the resurrection is the period of three days. Mark keeps this detail before the reader by means of the irony of the false witness at the trial of Jesus (14.58) and taunt at the cross (15.29), in both of which there is mention of three days. Then the empty tomb narrative is timed on the third day by implication (15.42; 16.1), and the resurrection is announced. Thus Mark is clear that the resurrection took place on the third day. But it does not at all follow that he believed that the risen Christ first appeared on the third day. In fact the journey of the disciples back to Galilee before his appearance would make this impossible.

Thus the passion predictions are also resurrection predictions. They therefore reflect the confession of faith which stands at the heart of the primitive kerygma. In recent years increasing importance has been attached to the confession of faith and summary of the resurrection appearances which Paul has incorporated in 1 Cor. 15.3–11.[4] This has features which mark it out as a pre-Pauline formula.[5] The prominence of Peter suggests that it is an official formulary of the Jerusalem church, which Paul received when he went to Jesusalem for consultation with Peter three years after his conversion (Gal. 1.18). If so, it must rank as one of the oldest confessional statements in the New Testament. Now the point which concerns us is that this statement of the death and resurrection of Jesus has several points in common with Mark's passion predictions. So it must be regarded as at least possible that a formula of this kind has exerted some influence upon the form of Mark's predictions. It is obvious that, if this is the case, it becomes very much more difficult to isolate the authentic basis (if any) of the passion predictions.

At this point it will be convenient to set out Mark's three predictions in parallel, and to subjoin the confession of faith in 1 Cor 15.3–4.

Mark 8.31	*Mark 9.31*	*Mark 10.33f*
And he began to teach them	For he was teaching his disciples, saying to them	'Behold we are going up to Jerusalem;
that the Son of man must	that 'The Son of man	and the Son of man
suffer many things	will be delivered	will be delivered
and be rejected by the elders	into the hands of men,	
and the chief priests and the scribes,		to the chief priests and the scribes
		and they will condemn him to death,
		and deliver him
		to the Gentiles;
		and they will mock him, and spit
		upon him, and scourge him,
and be killed	and they will kill him;	and kill him;
and	and when he is killed	and
after three days	after three days	after three days
rise again.	he will rise.'	he will rise.'

1 Cor. 15.3f

For I delivered to you as of first importance what I also received,
that Christ died for our sins in accordance with the scriptures,
that he was buried,
that he was raised on the third day in accordance with the scriptures.

It is clear from a first glance that Mark 9.31 gives the simplest of the three forms of the prediction. This, then, is likely to be the nearest to the underlying original saying. It can also be seen that the concluding prediction of the resurrection is virtually identical in all three cases, and that this is the part which accords most closely with the formula in 1 Cor. 15. Thus the first part, dealing with the passion, shows considerable variation, but the latter part is relatively fixed. Comparison with the parallels in the other gospels (Matt. 16.21; 17.23; 20.19: 'he will be raised on the third day'; Luke 9.22: 'and on the third day be raised'; Luke 18.33: 'and on the third day he will rise') shows that there is a tendency to conform this element to the confessional formula as it is given in 1 Cor. 15.4

(presumably, then, as it was current in the evangelists' own churches, as they probably did not have access to Paul's letters). In fact the two forms of the verb, 'rise' (active) in Mark and Luke 18.33, and 'be raised' (*sc.* by God, i.e., divine passive) in Matt., Luke 9.22 and 1 Cor. 15.4, are variant Greek renderings of one Aramaic original *yequm* (active, lit. = 'stand'). This is translated literally in the form known to Mark, but has been understood correctly in the other version as a substitute for the passive of the causative stem (= 'be caused to stand'), as in Syriac.[6]

The variations in the first part, however, are not due to the influence of the confessional formula, but relate to Mark's own narrative of the passion. It is precisely because he wishes his readers to see this element fulfilled in the ensuing narrative that he introduces exact details which can be easily verified. Thus 'the elders and the chief priests and the scribes' appear in connection with the plan to arrest Jesus in Mark 11.18, 27; 14.1, 10, 43, 53. The third prediction (10.33f) then continues with 'condemn him to death', which anticipates 14.64; 'deliver him to the Gentiles' anticipates 15.1; 'mock him', 15.20, 31; 'spit upon him', 14.65; 15.19; and 'scourge him' is reflected in 15.15, though a different Greek word is used.

A further influence upon the form of the predictions is the use of scripture in connection with the passion.[7] This is another feature which ties up with the formula in 1 Cor. 15.3–4, where the fulfilment of scripture is a constituent item of the confession of faith. It is probable that the verb 'to deliver' (*paradidonai*) is intended to allude to the prophecy of the suffering servant, Isa. 53, in which it occurs several times. This will be considered in greater detail below. But Mark creates his own link with scripture in the first prediction by using the word 'rejected' (*apodokimasthenai*). The only other place where he uses the same word is 12.10, where it occurs in a quotation of Ps. 118.22. The quotation has been added by Mark to the parable of the wicked husbandmen with the express object of emphasizing the application of it to the imminent arrest of Jesus by the Jewish authorities. But it seems likely that this scripture was used in conscious connection with the prophecy of Isa. 53. For when Mark repeats the first passion-prediction in the conversation following the transfiguration, he alters the verb (9.12): 'How is it written of the Son of Man, that he should suffer many things and be treated with contempt (*exoudenethe*)?' This is reminiscent of Isa. 53.3, where the same verb is used in the Greek versions of Aquila, Symmachus and Theodotion. This link becomes less tenuous when it is observed that, in the quotation of Ps. 118.22 which is ascribed to Peter in Acts 4.11, this verb is used instead of *apodokimazein*, which suggests that one text has been glossed in the light of the other. For our present purpose, however, it is not necessary to insist on this connection, which is bound to remain doubtful, because *exoudenein* is too common a word to permit certainty. It is sufficient that Mark uses *apodokimazein* only in these two places (8.31 and 12.10), for this fact alone shows that a scriptural allusion has influenced the form of the passion prediction in this case.

We have now discovered three factors which appear to have affected the passion predictions in Mark: the confession of faith, the form of Mark's own passion narrative, and the use of scripture in the primitive church. These factors show that the predictions relate to matters of central importance in the earliest formulations of the church's faith. A further glimpse at 1 Cor. 15.3–4 reinforces the connection beween Old Testament prophecy and the confessional formula. On the other hand, the repeated reference to the scriptures highlights the complete absence of any suggestion that the death and resurrection of Jesus had been predicted by Jesus himself. Are we to conclude that the predictions have been evolved entirely on the basis of the primitive confession? Have they arisen as *vaticinia ex eventu*, in the light of what actually happened?[8]

We seem to have lost sight of the Son of Man title in the complexity of these sayings. But it has an immediate bearing on the question of authenticity. So long as it was held that there was such a title in the background to the New Testament, it was naturally supposed to be a title of honour, and sayings which refer to the parousia of the Son of Man were regarded as representing its proper usage. Seen in this way, the Son of Man does not suit the passion predictions at all. Neither crucifixion nor resurrection can be proper actions of the Son of Man, who is more correctly spoken of as coming in glory. Hence the predictions could be accepted only in relation to the subsequent faith of the Church. The one who says that he must suffer and rise again is the one who, even then, was destined to be revealed as the Son of Man. Interpretation on these lines is bound to reduce the case for an authentic basis for the predictions.

According to the new approach to the Son of Man which is

adopted in this book, the connection with the parousia is not the starting point, but the conclusion, of the development of the usage in the sayings tradition. This begins with the *bar enasha* idiom, which we have found to be so illuminating in the last chapter. Only after these sayings have been translated into Greek does the Son of Man phrase begin to be treated as a title. Even at this stage it operates primarily as an exclusive self-reference on the part of Jesus. Though there may always be consciousness of the connection with Dan. 7.13 on the part of the evangelists in making use of the phrase, this comes to expression only in secondary developments where actual allusion to Daniel is indicated by the presence of other words and concepts. But it is never more than a quasi-title, because it had no currency outside the sayings tradition.

We must thus look again at the passion predictions to see whether the Son of Man functions in them according to the *bar enasha* idiom. Here we are hampered by the difficulty of reconstructing the original saying underlying them, free from the overlay of the various influences upon them which have been considered above. Casey has attempted a reconstruction on the basis of Mark 9.31, which he translates as follows, 'A man will die, but he will rise again at three days'.[9] Unfortunately at least three objections may be made against this reconstruction. Consideration of them may help towards a more satisfactory conclusion.

a. Because of his misunderstanding of the generic idiom, Casey has used the anarthrous form *bar enash* instead of the definite *bar enasha*. This makes the whole sentence an indefinite statement describing what is true of every man. That 'a man will die' in this sense is, as Casey himself says, 'an obvious commonplace'. Resurrection 'at three days' (a phrase designed to account for the bifurcation of the tradition into the two forms 'after three days' and 'on the third day') is certainly not a commonplace, even in a society, such as the main body of Judaism in the time of Jesus, which believed in the idea of resurrection. As an idiomatic expression for speedy renewal (cf. Hos. 6.2: 'After two days he will revive us; on the third day he will raise us up, that we may live before him') resurrection on the third day could perhaps be applied to every man.[10] A general statement of this kind is, however, extremely improbable, because it has left no trace in the rest of the New Testament. The idea is never applied to anyone except Jesus himself. Moreover, when it is understood in this general way, the reconstructed saying does not make a convincing statement on the part of Jesus. It remains a floating item, with no known context. For, of course, if the saying is a general statement it loses the ironical reference to the situation of Jesus himself. This requires the generic idiom, and it is bound to affect the way in which the verb is translated, as we have seen in several previous cases. This will help to explain why the word 'must' (Greek *dei*) appears in Mark 8.31, although it is very unlikely that it would be expressed in the underlying Aramaic, which does not have much capacity for modal expressions.[11] But the idea of necessity is not to be eradicated from the passion predictions, for it is reflected in a related Son of Man saying (Mark 14.21a), as we shall see later. Thus, leaving aside for the moment the remainder of Casey's reconstruction, we must at least modify it to begin as follows, 'A man may die . . . '. The *bar enasha* idiom would make excellent sense on this basis, if the completion of the sentence related to the achievement of Jesus' mission, e.g., 'a man may (must) die for the sake of God's chosen ones', or something similar. It would then suit a context in which the disciples are representing to Jesus the danger which he is courting by his open demonstrations in Jerusalem (cf. Mark 11.1–18). He replies that anyone who has the commission from God which he has is bound to incur such danger.

b. The second objection, however, is to the use of 'die' as the verb in the reconstructed form. This verb (Greek *apothneskein*) does not occur in any of the passion predictions, though it *is* used in the confessional formula of 2 Cor. 15.3, and Paul employs it fairly often when referring to the death of Jesus. But reconstruction of a single form underlying Mark's passion predictions cannot stray outside their range of vocabulary except with very good reason. In fact they include two excellent alternatives, and the only difficulty is to decide which is the right one.

(*i*) The first prediction (8.31; also 9.12 in dependence on it) has 'suffer many things' (*polla pathein*). This links up with the idiomatic use of *paschein* to denote, not just the endurance of pain, but the actual death of Jesus, which occurs quite commonly in the New Testament, especially in Luke–Acts, Hebrews and 1 Peter.[12] Some of the passages make allusion to Isa. 53, though the verb *paschein* does not occur in that prophecy. As we have already observed a connection between the first prediction and the passion scriptures, we may suspect that Mark has here used a word from the common stock of vocabulary relating to the passion. It is in fact employed here as an inclusive idea, comprising both rejection and execution, which accords well with the special use elsewhere in the New Testament.

(*ii*) The other alternative is 'be delivered' (*paradothenai*), which occurs in both the second and third predictions, and indeed in the third twice over. The double use in the third prediction, first to denote the betrayal of Jesus to the chief priests, and secondly to denote their handing him over to Pilate, brings a wide range of usage into play. For we not only find this verb used in connection with the death of Jesus in Paul,[13] but it also occurs with the Son of Man as subject twice more in Mark in connection with the betrayal by Judas Iscariot (14.21b, 41). In each case the verb is passive, but the real subject, or agent, of the action varies. Mark, as we have seen, has both Judas and the chief priests as agents. But Paul in Rom. 4.25 correlates the passive 'delivered' with the passive 'was raised' in such a way as to imply that the real subject is God, by whose will the acts of redemption have taken place. It thus seems likely that an original Son of Man saying circulated with this verb (Aramaic *mesar*), and was applied variously according to different ways of understanding the logical subject of the passive verb. It will be seen that this suggestion has the added advantage of bringing the betrayal sayings (Mark 14.21b, 41) into the scope of the reconstruction of the passion predictions.[14] Only one underlying saying is required to account for them all: *Ithmesar bar enasha*, 'A man may be delivered up . . .'.[15]

c. The prediction of the resurrection which concludes the saying falls under suspicion on two counts. It completes Mark's application of it to the gospel narrative, and it reflects the confession of faith. As it is clear that Mark has created an expanded text for his own purposes, there is no difficulty in regarding this element as part of the expansion. On the other hand it cannot be excluded *a priori*. It is not impossible that Jesus should have said, 'A man may be delivered up [to death], but he will rise again at three days', provided that the idea of resurrection after three days is not intended literally, but is used as a metaphor for speedy renewal or vindication. As a generic statement this would refer to any man faced with such circumstances, e.g., a mortal blow to his plans and expectations. Jesus finds himself in this position. Thus, though he faces the real possibility of death, he has faith that renewal can come out of it, which he expresses with the metaphor of resurrection. This could be said by any man in this position who could rise to the same quality of faith.

It is thus plausible to suggest that Jesus might have concluded the saying with a prediction of resurrection in this sense. But is it probable? One factor weighs heavily on the other side. By isolating 'deliver' (*mesar*) as the verb which goes with *bar enasha*, we have been able to point to a single saying which lies behind not only the passion predictions, but also the betrayal sayings. But the resurrection is missing from these sayings, and indeed could form no part of them. As it is very unlikely that the saying would circulate without the resurrection element, if that had belonged to the original form, it is better to regard it as an expansion in the light of the confession of faith, probably due to Mark himself.

It seems probable, then, that the resurrection prediction has a separate origin from the passion prediction. This does not exclude the possibility that it has its ultimate foundation in the words of Jesus himself. But it is notable that the confession of faith, as given in 1 Cor. 15.3–4, does not make appeal to Jesus' own sayings, but to the fulfilment of scriptural prophecy. This is said separately, and therefore emphatically, in connection with both the death of Jesus and his resurrection on the third day. Amongst the scriptures which apply to the death of Jesus we must certainly count the passion prophecy of Isa. 52.13–53.12. But we have already seen a link between this prophecy and Mark's passion prediction (cf. p. 64f above), and it will be shown below that the verb 'deliver' (*mesar*) also takes us to this prophecy. Thus a saying of Jesus which expressed his premonition of death points the way to the prophecy which explains the theological meaning of his death, and this is what is adduced in Paul's formula. Similarly the resurrection on the third day has its own scriptural basis,[16] and it is desirable to look for an item in the sayings tradition which would lead the way to that too. It cannot be the *same scripture* as that which explains the death, because the two items are kept separate. It is thus unlikely that it depends upon the *same saying* of Jesus, because this would not point to a different scripture (of course Isa. 52.13 speaks of the exaltation of the Servant, and this may be alluded to in John 3.14). Are there

69

any other sayings which can provide the clue? There are two possibilities.

(*i*) Luke 13.32–3 is an important text for the idiomatic use of the third day. Jesus is warned of the intention of Herod Antipas to kill him, and replies:

> Go and tell that fox, Behold, I cast out demons and perform cures today and tomorrow, and the third day (*te trite*)[17] I finish my course (*teleioumai*). Nevertheless I must go on my way (*poreuesthai*) today and tomorrow and the day following (*te echomene*);[18] for it cannot be that a prophet should perish away from Jerusalem.

This episode is unknown from other sources. In spite of several problems, there seems no reason to doubt its essential authenticity. The principal difficulty is the meaning of *teleioumai*, here translated 'I finish my course' (RSV; cf. NEB). It has been traditionally rendered 'I am perfected' (AV; cf. RV). The latter, if correct, would certainly be a veiled resurrection prediction. But though this use of the verb is not without parallel in the Epistle to the Hebrews, it is not found elsewhere in the gospel traditions, and it is most improbable that this would be the meaning if the saying has an authentic basis. For this reason Wellhausen argued that the saying has been expanded in order to introduce the reference to the resurrection. He proposed the omission of the words 'and the third day . . . tomorrow'. The shorter text then cuts out all the repetitions and removes the reference to the resurrection.[19] But once it is agreed that 'finish my course' is the better translation of *teleioumai*, this becomes unnecessary. The repetitions are required to introduce the final reference to the prospect of death in Jerusalem.[20] The third day is not the day of resurrection, but the day of completion, i.e., death, which brings the work of Jesus to an end. Jesus is determined to pursue his mission to the end, undeterred by present danger. He intends to go to Jerusalem, well aware that even greater danger is in store for him there. The saying is thus a valuable addition to the passion predictions, but does not support the idea that these included a forecast of the resurrection. On the other hand it attests the use of the third day in a context expressing a short space of time. The time referred to is the period of Jesus' ministry, and it is not clear whether the death which puts an end to it is to be on the third day itself, or on the day after that (i.e., the fourth day).[21] In any case the number of days is manifestly not intended to be taken literally. The saying thus gives evidence for this idiomatic usage in the diction of Jesus, and so supports the authenticity of the other saying in which this occurs.

(*ii*) Jesus prophesied the destruction of the temple, but claimed that he would rebuild it in three days. The astonishing thing about this saying is that Mark (followed closely by Matthew) does not actually place it on the lips of Jesus himself. He does record a prophecy by Jesus of the destruction in 13.2, but there is no mention of rebuilding. He then gives the saying in its fullest form in 14.58, 'I will destroy this temple that is made with hands, and in three days I will build another, not made with hands'. The words are spoken by the false witness at the trial of Jesus, and so it remains uncertain whether Mark thought that Jesus had actually said them or not. But it is very widely held that the saying is authentic. The witness is false in that the saying is misused to suggest a criminal intention on Jesus' part. But Jesus did not intend his words to be taken literally. Mark's trial narrative continues with the fact that the high priest challenged Jesus to respond to the evidence. But he remained silent. His silence indicated that he would not repudiate the saying. It may well be that this was the crucial point in the trial.[22] If the saying were held to constitute blasphemy,[23] then his refusal to retract it was all that was required to secure conviction. Mark repeats the saying in a shorter form in 15.29, where it is taken up by the crowd as a taunt against Jesus, as he hangs helpless on the cross.[24]

Once more we have here a feature of Mark's narrative which relates closely to his evangelistic concerns. The repetition of the saying by the crowd in 15.29 applies it ironically to the death and resurrection of Jesus. This is joined with an allusion to the confession of faith in 15.32, 'Let the Christ, the King of Israel, come down now from the cross, that we may see and believe'. This reflects the juxtaposition of the temple saying and the high priest's question in 14.58–62. Finally, both temple and confession are juxtaposed again at the moment of Jesus' death (15.38f): 'And the curtain of the temple was torn in two, from top to bottom. And . . . the centurion . . . said, "Truly this man was the Son of God!" '[25] The note concerning the temple interferes with the flow of the narrative so badly that it may well be Mark's own insertion into his source.[26] If so, it has all the greater value for exposing Mark's intentions as an editor. The death of Jesus breaks down the barrier between Jew and Gentile, as required by the prophecy (Isa. 56.7) which Jesus quoted in explanation of his action in cleansing the temple (Mark 11.17).[27] A Gentile then makes confession of faith.

It seems, then, that Mark at least understands the temple saying as a prophecy of Jesus' death and resurrection, which points to the meaning of these events for salvation. But it is very likely that Mark was not the first to see this connection, for the saying is included by John in his account of the cleansing of the temple and specifically applied to the resurrection (John 2.19–22). Here the first clause has imperative, 'Destroy this temple'. This has the force of a conditional clause ('even if this temple be destroyed . . . '). It points to the correct interpretation of the saying, even if it cannot be certainly claimed to be closer to the original text.[28] But it makes a less satisfactory connection with the preceding verse, which requires the action of Jesus himself, and so would be more suitably followed by Mark's 'I will destroy . . . '. Hence it is likely that the form of the saying goes behind John. It is therefore independent of the form in Mark.[29] John also informs his readers that the saying was remembered in connection with scripture as a prophecy of Jesus' resurrection (John 2.22).

At this point we are brought back to the confession of faith in 1 Cor. 15.4. Here the resurrection on the third day is said to be 'in accordance with the scriptures'. But there is no indication of the actual scriptural reference, any more than there is in John (unless Ps. 69.9, quoted by Jesus in John 2.17, is intended). Rabbinic references to Hos. 6.2 show that it was regularly applied to resurrection, usually to the general resurrection in the coming age. The same may be true of Jonah's escape from the whale, used by Matthew at Matt. 12.40.[30] In spite of the difficulty of dating the rabbinic literature, it may be safely assumed that these passages were in use in New Testament times, because the Pharisees were much concerned to promote the doctrine of resurrection. On the other hand it is not at all likely that the rabbinic use is derived from Christian influence, because in Christian usage the idea of resurrection on the third day is applied only to the special case of Jesus himself. It thus seems best to assume that the resurrection of Jesus on the third day is not an idea created within the primitive church on the basis of these scriptures. Rather, they have been adduced afterwards as current resurrection texts, to provide scriptural warrant for what happened. However, the claim that Jesus actually rose on the third day is not based on historical evidence. Mark, as we have already seen, gives only the angel's statement that Jesus has arisen when the women visit the tomb on the third day, and his account precludes the later tradition that Jesus actually appeared on the third day. Similarly 1 Cor. 15.4 simply states the fact that Jesus was raised on the third day. The resurrection appearances to apostles, beginning with Peter, are not dated, but it can scarcely be supposed that Paul means the same day. Thus the resurrection on the third day is purely theoretical. It is a way of expressing the church's conviction concerning Jesus in terms of a divine act, but the third day as such appears to be entirely unnecessary. There is thus much to commend the suggestion that this feature of the primitive confession has been derived from the temple saying, applied, as we have seen, to the death and resurrection of Jesus. From this point of view, Jesus spoke of speedy renewal in terms of resurrection in three days. But he was not himself the subject, because he was referring to the renewal of the temple. But this saying played a decisive part in his condemnation to death. The experience of resurrection shortly afterwards, attested in the appearance to Peter, drew attention to the element of renewal in the saying, and brought about the application of it to Jesus himself. The period of three days was not intended literally, but not unnaturally came to be treated as such, and the resurrection traditions in the gospels were shaped on this basis.

If this necessarily speculative reconstruction is approximately correct, it can account for the way in which a saying of Jesus pointed the way to the prophecies which explain the significance of the resurrection, and incidentally brought about the fixed tradition that the resurrection took place on the third day. Hence this became a feature of the confession of faith, as it has been preserved in 1 Cor. 15.4. The saying concerned, however, was the temple saying, not the passion prediction. Nevertheless, for evangelistic reasons, Mark has added this feature of the confession to his form of the passion predictions in Mark 8.31; 9.31 and 10.34. Thus there is no authentic Son of Man saying which includes mention of the resurrection. The Son of Man is confined to the basic passion prediction, 'A man may be delivered up', applied both to the betrayal of Jesus by Judas and to the commital of Jesus by the Sanhedrin to Pontius Pilate. Mark's forms of the prediction are complex because of his literary methods. He relates it to the purpose of his gospel by expanding it, firstly with anticipations of his own passion narrative, and secondly with the confession of faith in the resurrection, which it is his aim to promote, but which will actually be left undescribed.

The underlying form is incomplete. To say that 'a man may be delivered up' is not enough, though that is as much as is quoted by Mark in 14.21b, 41. The conclusion of the saying cannot be reconstructed, because of the overlay of expansions in the passion predictions. We can, however, gain some idea of Jesus' meaning when we turn to the other forms of passion saying in which the *bar enasha* idiom is used.

2 Bar enasha *goes according to his destiny*

Mark 14.21a	*Luke 22.22a*
For the Son of Man goes (*hupagei*) as it is written concerning him.	For the Son of Man goes (*poreuetai*) according to what has been determined.

A moving feature of the account of the Last Supper is Jesus' dreadful premonition of betrayal by one of his own friends. In the Fourth Gospel this has been built up by John with consummate skill, so as to draw out the irony of the situation to the uttermost (John 13.21–30). We are not concerned here with the historical basis of the tradition,[31] but in Mark's simpler account of it there is a double Son of Man saying (14.21), 'For the Son of Man goes as it is written of him, but woe to that man by whom the Son of Man is betrayed!' The repetition of Son of Man in this verse suggests that two separate sayings have been brought together by the evangelist. The second we have dealt with already, for it was the basis of Mark's passion predictions. It now provides the theme of the whole paragraph ('one of you will betray me', verse 18).[32] The first is found only here, but has links with other passion sayings, as we shall see.

This short saying has two distinctive features. First there is the word 'goes' (*hupagei*, Mark 14.21 = Matt. 26.24, but *poreuetai* in Luke 22.22). The two Greek words are not quite identical, as *hupago* means to go away, and so to take leave of someone, while *poreuomai* means to go on a journey. Mark's verb thus suggests taking leave, and must certainly be regarded as a euphemism for 'to die'. The change in Luke may be due to reminiscence of Luke 13.33, which, as we have already seen, must be classed with the passion predictions. There the verb *poreuesthai* was used to denote the course of Jesus' ministry leading up to his death at Jesusalem. It is thus unlikely that Luke has changed the verb here in order to remove the implication of death in Mark's *hupagei*. The fact that we have here a genuine memory of Jesus' ironical use of 'go' is supported by the Fourth Gospel, where it is used very effectively to express the passage of Jesus to the Father by way of the cross; cf. John 7.33, 35; 8.14, 21, 22; 13.3, 33, 36, etc. In these passages both *hupago* and *poreuomai* are used without clear distinction of meaning.

The second feature is the phrase 'as it is written of him'. If the Son of Man is taken to be an exclusive self-reference on the part of Jesus, it is natural to suppose that this is concerned with the fulfilment of prophecies which may be applied to the Messiah's death. But this is not how Luke took it. He has altered Mark's phrase, but not in the manner which we should expect if he understood it to refer to prophecies of the suffering Messiah, for which he would certainly have used Mark's verb, as he does frequently in both the gospel and Acts. But here exceptionally he has changed it to 'according to what has been determined' (*kata to horizomenon*), a verb which he uses five times in Acts, though it never occurs elsewhere in the gospels.[33] This shows that he understood the phrase to refer, not to the scriptures, but to the predetermined plan of God. Of course it is not excluded that God's plan may be discovered in the scriptures, but this is not the primary meaning of the phrase. It thus means 'according to his destiny', and carries with it the notion of necessity which is expressed by 'must' (*dei*) in both Mark 8.31 and Luke 13.33.

Luke arrived at this interpretation of the saying without necessarily recognizing the idiomatic use of *bar enasha* which lies behind the Greek. But when this is given its proper value, the interpretation in terms of destiny becomes indispensable, because the scriptures do not provide details of everybody's destiny. When Jesus says, 'A man goes according to his destiny', he is not saying that everyone's destiny may be found in scripture. Moreover, he is not making a statement which refers to *everyone* at all, even though what he says might be true of everyone. The generic *bar enasha* limits the application to those whose lives are apparently contradicted by an inexorable fate, or circumstances beyond their control, which must be accepted as the will of God. Thus the saying is not simply equivalent to the general assertion, 'No man can escape death'. It is rather a way of saying, 'When a man is faced with death, he must accept it, if it is God's will, for God's plan for him must be fulfilled'. The context of the saying is exactly the same as that of the passion predictions which we have already considered. The danger of death facing Jesus is only too apparent to the disciples. The resolution which was expressed in his message to 'that fox' Herod (Luke 13.32f) is here put in the form of a readiness to accept the necessity to die, if that is demanded of him. He speaks in a proverbial manner, not confining his attention to himself. This has the effect of placing his personal danger in a wider perspective. Anyone else in the same situation would have to do the same. There is an ironical glance at the disciples themselves, who must also be ready to face danger. Jesus is not the only one whose life is at risk. The irony of the *bar enasha* saying is thus quite similar to that of the 'foxes' saying which we considered in the last chapter (Matt. 8.20 = Luke 9.58).

3 'Bar enasha *will give his life for many*'

One more prediction of the passion remains for our attention, and that is the inspiring saying of Mark 10.45, 'For the Son of Man also came not to be served but to serve, and to give his life as a ransom for many'. This saying has been the subject of endless controversy. In the first place, although the two halves of the saying interpret each other, there is no essential connection between them, so that the juxtaposition appears to be artificial. This impression is confirmed by the parallel in Luke 22.27, '. . . But I am among you as one who serves'. Luke has no parallel to the second half. The saying in both gospels forms the conclusion of teaching in relation to a dispute of the disciples over greatness in the coming kingdom. In Mark this takes the form of the request of the sons of Zebedee (10.35-40), which is then followed, after an editorial connecting verse, by the teaching on service (10.41-5). Luke's version comes in a different context, the Last Supper. An editorial introduction mentions the strife among the disciples, and then comes the teaching on service (Luke 22.24-7). Verbal links between the two versions are slight, and it is widely held that they depend on separate traditions. Yet another version of this teaching occurs in the Last Supper narrative of the Fourth Gospel, in which Jesus' claim to be a servant is acted out in the washing of the disciples' feet (John 13.4–17). The episode concludes with sayings on service which have links with the Synoptic sayings.[34] It is unlikely that John has built up the episode directly out of the Lucan version, because John's distinctive touches have clearly been added to a simpler form which is already in the form of a story.[35] The remarkable thing about his treatment of the tradition is that his principal insertion is almost certainly aimed at introducing the idea of atonement for sin, but without a hint of the ransom theme with which Mark 10.45 alludes to the same idea. Nevertheless, John does have a phrase which is related to the ransom saying elsewhere in his gospel, as will be shown below. On these grounds it is reasonable to conclude that the ransom half of Mark 10.45 is an addition to the original saying on service.

Secondly, if the two halves of Mark 10.45 are to be separated, to which half does the Son of Man belong? As none of the parallels to the saying on service are Son of Man sayings, it seems probable that it belongs to the ransom half. The point is strengthened by the fact that, if the Son of Man is subject of the service half, it can only be an exclusive self-reference on the part of Jesus, because there is a formal contrast between him and the disciples. The idiomatic use of *bar enasha* is impossible here. On the other hand, this difficulty does not arise with the second half of the saying, so that there is no compelling reason to exclude it from the second half, if it is taken to be a separate tradition.

Thirdly, Mark's use of 'ransom' (*lutron*) is unique in the gospels, and raises acute problems.[36] The word occurs nowhere else in the New Testament, but cognate words in Luke–Acts[37] take up the Old Testament idea of redemption from slavery, and in other New Testament writings these expressions sometimes have definite sacrificial significance.[38] The sacrificial significance of *lutron* in the present passage is fixed by the words which immediately follow it, 'for many' (*anti pollon*). An astonishingly similar phrase occurs in the formulaic passage 1 Tim. 2.6, 'who gave himself a ransom for all' (*ho dous heauton antilutron huper panton*); cf. Titus 2.14. Seeing that the sacrificial connotation of *lutron* derives from the idea of a ransom-price (e.g., for manumission of a slave), the most likely Aramaic equivalent would be *kopher* (so Barrett).

Fourthly, it has been argued that these passages, including Mark 10.45, must be later than the time of Jesus, because the idea of self-sacrifice is distinctively Greek, and is notably absent from Jewish traditions. This seems to be borne out by the fact that in any case most of the relevant passages belong to the later strands of the New Testament. The application of this idea to Jesus could then be due to the contemporary interest in the Maccabean martyrs, whose death was regarded in Hellenistic Jewish circles as an atonement on behalf of the people.[39]

The cogency of the argument depends upon another facet of the problem. For most modern readers the sacrificial language of Mark 10.45 calls to mind the suffering servant prophecy of Isa. 53, in particular verse 10, 'when he makes himself [Heb., thou makest his soul] an offering for sin (*asham*) . . . '. This chapter stands outside the general Jewish reluctance to think of a man's death as acceptable to God, and therefore capable of being a prevailing sacrifice.[40] But the reason for this reluctance was the fact that Sheol, the abode of the dead, was held to be outside God's realm, so that death was always thought of in terms of misfortune.[41] But the case of the Maccabean martyrs, coinciding with the beginnings of the doctrine of resurrection, began to change this. There is thus no great difficulty in the supposition that Jesus might have been inspired by Isa. 53 to express his vocation to a sacrificial death in this way. Unfortunately the connection between Mark 10.45 and Isa. 53.10 does not survive closer scrutiny. As Barrett has pointed out, the Greek *lutron* and its cognates do not occur anywhere in the Septuagint version of the prophecy. In any case *lutron* is not a proper equivalent of the Hebrew *asham* (= a compensation offering), which belongs to the sphere of restitution, to put right an offence.[42] As *lutron* is not found in any Greek translation of Isa. 53.10 and does not correspond in meaning with *asham*, it is hazardous to build any argument on the connection.

None of these difficulties is insuperable. Mark 10.45b should be detached from the saying on service on critical grounds, but the Son of Man should be retained as subject of the saying, because it does not belong to the service material. The word 'ransom' (*lutron*) should be regarded as interpretative. It is not a quotation from Isa. 53.10, but connection with Isa. 53 should not be ruled out altogether, because the ransom idea is a legitimate way of interpreting the prophecy as a whole.[43] Evidence that 'ransom' belongs to the form of the saying which Mark received is provided by 1 Tim. 2.6, already referred to above. For, late as this epistle is, the formula which is quoted here may be independent of Mark.[44]

Nevertheless, it is doubtful if 'ransom' belongs to the saying in its original form. As already pointed out above, it owes its sacrificial significance to the prepositional phrase 'for many (all)'. It can thus be omitted without seriously affecting the essential meaning of the sentence. It is a useful addition, because it draws attention to the implied sacrificial metaphor, and so helps to enrich the understanding of Jesus' death (cf. Rom. 3.24). But there is evidence that the saying was current without 'ransom' in both Paul and John. As it is unlikely that 'ransom' should be dropped, if it is an original part of the saying, it seems best to regard it as a primitive interpretative addition.

The evidence is provided by the verb 'give', which in this context represents Aramaic *mesar*. This verb (Greek *didonai*) is the one point of agreement between Mark 10.45b and 1 Tim. 2.6. But we have already had the compound form *paradidonai* corresponding with *mesar* in the passion predictions, where it was in the passive form, meaning 'to be delivered up' or 'be betrayed'. Paul has this same word in the active form in Gal. 2.20, where he speaks of 'the Son of God, who loved me and *gave himself for* (*paradontos heauton huper*) me'. Precisely the same words are echoed in Eph. 5.2, 25. There is a tendency for the two forms to interchange; cf. Rom. 4.25a, 'who *was delivered up for* (*paredothe dia*) our transgressions'; Rom. 5.8, 'Christ died *for* (*huper*) us (the ungodly)'. In all these places the sacrificial idea is secured by the prepositional phrase, and there is no word corresponding with 'ransom'.

The Fourth Gospel also attests an active form of *mesar* with preposition 'for', but without 'ransom'. In John 10.11 Jesus says 'the good shepherd *lays down his life for* (*ten psuchen autou tithesin huper*) the sheep'. Thereafter the same phrase occurs in relation to the passion in 10.15, 17–18; 15.13. But it is taken up by Peter in imitation of Jesus in John 13.37–8, and it is applied first to Jesus and then to the disciples in general in 1 John 3.16. As the epistles of John were probably written by a different author from the gospel, the phrase can be regarded as characteristic of the Johannine community.[45] In all these places the Greek verb is *tithenai*. But this would also fittingly translate Aramaic *mesar*.

Finally, it may be observed that the feature which gives to the saying its sacrificial connotation, i.e., the prepositional phrase 'for many' (*anti pollon*), also occurs in Mark's version of the eucharistic blessing of the cup (Mark 14.24, *huper pollon*), and this is reflected in Paul's version of the blessing of the bread (1 Cor. 11.24, *huper humon*, 'for you'). Of course these are distinct traditions, and their value is that they help to place Mark 10.45b in a wider context of Jesus' teaching.

There thus seems to be good reason to suppose that Jesus was remembered to have said, 'A man may give his life for many', and this was used especially to interpret the death of Jesus as an atoning sacrifice. It occurs in a number of forms. A form with 'a ransom' added may have been current in Aramaic at an early stage in the Church's life. It remains to consider what may have been the original meaning of it, taking into account the *bar enasha* idiom. But it must also be pointed out that the Aramaic 'to give (lay down) one's life' (*mesar naphsheh*) is used idiomatically for 'to risk one's life', without necessarily implying that death will actually occur.[46] Thus in Rom. 16.3–4 Paul commends his fellow-workers Prisca and Aquila, because 'they have risked (*hupethekan*) their neck for my life'. The verb is a compound of *tithenai*, which makes it possible to distinguish between risking one's life and actually laying down one's life. But Aramaic would use *mesar* for both cases. Moreover, a similar phrase occurs with *paradidonai* in Acts 15.26.[47] This gives an even closer parallel to the present phrase.

It may well be the case that this is what Jesus meant when he used the phrase. As before, the *bar enasha* idiom forbids us to interpret the saying either of Jesus exclusively or of mankind in general. It makes sense as an ironical reference to the situation of Jesus, if the setting is a remonstrance on the part of the disciples. They are alarmed at his seemingly foolhardy disregard of imminent danger. But he refuses to be deflected from his purpose. When the eternal salvation of many people is at stake, then 'A man may risk his life for the sake of the many'. Such a situation is consistent with the determination of Jesus and his commitment to his prophetic task on behalf of God, which we have seen repeatedly in the Son of Man sayings already considered. The possibility that the disciples did try to remonstrate with Jesus is implied by features of the tradition which are not likely to have been invented groundlessly. Besides Peter's famous rebuke of Jesus after the first passion prediction (Mark 8.32), there is Jesus' prophecy that 'you will all fall away' and that even Peter 'will deny me three times' (Mark 14.27–31). This implies that Jesus has reason to believe that they do not possess the same measure of resolution with which he faces the coming ordeal himself.

4 *Jesus and the Suffering Servant*

Our study of the passion predictions has led to the conclusion that three Son of Man sayings are likely to be authentic. In each of them the *bar enasha* idiom is correctly used. But the matter has been complicated by the close relationship which they bear to the primitive confession of faith and to the process of unfolding the meaning of that faith in greater detail. The crucifixion would have been the end of the Jesus movement, if his followers had not had experience of him as the risen and glorified one, and so proclaimed him to be the Christ. Jesus had insisted that *a man may be delivered up to death in the course of his duty*, and that is what had in fact happened in the case of Jesus himself. But the Easter proclamation is not merely that *Jesus* was delivered up (or died), but that the *Christ* was delivered up. Contrary to current messianic expectations, Jesus had died as the Christ. Such an assertion required a fresh examination of the prophecies on which messianic expectations were based. It was not difficult for the disciples, possibly following a lead given by Jesus himself, to find sufficient grounds for the claim that 'Christ died . . . according to the scriptures' (1 Cor 15.3). Jesus also said that *a man goes according to his destiny* (as it is written of him). Here again it could be claimed that Jesus' destiny was not only written in the predetermined plan of God, but also revealed in advance in prophecies concerning the Messiah. When Jesus spoke of the danger which faced him in Jerusalem, he pointed out that *a man may risk his life on behalf of many*, and if the last word 'many' is authentic, it could scarcely fail to recall the prophecy of the Servant of the Lord, who 'bore the sin of many' (Isa. 53.12).

The Easter proclamation of the death and resurrection of Jesus did not take the form of a claim that Jesus' own words had come true. He had spoken of the risk to his life, and this would have posed an insuperable problem for the church's faith in him as the Christ, if it had not been possible to find scriptures in which the suffering of the Messiah was foretold. The kerygma, then, takes the form of a claim that in this particular the scriptures have been fulfilled.

Similarly there is never any appeal in the New Testament to the sayings of Jesus in connection with the resurrection. It has been argued above that Jesus never foretold his own resurrection in such a way as to make this possible but that the 'temple' saying, quoted as evidence against him at his trial before the Sanhedrin, was interpreted in the light of the resurrection experience of the disciples, and provided the origin of the 'third day' formula. This also was supported from scripture, and thereby brought within the scope of messianic prediction (1 Cor. 15.4).

The resurrection predictions need not be pursued further. But there is enough in common between the three passion sayings and the prophecy of Isa. 53 to require further examination. If Jesus intended his words to allude to this prophecy, it may be concluded that his ideas concerning the inevitable approach of death were shaped in the light of it. There could then be no doubt that Jesus did go to his death with the idea that he was undertaking an expiatory sacrifice on behalf of the people. Otherwise it might then be more prudent to conclude that this aspect of the kerygma is the result of subsequent reflection upon the death of Jesus. His death was seen to be a sacrifice for sin, although Jesus had not actually said that that was his intention.[48]

Our three Son of Man sayings relating to the passion all open the possibility that Jesus did have Isa. 53 in mind when he spoke, but fail to furnish absolute proof.

a. The significant feature of the first saying is the passive verb, 'be delivered up'. The same verb is used in the active form in the third saying. The principal Greek verb here is *paradidonai*, though *didonai* and *tithenai* are also used for the active form. The Aramaic word corresponding with all these is *mesar*. This at once suggests a connection with Isa. 53, for *paradidonai* occurs three times in the Septuagint version, and *mesar* also occurs three times in the Targum, though not quite at the same points.[49] With the aid of this prophecy the transformation of the first saying ('a man may be delivered up') into the confession of faith ('the Christ was delivered up for our sins') could be easily achieved. In this connection it may be observed that Rom. 4.25a, 'who was delivered up on account of our transgressions', corresponds exactly with the Targum *ithmesar ba-awayathana* (= 'he was bruised for our iniquities', Isa. 53.5).[50] But the first Son of Man saying, deduced from Mark's passion prediction, does not have 'for our sins', and without such a phrase the use of 'delivered up' is insufficient to establish the link.[51] It allows the possibility, but lacks anything sufficiently distinctive to prove it.

b. With regard to the second saying, it has been argued above that 'as it is written of him' does not necessarily refer to the scriptures, but rather to the predetermined plan of God. But as this is made known in the prophetic scriptures, a reference to them cannot be excluded altogether, and the natural passage to appeal to is Isa. 53. If the saying were merely a general statement about all men, such a connection would be very remote. But the irony of the saying, which appears when the *bar enasha* idiom is given full value, places it in a context of personal danger. Jesus is tempted to escape his destiny. To say in these circumstances that 'a man goes according to his destiny' may appear to be nothing more than fatalism. But the implied rebuke to the disciples and the dramatic quality of the Gethsemane tradition argue for a more positive interpretation. Jesus is expressing his resolve to go through with whatever is laid upon him by the will of God, and he wishes the disciples to do the same. Seen in this light, the saying refers to a clearly defined sense of personal destiny, which makes acceptance of it purposeful and deliberate, rather than fatalistic. If Jesus did see the danger to his life in this purposeful way, there is much to be said for the suggestion that he found his destiny in Isa. 53, whether or not he thought of himself as the Messiah. Thus, though the second saying has no verbal connection with Isa. 53, it provides circumstantial evidence for the possibility that Jesus had this prophecy in mind.

c. The 'ransom' saying supplies the strongest indication that Jesus was indebted to Isa. 53. This is not because of the word 'ransom' itself, which, as we have seen, does not furnish a direct link with Isa. 53.10, and is best regarded as a very early addition to the saying in order to bring out the sacrificial meaning of Jesus' death. But, apart from this word, the whole of the saying is found in Isa. 53.12ce, 'because he poured out his soul to death, . . . yet he bore the sin of many'. Here the Septuagint has, 'because his soul was delivered up to death, . . . and he himself bore the sins of many' (*anth' hon paredothe eis thanaton he psuche autou, . . . kai autos hamartias pollon anenenken*). The Targum reads, 'because he delivered up his soul to death, . . . and he shall make intercession for many sins' (*halaph dimsar le-motha naphsheh . . . we-hu al ḥobin saggiin yibᶜe*).[52] This is very close to the Aramaic which, we have suggested, lies behind Mark 10.45b, and perhaps also 1 Tim. 2.6. This is at first sight very impressive. But we have seen that 'to give one's life (soul)' is a common expression for to risk one's life, and so the whole weight of the argument for a connection with Isa. 53.12 falls on the final phrase 'for many'. Here too the phrase is not sufficiently distinctive to prove dependence,[53] and we are left with the juxtaposition of the two phrases as the only significant basis for this supposition. Slight as this is, it receives some support from the eucharistic words of Jesus, as noted above. Again, a connection with Isa. 53 which at first seemed very promising turns out to be incapable of being proved, though it remains very probable.

Whether Jesus' thought concerning the danger to his life was influenced by Isa. 53 is not a matter of great importance. It is absolutely certain that the primitive church rapidly made use of this prophecy in order to express the significance of his death. But whether he was referring to it or not, Jesus was certainly aware that he was liable to be put to death. The three Son of Man sayings which we have isolated in this chapter testify to the resolution and deliberation with which he faced the inevitable march of events. This was no Stoic indifference, but a deep sense of responsibility and commitment to the mission which he had undertaken in the name of God. Thus, if death is to be chosen rather than repudiation of his message, it is a sacrifice for the sake of those to whom the message is addressed, the 'many'. It thus seems likely that Jesus did see the necessity of death in terms of sacrifice in spite of what was said above. Jesus' sacrificial approach to his death does not need to be dependent on Isa. 53, but it is certainly consistent with it. And it was a right instinct on the part of the post-Easter community to turn to this prophecy to support their claim that it was as Messiah that he died.

5

The Future Son of Man in Q

The Son of Man sayings which we have analysed in detail in the last two chapters comprise only a fraction of the total of such sayings in the gospels. But only these sayings, numbering nine altogether, reproduce traditions in which the underlying *bar enasha* idiom can still be detected. As the use of *bar enasha* is incorrect for an exclusive self-reference, it is probable that those sayings in which the Son of Man functions in this way have been developed only after the transference of the sayings tradition into Greek. Consequently all the other sayings apart from the nine which we have already accepted must be regarded as inauthentic. This, however, does not justify us in rejecting them out of hand. Their presence in the tradition still has to be accounted for. If a proper appreciation of the authentic sayings casts new light upon the historical Jesus himself, study of the development of the tradition may be expected to make some contribution to the perennial problem of bridging the gap between Jesus and the faith of the church.

Moreover, the process of development can be discerned in all the gospels, including the source Q. It thus happened at a comparatively early stage in the church's existence. It would be wrong, however, to suppose that this was done in the interests of a primitive Son of Man Christology. There is no evidence that such a Christology ever existed. That idea is part of the modern myth, which we have seen to be untenable.

So also, if we now have to explain the origin of inauthentic sayings, it will not be possible to adopt Käsemann's idea that they are to be regarded as 'sentences of holy law', spoken by Christian prophets in the eucharistic assembly.[1] This is intended to explain why the Son of Man is confined to the sayings tradition, for of course the concept of sentences spoken by prophets is that of a continuation of the sayings tradition, as opposed to catechesis and paraenesis, and other forms of teaching and theological expression in the New Testament. For this still does not explain the almost conspiratorial way in which the Son of Man has been kept out of all the other literary forms of the New Testament.

The starting point for our enquiry must be the great importance which the few authentic sayings had in the primitive Christian community. On the one one hand, the six sayings which we considered in chapter 3 demonstrated that the *bar enasha* idiom was a feature of Jesus' personal style. Such a feature would not be quickly forgotten, because it was rather unusual and was used to very good effect. On the other hand, three of Jesus' Son of Man sayings, the passion sayings considered in chapter 4, played a fundamental part in the first attempts at formulation of the faith. Jesus may not have predicted his death and resurrection as straightforwardly as Mark would have us believe, but relevant sayings of his were related to scriptural testimonies, and so produced such a statement of faith as Paul quotes from the Jerusalem church in 1 Cor. 15.3–4.

Thus the tradition starts with the Son of Man, not as a recognized title for Jesus, but as a style-feature belonging to important sayings of Jesus concerning himself. It may thus be taken as axiomatic that it was accepted as a self-reference on his part. But it is also only natural that the subtlety of the generic usage should be neglected, and this is what happened when the sayings were translated into Greek. Reference to the Danielic Son of Man, which plays no part at all in the authentic sayings, was soon incorporated, if it was not already implied by the translation *ho huios tou anthropou* itself. Thus the characteristic feature of the inauthentic sayings is that the phrase is used as an exclusive self-reference; and these sayings show a tendency to make the allusion to Dan. 7.13–14 explicit. We shall see that most of these sayings can be best explained as the work of the evangelists themselves. Thus it is not necessary to suppose that there was a considerable number of floating Son of Man sayings of this type. We have already observed Mark's deliberate repetitions of the passion predictions for the christological purpose of his gospel. This means that nearly half the Son of Man sayings in Mark can be attributed to the evangelist. The same is true of the other evangelists. This observation is consistent with the fact that there never was a Son of Man Christology in the early church, so that the prevalence of the phrase in the sayings tradition is a feature of the presentation of Jesus by means of a biography.

Not all the sayings can be explained in this way. In particular the Q source, in so far as it can be identified as a coherent work, scarcely ranks as a biographical work, even if it is to be regarded as more than a random collection of sayings attributed to Jesus.[2] Thus the remaining Son of Man sayings in Q must have first claim on our attention.

1 *The Son of Man in Q*

In keeping with its character as a collection of sayings, the Q source has already contributed four, or possibly five, Son of Man sayings in which the *bar enasha* idiom is preserved. These are Matt. 8.20=Luke 9.58; Matt. 11.19=Luke 7.34; Matt. 12.32=Luke 12.10; Luke 11.30; Matt. 10.32f=Luke 12.8f. Out of these five, the second forms part of a longer sequence on John the Baptist, which provides an example of a thematic principle of collection in the source. The fourth also belongs to a thematic sequence on the sign of Jonah, and is important because it is concerned with future judgement. The last one, on confessing and denying Jesus, has even greater importance, partly because it has an independent parallel in Mark 8.38, but chiefly because it is the one example among the authentic sayings which actually speaks of the eschatological function of the Son of Man. It thus paves the way for the identification of the Son of Man, assumed to be an exclusive self-reference on Jesus' part, with the Danielic Son of Man figure. However, it has been argued above that the Q form of this saying may have had the first person, as in Matthew. In this case it would not count as a Son of Man saying in the Q collection, and therefore it could not have influenced the compiler of Q in this respect.

The remaining Son of Man sayings in Q consist of (*a*) Matt. 5.11 = Luke 6.22, which is another case where Matthew has the first person form against Luke's Son of Man; (*b*) Matt. 19.28=Luke 22.28–30, where on the contrary Matthew has the Son of Man against Luke; (*c*) a series of eschatological references, four in Matthew and five in Luke, in which Jesus appears as the apocalyptic Son of Man and the main subject is 'the day of the Son of Man'. The lack of agreement between Matthew and Luke in (*a*) and (*b*) raises the question whether the Son of Man belongs to Q, or

has been substituted for the first person by the evangelist himself.
(*a*) The first of these is quite similar to the 'advocate' saying (Matt.
10.32f= Luke 12.8f), in which the Son of Man appears to have
been inserted by Luke from the Marcan parallel. It will therefore be
considered later, when we review all the Son of Man sayings that are
peculiar to Luke. (*b*) In the second case the differences between
Matthew and Luke are more far-reaching, and there is good reason
to believe that Matthew has recast the material, introducing the
reference to the Son of Man at the same time. So this must also be
left for consideration later, when we deal with the Son of Man in
Matthew. (*c*) This leaves only the eschatological series, and to this
we now turn.

2 *The eschatological sayings in Q*

Although Matthew has all these sayings in one chapter (Matt. 24),
there are in fact two separate traditions involved, which appear in
distinct contexts in Luke. Characteristically, Matthew has fused
them both with the corresponding material in Mark, the Little
Apocalypse of Mark 13. A central feature of Mark's composition is
the appearance of the Son of Man on the clouds (Mark 13.26). This
is the climax of the piece, following the description of woes and
portents which will precede it. It is thus very natural that Matthew
should incorporate into it the Q sequence on 'the day of the Son of
Man'. He divides it up, with the part corresponding with Mark
13.26 in between.

Luke, on the other hand, keeps the sources separate, though he is
aware of the similarity of the material, and it cannot be assumed that
his presentation of the Q material is entirely free from Marcan
influence. He has the main Q sequence in Luke 17.22–37, following
a unique piece about the coming of the kingdom of God. This may
be quoted here, as it will be relevant to the subsequent discussion
(Luke 17.20f):

> The kingdom of God is not coming with signs to be observed; nor will
> they say, 'Lo, here it is!' or 'There!' for behold, the kingdom of God is in
> the midst of you.

The other Q piece is the parable of the thief. Luke has already
used this at an earlier point in his narrative (Luke 12.39f).

It is characteristic of this material that the Son of Man sayings cannot be detached from their contexts and treated as isolated traditions. There are also significant differences between Matthew and Luke. For this reason it is necessary to set out the relevant verses in parallel as a basis for comparative study (see table on pp. 90–2).

A quick, broad comparison shows that this is another case where Mark and Q preserve parallel, but independent traditions. In the section of the Marcan apocalypse with which we are here concerned, there is a reasonably coherent scheme. First there is a warning of tribulation, in which the disciples are not to be misled by false messianic claimants (Mark 13.19–23). Then comes the climax (not included in the synopsis below), when 'you will see the Son of Man coming in clouds with great power and glory' and the gathering of the elect takes place (Mark 13.24–7). This is followed by various assurances concerning this plan of the future and the impossibility of predicting it exactly (Mark 13.28–32), ending with the parable of the master of the house and its application (Mark 13.33–7).

The Q sequence, best preserved in Luke 17.22–37, is not chronologically ordered like Mark's apocalypse, but is rather a collection round a theme, the suddenness of the day when the Son of Man is revealed. This makes it roughly parallel with the climax of Mark 13.24–7. It is thus easy to see why Matthew fused the two pieces together, creating a literary harmony comparable to Tatian's Diatessaron in the next century.[3] The first part of the Q sequence has a close parallel to Mark's warning of false messianic claimants, and so Matthew has brought the two together. The repetition of this element betrays his dependence on two sources.[4] Then the lightning simile for the appearance of the Son of Man anticipates the Marcan climax, so that Matt. 24.27 and 24.30 are virtually doublets. The further simile of the vultures (Matt. 24.28) suggests that the Son of Man's appearing is for judgement and destruction of the wicked, though the main point is the same as the lightning: it is something that cannot be missed when it happens. Luke has moved this verse to the end of the sequence (Luke 17.37),[5] presumably because he wishes to associate the Son of Man with God's vindication of the elect rather than with destruction (hence the parable of the unjust judge immediately follows, Luke 18.1–8a, rounded off by a Son of Man saying in verse 8b, which we shall consider along with other Son of Man sayings which are peculiar to Luke). Instead, Luke has inserted a reference to the passion of

Matt. 24.21-44

21 Then there will be a great tribulation . . .

(*verses 21-22*)

23 Then if anyone says to you, 'Lo, here is the Christ!' or 'Here!' do not believe it. 24 For false Christs and false prophets will arise and will give great signs and wonders, so as to lead astray, if possible, even the elect. 25 Lo, I have told you beforehand. 26 So if they say to you, 'Lo, he is in the wilderness,' do not go out; 'Lo, he is in the inner rooms,' do not believe it. 27 For as the lightning comes from the east and shines as far as the west, so will be the parousia of the Son of Man.

Mark 13.19-37

19 Those days will be a tribulation . . .

(*verses 19-20*)
(*on the tribulation in 'those days'*)

21 And then if anyone says to you, 'Look, here is the Christ!' 'Look, there!' do not believe it. 22 But false Christs and false prophets will arise and will perform signs and wonders, in order to lead astray, if possible, the elect. 23 But take heed; I have told you all things beforehand.

Luke 17.22-37; 12.39f

22 And he said to the disciples, The days are coming when you will desire to see one of the days of the Son of Man, and you will not see it.

23 And they will say to you, 'Lo, there!' 'Lo, here!'; do not go out, and do not follow [them]. 24 For as the lightning flashing from the [one side] under heaven lights up to the [other side] under heaven, so will be the Son of Man in his day. 25 But first he must suffer many things and be rejected by this generation.

Matt. 24.21-44

28 Wherever the body is, there will the vultures be gathered together

(*verses 29-36*)

37 For as [were] the days of Noah, so will be the parousia of the Son of Man. 38 For as in those days before the flood they were eating and drinking, marrying and giving in marriage, until the day when Noah entered the ark, 39 and they did not know until the flood came and swept them all away,

so will be also the parousia of the Son of Man.

40 Then there will be two men in the field; one is taken and one is left. 41 Two women will be grinding at the mill; one is taken and one is left.

Mark 13.19-37

(*verses 24-32*)

(*final portents and the coming of the Son of Man*)

Luke 17.22-37; 12.39f

(*cf. verse 37*)

26 And as it was in the days of Noah, so will it be also in the days of the Son of Man.

27 They ate, they drank, they married, they were given in marriage, until the day when Noah entered the ark, and the flood came and destroyed them all. 28 Likewise as it was in the days of Lot - they ate, they drank, they bought, they sold, they planted, they built, 29 but on the day when Lot went out from Sodom it rained fire and brimstone from heaven and destroyed them all. 30 In the same way it will be on the day when the Son of Man is revealed.

(*verses 31-33*)

(*sundry warnings*)

34 I tell you, in that night there will be two men in one bed; one will be taken and the other left. 35 There will be two women grinding together; one will be taken and the other left. [36]

Matt. 24.21–44	*Mark 13.19–37*	*Luke 17.22–37; 12.39f*

Luke 17.22–37; 12.39f

37 And they said to him, Where, Lord? He said to them, Where the body is, there also the vultures will be gathered together.

Mark 13.19–37

(*verses 33f*)
(*parable of absent master*)
35 Keep awake therefore – you do not know when the master of the house is coming, in the evening, or at midnight, or at cockcrow, or in the morning – 36 lest he come suddenly and find you asleep. 37 And what I say to you I say to all: Keep awake.

Luke 12.39f
39 But know this, that if the householder had known in what hour the thief was coming he would not have let his house be broken into. 40 You also must be ready, because the Son of Man is coming at an hour you do not expect.

Matt. 24.21–44

(*cf. verse 28*)

42 Keep awake therefore, for you do not know on what day your master is coming.
43 But know this, that if the householder had known in what watch the thief was coming, he would have kept awake and would not have let his house be broken into. 44 Therefore you also must be ready, because the Son of Man is coming at an hour you do not expect.

Jesus, based on his own version of the first passion prediction (Luke 9.22 = Mark 8.31). This explains how Jesus comes to be in heaven, though the kingdom is in a sense already present, 'in the midst of you' (Luke 17.21). The elect must wait in faith until the unknown moment when he comes to vindicate them. The rest of the Q sequence (Luke 17.26–35, including some further Lucan expansion in verses 31–3)[6] is concerned with the suddenness of this moment (seen as a moment of destruction) and of the peril of heedlessness. This takes the form of a comparison with the flood, and (in Luke only) with the destruction of Sodom.[7] From Matthew's point of view this corresponds with the remarks on the impossibility of predicting the time of the Son of Man's coming in Mark 13.32, and so he places these final verses immediately after his version of it. So once again there is a thematic parallel between Mark and Q.

Finally, the other Q tradition consists of the parable of the thief (Luke 12.39), which Matthew has conflated with Mark's parable of the absent master under the slogan 'Keep awake!' (Matt. 24.42f = Mark 13.35f). It will be observed that the application to the coming of the Son of Man (Matt. 24.44 = Luke 12.40) is almost identical in Matthew and Luke, though it is much more suitable to the Marcan parable of the returning master than to the Q parable of the thief. It should thus be considered as a serious possibility that this is Matthew's own addition to the conflated parable, and that it should not be accepted as an authentic part of Luke's text.[8] If so, it belongs with Matthew's special use of the Son of Man title, and does not contribute to our knowledge of the usage in Q. As this suggestion falls short of proof, it will be assumed nevertheless that it accompanied the parable of the thief in Q.

3 *Analysis of the Son of Man sayings*

Our next task is to see how the Son of Man functions in this material, in order to trace the relationship with Q's use of the phrase in the sayings already studied in chapter 3.

a. The first mention of the Son of Man comes in Luke's introduction to the Q sequence, and has no parallel in Matthew (Luke 17.22). Doubts immediately arise whether this really represents the Q opening, because the verse forms the link between the publicly spoken saying on the kingdom of God in Luke 17.20f and Luke's presentation of the Q material as further teaching on the same subject, given to the disciples privately. Moreover the phrase 'one of the days of the Son of Man' is so strange that it suggests that Luke had difficulty in integrating the material. The fact is that he had to effect the transition between the concept of the kingdom as an ongoing state in verse 21 and the particular day of the revelation of the Son of Man to perform the judgement (whether at the beginning or at the conclusion of the time of the kingdom remains unclear). From this point of view 'the days of the Son of Man' is an alternative expression for the kingdom of God, comparable to the 'days of the Messiah' in rabbinic sources.[9] The connection between the two expressions is made clearer by Luke's repetition of the 'Lo, here!' theme in verses 21 and 23. On these grounds it does not seem safe to attribute verse 22 to Q.[10] The use of the Son of Man in this verse is thus derived from what follows. Luke's redactional use of it in this way shows clearly that he regards the phrase as equivalent to the Messiah, referring exclusively to Jesus himself.

b. Next, there are three verses in which Matthew and Luke are agreed in referring to the Son of Man, and these may be confidently assigned to the Q sequence which underlies both. In each case Matthew has streamlined the expression ('so will be the parousia of the Son of Man', Matt. 24.27, 37, 39) so as to correspond with his redactional opening (the disciples ask, 'What will be the sign of your parousia and of the close of the age?', Matt. 24.3). Although the word *parousia* does not occur in the gospels outside these four verses, it is a natural word for 'coming' in this kind of context, and is so used elsewhere in the New Testament, both for the prophetic–eschatological 'coming of the Lord' (Jas. 5.7f, unless it refers to Christ; 2 Pet. 3.12, the coming of the day of God) and for the Christian application of this notion to the exalted Christ (1 Cor. 15.23; 1 Thess. 2.19; 3.13; 4.15; 5.23; 2 Thess. 2.1; 2 Pet. 1.16; 1 John 2.28). Thus, as far as Matthew is concerned, the Son of Man here certainly refers to Jesus as the messianic figure of Dan. 7.13–14.

In Luke, however, the expressions are varied. In Luke 17.24 no action of the Son of Man is described: like a flash of lightning, 'so will be the Son of Man in his day'.[11] Whatever he does, it will be sudden and unmistakable. But the comparison to lightning certainly favours the supposition that the reference is to the revelation of the Son of Man, as in verse 30. In view of Luke's opening verse, it would seem to be his intention to refer to the appearance of the Son of Man for the release and vindication of the oppressed faithful. The original was no doubt more concerned with the judgement. This is clear in the second instance, verse 26, where the 'days of Noah' are compared with the 'days of the Son of Man'. Here the plural 'days' refers to the period within which the cataclysm occurred, rather than the specific day of the disaster, which is then mentioned in verse 27. The same distinction is made between the 'days of Lot' and the day of the destruction of Sodom in verses 28–9. Consequently the conclusion in verse 30 speaks of the particular day of the corresponding event in the history of the Son of Man. Thus there is no contradiction between the 'days' in verse 26 and the 'day' in verse 30, because they refer to different things. And if 'in his day' is rightly excluded from verse 24 on textual grounds, the sequence shows an artistic progression from bare mention of the Son of Man in verse 24, through the period in which he is expected in verse 26, to the actual date of his appearance in verse 30. It is thus a mistake to take the lead of Matthew and to attempt to co-ordinate the expressions in these three verses. It may be noted further that 'revealed' in verse 30 not only brings the sequence to its climax, but also makes an inclusion with verse 24, where the lightning simile has suggested revelation.

Luke's version may be accepted as reproducing the source with a fair degree of fidelity. Luke is not responsible for introducing the confusing references to 'days' and 'day', and indeed his retention of this feature is the reason why he worded the opening verse 22 so awkwardly. Matthew is correct in assuming that the event, described in terms of revelation in Luke 17.30, is a heavenly coming. The point is that it is a coming that can be seen. Thus the actual meaning of the passage has the crucial features for postulating an allusion to Dan. 7.13–14.[12] The Marcan parallel, where the allusion to Daniel is incontrovertible, begins, 'Then you will see the Son of Man coming . . . ' (Mark 13.26). Thus there can be no doubt that, in this sequence at any rate, the titular use of the Son of Man to denote the Danielic figure is already found in Q. This causes no difficulty, because consciousness of the allusion may have been a factor in the Greek translation of *bar enasha* anyway. Nothing is gained by trying to maintain that he who was proclaimed as the exalted Messiah in terms of Ps. 110.1 was not also recognized as the Danielic figure, even if identifiable allusions to Daniel in the New Testament are rare.[13]

What is more difficult is to see how this Q sequence relates to the teaching of Jesus himself. It cannot be regarded as an extraneous piece about the Son of Man, which has been incorporated into the Jesus tradition. Any solution on these lines is excluded by the fact that the Son of Man was not a title in Judaism outside the sayings of Jesus. To speak of 'the day when the Son of Man is revealed' would be meaningless outside this context. Thus the form of the sequence in Q has been built up as part of the process of collecting and editing the sayings of Jesus.[14] It is therefore proper to see it in relation to other similar items within the sayings tradition. Here we can adduce the quite sizable number of sayings and parables on watchfulness, which give warning of a coming event.[15] The nature of the eschatological teaching of Jesus is too big a question to go into here. But we have already come across references to the judgement in the 'advocate' saying, and this must be seen in relation to the fundamental proclamation that 'the kingdom of God is at hand' (Mark 1.15). Moreover the material on the 'sign of Jonah' brings in the warning of judgement. Thus the idea contained in the present passage, that judgement will fall suddenly upon the heedless, is not foreign to the sayings tradition. References to the eschatological days or day can be found outside the range of Son of Man sayings, notably in 1 Thess. 5.2–3, which reflects this eschatological teaching:

> For you yourselves know well that the day of the Lord will come like a thief in the night. When people say, 'There is peace and security', then sudden destruction will come upon them as travail comes upon a woman with child, and there will be no escape.

These thoughts may be the stock-in-trade of the contemporary Jewish apocalyptic, but they bear a remarkably close resemblance to the eschatological sayings attributed to Jesus.

But when Jesus spoke of the coming of the kingdom, what he meant was the coming of God.[16] Similarly the idea of the eschatological day is a continuation of the day of the Lord, which features in Old Testament prophecy. It is thus reasonable to suggest that the teaching with which we are now concerned originally referred to the expected day in this sense. But—in keeping with a tendency which is found throughout the New

Testament—functions ascribed to God in the Old Testament were attributed to the exalted Jesus as his agent in the teaching of the primitive church. Thus the day of the Lord becomes the day of the exalted Christ, or, in terms of the Christian messianic understanding of Dan. 7.13–14, the day of the Son of Man. On this basis it may be conjectured that the tradition lying behind Luke 17.24, 26, 30 read 'so will it be on that day', 'so will it be also in those days', and 'in the same way it will be on that day'. The lightning flash in verse 24 suggested an appearance in glory, and this helped the compiler to introduce specific allusion to Dan. 7.13–14. But his principal motive was the desire to integrate this eschatological picture into the Church's christological understanding of it. From his point of view, specification of the day as the day of the Son of Man was no more than making explicit the actual meaning of the text.[17]

c. The same considerations apply to the parable of the thief (Luke 12.39), if the Son of Man saying which follows it is to be regarded as part of the Q material. As already mentioned, the latter saying is far more suitable to Mark's parable of the returning master of the house. The proper comparison to the thief breaking in at night is not the Danielic Son of Man, who is of course a figure of honour, but the day of the Lord, i.e., a happening rather than a person. This is precisely the comparison that is drawn in 1 Thess. 5.2, quoted above, and also in 2 Pet. 3.10, and the parable is echoed again in Rev. 3.3; 16.15.[18] It has often been supposed that Paul deliberately dropped the Son of Man title as unsuitable for a Gentile audience, but our argument suggests that he had never heard of such a title because it did not exist when he was writing. The titular use of the Son of Man came about as a feature of the literary editing of the sayings tradition, and was never used outside it in the primitive Christology. Actually the parable of the thief in Luke 12.39 does not use the Son of Man title, which belongs solely to the application in verse 40. Thus a connection between the parable and the 'thief' sayings in 1 Thess. and Rev. can be accepted without any reference to the Son of Man.

Comparison of the application in Matt. 24.44=Luke 12.40 with Mark's parable on the returning master or lord (Greek *kurios*) is more fruitful. Mark's 'you do not know when the master . . . is coming' (*ouk oidate gar pote ho kurios . . . erchetai*) is almost identical with 'at an hour when you do not expect the Son of Man is

coming' (*he ou dokeite hora ho huios tou anthropou erchetai*). In his
parallel to Mark at Matt. 24.42 Matthew has specified Mark's
'when' as 'on what day', but this is for the sake of continuity with
the preceding section on the parousia of the Son of Man (and
incidentally suggests that he was working on a form of Q in which
'day' rather than 'parousia' was used, as in Luke 17). But 'hour', as
in verse 44, is obviously much more suitable, because the Marcan
parable goes on to suggest the four divisions of the night
(represented in Matthew's conflation by 'watch', Greek *phulake*,
Matt. 24.43). Mark's parable does not have an application. It is left
to the hearer to make the identification between the master's return
and the eschatological time, and it is obvious that the original
reference is likely to have been to the coming of God himself ('the
lord'). So here again the Q source has spelled out the christological
transformation of conventional eschatological sayings, and the
kurios is identified with the Danielic Son of Man. However, it
cannot be supposed that Q provides the interpretation of a parable
that is only found in Mark! It is for this reason that the suggestion
that Luke 12.40 is not an original part of Luke's text should be
considered a serious possibility. For it is easy to see how Matthew
can have composed this verse on the basis of his conflation of the
two parables, so as to round off the whole Son of Man sequence. On
the other hand there is really no compelling reason to deny it to Q.
This may be seen if Luke 12.39–40 are punctuated in such a way as
to isolate the proverbial (parabolic) material from its frame and
'master' is substituted for 'Son of Man':

> But know this, that 'If the householder had known in what hour[19] the
> thief was coming, he would not have let his house be broken into'. You
> also must be ready,[20] because 'The master is coming at an hour you do
> not expect'.

Set out in this way, the two verses can be seen to be a pair of
parables, rather than one parable with appended interpretation. In
this case the second parable is the Q equivalent of Mark's parable of
the returning master. As before, the motive for introducing the Son
of Man was to identify the master with Jesus himself. And the use of
the verb 'comes' was sufficient to give the hint that the Son of Man
phrase was not only a characteristic form of self-reference on Jesus'
part, but also intended to refer to him as the future fulfilment of
Dan. 7.13–14.[21]

Our findings on the Son of Man in Q may now be summarized. This collection contained at least four, and possibly five, sayings which preserve the authentic *bar enasha* idiom. The Greek translation, however, makes the phrase appear to function as an exclusive self-reference on Jesus' part, and thus makes it virtually a title. As such, it is inevitable that its christological content should be supplied by Dan. 7.13–14, not only because of the description there of *ke-bar enash*, one like a son of man, but also because the person so described precisely fitted the idea of Jesus in the primitive church's Christology. A pointer in this direction was already afforded in the authentic nucleus by the 'advocate' saying, though this may have been in the 'I' form in Q, and so should perhaps not be regarded as directly influential on Q's usage. But another authentic saying which may have exerted direct influence in this way is the 'sign of Jonah' saying. For this stands in a short sequence which could easily suggest that Jesus is to be God's agent in the eschatological judgement. This suited the situation in the development of Christology, because there was a tendency to ascribe to Jesus, as the exalted Lord, the functions of God in the coming eschatological events. The Q sequence in Luke 17.22–37, and the saying in Matt. 24.44, if it is properly to be attributed to Q, provide examples where the teaching of Jesus is best understood in terms of the coming of God, but the christological tendency of the time of the Q collection requires that they should refer to the coming of Jesus himself. This is done by incorporating the Son of Man, as a characteristic self-reference of Jesus, and from this point of view it is no more than extension of his style. But in fact the Danielic reference is deliberate, and this has dictated the introduction of this feature into these particular contexts.

The Christology of Q is not easily determined. But because Q does appear to have a narrative opening (John the Baptist, the baptism of Jesus, the temptations) but yet lacks a passion narrative altogether, it has all too easily been assumed that Q presents a Son of Man Christology. Jesus announces the kingdom, and warns the people that he will be present at God's intervention in which it is set up.[22] Apart from the fact that any reconstruction of Q is too tenuous to allow conclusions from what the source apparently did *not* contain (the dangerous argument from silence), it should now be clear that such an idea of the Son of Man in Q is confined to Luke 17.22–37 and Matt. 24.44, and that outside these passages Q is more

notable for the variety in the small number of Son of Man sayings
which it contains and for the fidelity with which they preserve the
underlying idiom. The idea that Q has a Son of Man Christology is
not really warranted by the facts. In any case it depends on the
contention, which we have seen to be erroneous, that the Son of
Man was current as a messianic title outside the development of the
sayings tradition.

6

The Son of Man in the Christology of Mark

Introduction

Much the same phenomena can also be detected in Mark. The Son of Man, assumed to be an exclusive self-reference, is recognized as a style-feature of Jesus, and exploited in relation to the growth of Christology. Thereby Jesus can be made to refer darkly to his 'real' status, as understood by the evangelist. Thus Mark offers a parallel to what we have just seen in Q. But he goes about it in his own individual way. Whereas the aim of Q is as difficult to determine as the Christology, Mark's aim is clear and forthright. It is to present Jesus as the Son of God. Thus Mark has a conscious interest in the christological implications of his narrative. This has already been outlined to some extent in connection with the passion predictions. It is now our task to see how the rest of Mark's Son of Man sayings relate to these passion sayings, and are integrated into his christological design.

Mark has three main types of Son of Man sayings, which in fact correspond with the groupings generally employed in studies of the Son of Man in the Gospels as a whole. These are:

a. Sayings concerning the present, earthly position of Jesus: all six sayings considered above in chapter 3 come under this heading, apart from the ambiguous 'advocate' saying. These included one only from Mark (i.e., Mark 2.10), and we have yet to examine Mark 2.28, which belongs to this class.

b. Secondly there are the passion sayings, which need not now be reviewed again. But it will be relevant to notice Mark's technique. He has in these sayings material for his theme of the necessity of the passion, and he exploits it to the full by repeating the sayings and expanding their contents. Thus we should be prepared to find that Mark is capable of increasing the stock of Son of Man sayings in ways which he feels to be legitimate, because from his point of view it does not do violence to the tradition which he has received.

c. Finally, there are sayings which refer to the future coming of the Son of Man. These comprise Mark's version of the 'advocate' saying (Mark 8.38), which is notable for the way in which allusion to the text of Dan. 7.13 has been made explicit, and two further sayings, Mark 13.26 and 14.62, in which Dan. 7.13 is actually quoted. Thus this group of sayings gives a parallel with the development which we have seen in Q.

1 *The Authority of the Son of Man*

The first class of sayings consists only of two which come quite close together near the beginning of Mark's Gospel. These are 2.10 and 2.28. The first of these was found, in our study of it in chapter 3, to preserve the *bar enasha* idiom in a very telling way within the setting of the memorable story of the paralysed man who was let down through the roof. It was concerned with the authority to forgive sins on behalf of God. The idiom requires that the true meaning of the saying is 'that a man (i.e., anyone so called by God) may have power on earth to forgive sins'. But of course Mark, using a tradition already put into Greek, assumed that the Son of Man was an exclusive self-reference. Thus to him the story was concerned with the authority of Jesus over against all other people. It thus reinforces the opening impression of Mark's account of Jesus' ministry, which establishes that Jesus is a figure of authority (cf. 1.27).[1] Seeing that Mark will later make explicit reference to Dan. 7.13, it can be safely assumed that Mark values this attribute of Jesus as a hint of the full authority which he is destined to exercise after his death and resurrection. In fact Matthew has perhaps correctly perceived that this is the christological point of the whole pericope (cf. Matt. 9.8).[2]

The other saying in this class, Mark 2.28, is also concerned with authority: 'So the Son of Man is lord even of the sabbath'. This comes at the end of the story of an infringement of the sabbath by Jesus' disciples. They have been seen to pluck ears of corn and to thresh them in their hands (as Luke 6.1 explains), while walking through the cornfields. As a religious teacher, Jesus should have restrained them from this activity on the sabbath day. Jesus defends their action by adducing the case of David, who infringed the law of purity by taking the shewbread from the sanctuary at Nob (1 Sam. 21.1–6). The modern reader is likely to feel that the cases are not really parallel, because David was in real need, and the disciples are idly nibbling to satisfy their appetite. But, for our present purpose, the important thing is the conclusion to which it leads. Here Mark sums up the principle with a proverbial saying which gives every impression of being the correct conclusion of the pericope (verse 27), 'And he said to them, "The sabbath was made for man, not man for the sabbath" '. Verse 28 immediately follows this as a further conclusion, that the Son of Man is lord (and therefore has authority to dispense the rules) even of the sabbath.

It will be seen at once that this conclusion usefully enhances the impression already given that Jesus is a man with special authority. It thus suits Mark's editorial purpose excellently. But is it simply an addition to the pericope composed by Mark himself? Or can it be defended as an integral part of the parable? If not, has Mark received it from some other strand of tradition, and if so can it be regarded as authentic?

a. The case for regarding the saying as the original conclusion of the parable is supported by the parallels in Matt. 12.1–8 and Luke 6.1–5. Both omit verse 27, so that the Son of Man saying becomes the only conclusion to the dispute.[3] This degree of agreement between the two evangelists is not as impressive as it seems at first sight, because Matthew has expanded the text with a further Old Testament case in point (Matt. 12.5f, referring to the action of the priests on the sabbath; cf. Lev. 24.28; Num. 28.9f),[4] and has provided his own substitute for the general principle enunciated in Mark 2.27, in the form of his favourite quotation of Hos. 6.6 (Matt. 12.7; cf. 9.13). Luke on the other hand simply omits the verse, presumably because he finds the other sufficient as an explanation of the point.[5] There is thus no strong reason to regard Mark 2.27 as intrusive, in spite of the omission of it by Matthew and Luke, and its value as the proper conclusion to the pericope should be recognized.

b. If Mark 2.28 is retained as original, it must be taken in conjunction with verse 27, not as an alternative to it. So the general principle of man's superiority to the sabbath enunciated in verse 27 is then taken up as the grounds for a personal claim on the part of

Jesus to have authority over it. This becomes more plausible in the light of a rabbinic parallel (Mekhilta Ex. 31.14 (109b)), 'The Sabbath is given over to you and not you to the Sabbath'.[6] The reference here is to Israel as the chief beneficiaries of the institution of the sabbath. For it can be argued on this basis that Jesus, as the Son of Man, is the representative of God on behalf of the people, and that therefore he has authority to give guidance concerning such matters as the law of the sabbath. But this presupposes that the Son of Man is a recognized messianic designation, which is no longer a tenable position. Consequently, if this argument is to be accepted, verse 28 must belong to a stage in the history of the tradition when the Son of Man, understood as a self-designation of Jesus, is already identified with the Danielic figure. This makes it impossible for verse 28 to be an original part of the pericope and to go back to Jesus himself.

c. The difficulty might be overcome, if the Son of Man in verse 28 can be shown to be capable of bearing the *bar enasha* idiom. Comparison with Mark 2.10 suggests a possible interpretation. Seeing that the sabbath was made for man, etc. (the general principle), *a man may be* lord even of the sabbath, i.e. authorized by God to override it (the particular case). It is exactly the same as the authority to forgive sins. This interpretation avoids the weakness in the position of Wellhausen and others, who have taken Son of Man to mean any man, thus giving to *bar enasha* a general and universal application which is foreign to the idiom.[7] For it is not at all likely that Jesus would have expressed such a view, and it would certainly have ruined his argument with the Pharisees.

d. Unfortunately, though this interpretation is attractive at first sight, verse 28 still remains foreign to the purpose of the pericope, by contrast with Mark 2.10, where it is the central and indispensable feature. The point is to show Jesus' defence of the disciples as an example of his skill in opposing the extremely strict interpretation of the law required by the Pharisees. It is not to hold up Jesus as a superior person, who has authority to override the law. Jesus does not require a special position in order to make his point, because it is valid without that. The case of David, which Jesus actually cites, is sufficient to support the general principle which can cover the disciples' action. Thus, even if verse 28 is accepted as an authentic saying, interpreted along the lines suggested above, it must be regarded as out of context here. Moreover the phrase 'lord of the sabbath' is very strange, and seems as improbable for the generic interpretation of the saying as it does for the universal interpretation. (A further difficulty is that verse 27 is a good candidate for a possible case where Aramaic *bar enasha* has been rendered by simple *ho anthropos* in Greek, but it would be very unlikely that the same phrase would be translated *ho huios tou anthropou* in the very next sentence, if the two verses belonged together in the original form. This is not a strong argument, because it cannot be proved that *bar enasha* was used in the underlying text of verse 27.)

e. If verse 28 was a floating saying, as some commentators suppose,[8] it still fails to convince as an authentic tradition, because of the difficulty of the expression 'lord of the sabbath'. This really makes sense only when the Son of Man is taken to be an exclusive self-designation, denoting Jesus as an authority figure. It thus finds its most natural explanation within the literary process, in which the Son of Man, in the Greek form, has come to be regarded as an exclusive self-reference and identification of Jesus with the Danielic figure is presupposed. It is thus best regarded, not as a floating item of which the true context is lost, but as a deliberate addition to the pericope, aimed at bringing out the christological implications of it. For the Son of Man is comparable to David, whose example is held up as justification of Jesus' failure to rebuke the disciples. This is no doubt the reason why both Matthew and Luke have retained verse 28, in spite of abandoning the original conclusion in verse 27. And if this is the reason for the addition of verse 28, it does not seem necessary to attribute it to the pre-Marcan stage of transmission, because a good case can be made out for Mark's own responsibility for composing it and incorporating it into his redaction of the pericope.

Mark does not compose Son of Man sayings indiscriminately, but we have already seen several characteristics of his writing which can explain why he has done so here. The controversy sequence of Mark 2.1—3.6 is essentially concerned with the conflict between Jesus and the Pharisees over the interpretation of the law. But Mark is also interested in it as evidence for the position of Jesus as a figure of authority. This came to expression in connection with a Son of Man saying in 2.10. Now the reference to David suggests the same theme. It will come up again by implication in the very next scene, the healing of the man who had a withered hand, in which the question of authority is expressly raised (3.4), and the editorial conclusion tells of the intention of the Pharisees and Herodians to get rid of Jesus (3.6). Thus, to say at the conclusion of the present pericope that '*therefore* the Son of Man is lord *also* of the sabbath' can be taken as an extension of 2.10, where his authority to forgive sins was mentioned. Mark's technique here is not dissimilar to his handling of the passion sayings, which he expands and repeats for the sake of his christological aims. Moreover, it is well known that Mark does introduce comments of his own from time to time. For instance, the final words of 7.19 ('thus he declared all foods clean') are widely held to be Mark's own comment, and there is good reason to believe that the conversations between Jesus and the disciples in 8.14–21 and 9.9–13 are largely the work of Mark himself, building on more fragmentary items of tradition.[9]

On this view, Mark's creation of 2.28 is a repetition of the substance of 2.10, prompted by the implications of the appeal to David in the pericope, and adapted to the issue of the sabbath. It is motivated by Mark's christological concerns. But it is important to realize that this does not mean that Mark is treating the Son of Man as a recognized messianic title. It is precisely because of its lack of specificity that it is so useful to Mark's purpose. For Mark and his readers it is a self-designation of Jesus without particular christological content. That is provided only by the context. Thus, at this early stage in his gospel, Mark can give some first hints of the truth about Jesus. Jesus is a person entrusted by God with special authority in religious matters. This fact is likely to raise the question of his real identity, and so there is the questioning in 6.14–15; 8.27–8, leading to the confession of Peter, 'You are the Christ'. No one suggests the answer, 'You are the Son of Man', of course. The Son of Man is Jesus' way of referring to himself, and it is what he says *about* himself which leads to the conclusion that he is the Christ.

2 *The Future Son of Man*

It is now possible to see what Mark is doing when he incorporates Son of Man sayings from the tradition. He seizes on these items as a means of conveying his christological teaching. So the next thing he does, after Peter's confession, is to use one of the passion sayings, the first prediction in 8.31. This has been shaped in the light of the kerygma of the death and resurrection of Jesus, and so supplies essential Christian content to the claim that Jesus is the Christ. It is followed up by teaching on discipleship after the example of the cross, ending with the climax of the process in the judgement (8.38) and the kingdom (9.1).

We are already familiar with 8.38, for it is Mark's version of the 'advocate' saying:

> For whoever is ashamed of me and of my words in this adulterous and sinful generation, of him will the Son of Man also be ashamed, when he comes in the glory of his Father with the holy angels.

Here we are concerned with it only from the point of view of Mark's use of the Son of Man title. The most striking feature is the clear allusion to Dan. 7.13–14 in the last clause, omitting the ancillary role of Jesus and by implication making him to be the judge himself. Here, then, is the complete identification of Jesus with the Danielic figure, reflecting the Christology which we have also seen in the Q source at Luke 17.22–37. So, after death and resurrection, Jesus will come as judge, and then the kingdom of God will be set up (9.1).

That is the programme which is set before Mark's readers at this turning-point in his gospel. It is reinforced in what follows, not only by the conversation in 9.9–13, the repetition of the passion predictions, and the 'ransom' saying of 10.45, but also by the preview of the future glory of Jesus which is provided by the Little Apocalypse of Mark 13. So, when we discover that the climax of the signs of the end (verse 4) is that men 'will see the Son of Man coming in clouds with great power and glory' (verse 26), we are entitled to conclude that this is yet another case of Mark's extension and expansion of his christological material, and to take it very closely with his version of the 'advocate' saying in 8.38. The same can also be said of the comparable climax in the account of the trial of Jesus before the high priest. When the high priest asks Jesus, 'Are you the Christ, the Son of the Blessed?', Jesus replies (Mark 14.62), 'I am; and you will see the Son of Man sitting at the right hand of Power, and coming with the clouds of heaven'.

Because of the obviously close connection of these three sayings, it will be helpful to consider them together. All three reflect Dan. 7.13–14:

> *I saw* in the night visions, and behold, *with the clouds of heaven there came one like a son of man*, and he came to the Ancient of Days and was presented before him. And to him was given *dominion and glory* and kingdom . . .

However, none of our three sayings include the idea of coming *to* the Ancient of Days or of *receiving* dominion and glory. Thus, although a great deal has been made of this feature of the Daniel vision,[10] it is likely to be a false track. It is something that is deliberately excluded, and therefore it should not be used to control the interpretation.

a. The reason for this can be seen in the first of the three, the 'advocate' saying. For here the Son of Man is represented as coming (not to God, but to mankind) in judgement. The reference to the judgement, which belongs to the original form of the saying as preserved in Q, has been conformed to the current Christology, in which Jesus himself is to be the judge at the parousia.

b. In the second saying, Mark 13.26, the purpose of Jesus' coming is not stated, but it can easily be deduced from the context. He comes to deliver the elect from their tribulation and this is done by sending out the angels to gather them up from all points of the compass (verse 27). The fact that he has the angels at his command suggests that his position and functions are pictured in accordance with the contemporary apocalyptic idea of the coming of the Lord, based on Zech. 14.5: 'Then the Lord your God will come, and all the holy ones with him.' This had already been taken up in the earliest strand of the Book of Enoch, well before New Testament times (1 Enoch 1.9): 'And behold! he comes with ten thousand holy ones to execute judgement upon them . . .', and this is quoted in the New Testament in Jude 14, 'Behold, the Lord came with his holy myriads, to execute judgement on all . . . '.[11]

Thus, once again the clue to understanding the Son of Man saying in the apocalyptic discourse is the christological identification of the coming of the Lord with the parousia of Jesus. This explains how this feature, which cannot go back to Jesus himself on account of the titular use of the Son of Man, has come into the apocalyptic discourse. Mark 13 is certainly based on items from the sayings tradition, some of which have a good claim to be regarded as authentic. But the overall structure, and therefore the arrangement of the various elements into a chronological sequence, belongs to the editing of Mark himself. Those elements which are concerned with discipleship and watchfulness have the best claim to be accepted as genuine sayings of Jesus. The more programmatic verses, largely concerned with portents, differ from these in being replete with Old Testament phrases and allusions. This is a well known feature of apocalyptic writing, exemplified throughout the book of Revelation, but is not characteristic of the sayings tradition. Thus, in building up the apocalyptic discourse, Mark has taken the liberty of placing the traditional material within a framework of Old Testament prophecy, which accords with the basic idea of Jesus' message of the coming kingdom, but differs in specifying details of the apocalyptic programme.

Seen in this light, Mark 13.26 has no particular claim to be considered an isolated saying drawn by Mark from the traditions available to him. The whole of the climactic paragraph, Mark 13.24–27, is a mosaic of Old Testament passages, and our verse takes its place among them. The present verse can thus be seen to be a repetition of the idea already contained in Mark's version of the 'advocate' saying, Mark 8.38, but now worded in closer conformity with Dan. 7.13–14. This is deliberate, because it is an essential part of Mark's purpose to present Jesus as the agent of God for the eternal salvation of the elect (cf. verses 20, 27). Similarly, when Matthew takes over this composition, he adds further Old Testament quotations and allusions to make the picture more complete. In his version of verse 26 Matthew introduces the mourning of the tribes (Matt. 24.30; cf. Zech. 12.10–14) in words which are almost identical with the conflation of Dan. 7.13 and the Zechariah passage in Rev. 1.7.[12] Then in the next verse he adds the trumpet (Isa. 27.13) to Mark's account of the sending out of the angels, which is also a feature of Paul's apocalyptic expectations; cf. 1 Cor. 15.52; 1 Thess. 4.16. These facts show that Matthew's expansion of Mark is not merely the result of his own biblical studies, but reflects the wider use of such ideas in the church of his time. In the same way Mark's use of Dan. 7.13–14 here is a reflection of the process which we have observed already behind the eschatological material in Q. Jesus' use of the Son of Man phrase now carries with it overtones of the Danielic figure in the minds of

Mark and his contemporaries, even though the fact remains that the Son of Man never became a christological title outside the sayings tradition.

(c) Mark returns to the passion sayings in the next chapter (14.21, 41), but the last and most impressive of the Son of Man sayings is the answer of Jesus to the high priest in 14.62. Though the authenticity of this saying has frequently been challenged, there has been a strong impetus to defend it on account of its great importance for Christology. Here there can be no doubt about the literary dependence on Dan. 7.13.[13] But the words 'sitting at the right hand of Power' are universally recognized to be dependent on Ps. 110.1, which has already been quoted by Mark at 12.36. The significance of this addition to the Danielic saying has not always been correctly appreciated. It is precisely because the coming of the Son of Man is a coming *to earth* for judgement that his heavenly session has to be described in words other than Dan. 7.13f, and also has to be mentioned *first*. The two parts of the saying are not virtual equivalents, but are distinct ideas, and are placed in the right order.[14] The exaltation of Jesus is a fundamental feature of the primitive kerygma, because the resurrection experience was not just a conviction of Jesus' return to life, but an assurance of his continuing presence with God. This point was expressed with the aid of Ps. 110.1 from the earliest days, with the consequence that it has left its mark on the New Testament more than any other Old Testament quotation.[15] Much more than Dan. 7.13, it is a text which was readily available to Mark from common use among Christians in the expression of their faith.

There is thus no difficulty in the supposition that the composition of this conflate quotation goes back to Mark. It fits nicely into the series, beginning with 8.38, and continuing with 13.26, in which identification of Jesus with the Danielic figure is complete. Hence it must be regarded as at least possible, if not probable, that Mark's choice of 'Power' (*dunamis*) as a periphrasis for God is derived from his own quotation of Daniel in 13.26.[16] It is also easy to see why Mark should have inserted this saying at this point in his narrative of the trial. For the trial before the high priest he has used the tradition of the false witness concerning the 'temple' saying (Mark 14.57–61a). His material for the trial before Pilate presupposes that the charge against Jesus is a claim to be 'the king of the Jews' (Mark

15.2–20). The discrepancy can be removed by the insertion of a direct question on the part of the high priest whether he is the Christ. The answer needs to be suitably impressive, because it embodies the faith which Mark wishes his readers to hold. The heavenly session and the parousia express the faith and hope of everyone who acknowledges Jesus as the Christ. Thus, at the only point in the gospel where Jesus says 'I am' in reply to a direct question concerning his messiahship, the answer is defined further by words drawn from the Old Testament which are used in current christological teaching. It takes the form of repetition and expansion of 13.26, like the passion predictions.

On this showing both the high priest's question and Jesus' answer have to be regarded as the work of Mark, as he welds the traditions together to create a continuous narrative, at the same time as relating the whole to his overall evangelistic purpose. There is, of course, nothing new in the suggestion that Mark 14.61b–2 should be regarded as Mark's interpolation into his source.[17] The opening word 'again' is a recurring sign of a suture in Mark's text.[18] Moreover omission of these verses eases one of the intractable problems of the trial narrative, and that is the verdict that Jesus has been guilty of blasphemy (verse 63). It has always been difficult to see what was blasphemous in Jesus' reply in the preceding verse, as he appears to say nothing to the dishonour of the name of God, and the periphrastic 'Power' gives the impression of care to avoid doing so.[19] The usual explanation is the form of messiahship which he claims, involving virtual equality with God on account of sharing his throne. But this is rendered doubtful by the fact that the words used are those of Ps. 110.1, as we have seen, so that the messianic claim is expressed in scriptural terms. Two other possible causes for the accusation of blasphemy may be suggested, though they are not mentioned in the Mishnah: *i.* A claim to divine prerogatives might constitute dishonour to God. This seems to be the point at issue in the question of Jesus' authority to forgive sins in Mark 2.9, and we have seen how Jesus was able to maintain his position without denying the fundamental principle; *ii.* Words dishonouring God indirectly through abusing that which lies very close to God's honour might be considered to be blasphemous (the more restricted ruling of the Mishnah might well be directed against such a dangerous enlargement of the concept). In this case the prophecy of Jesus against the temple might be taken as blasphemous. Though this may not appear probable at first sight, it is supported by the treatment of Jeremiah (Jer. 26.1–11) and by the case of Stephen (Acts 6.11–14). If this is allowed for the case of Jesus, the continuity between verses 61a and 63f appears to great advantage. Jesus has been challenged to repudiate the 'temple' saying, but he has remained silent (61a). The high priest rends his clothes (as required by the Mishnah after hearing all the evidence and before giving sentence), and suggests that no further witness is required (63). The sanhedrin concur in his opinion and declare Jesus guilty of death (64). Thus the silence of Jesus, instead of appearing merely obtuse and being immediately negated by his reply to the high priest, becomes a crucial factor in the trial. It is precisely because Jesus refuses to deny that he said the words which have been quoted, in spite of the claim that they are blasphemous, that no further witnesses need to be called and the case against him can be regarded as proved.

It is, of course, possible that Mark derived 14.61b–62 from another source. But this suggestion does not overcome the obstacles which stand in the way of accepting it as authentic, and breaks the connection with 8.38 and 13.26, which has been shown to accord well with Mark's method and purpose. If Jesus did not actually speak these words, nothing is gained by attributing them to an unknown source rather than to Mark himself.[20]

d. Mark has no further Son of Man sayings, but the question must be asked whether his absolute use of 'the Son' in Mark 13.32 is intended to be an equivalent to the Son of Man. The verse opens the final exhortation to watchfulness in the Little Apocalypse, and states that 'that day or that hour' is unknown to anyone—to neither man nor angels nor 'the Son'— but only to 'the Father'. The theme of the verse fits well with the unexpectedness of the coming judgement, which we found in the Q material about the day of the Son of Man, though it conflicts with the careful programme previously outlined in the chapter. But the use of 'the Son', with the correlative 'the Father' without further description, is unique in Mark. Thus it is not sufficient to bracket 'nor the Son' as a doctrinal insertion into Mark's text, based on the Father/Son correlation of developing christology, because the absolute use of 'the Father' also has to be explained.[21] Moreover it is extremely unlikely that a dogmatic interpolation would take the form of an assertion of the ignorance of the Son (naturally these words were the centre of immense discussion in the later Arian controversy). The lack of a good connection with the preceding description suggests that the verse should be regarded as coming from another source. Nineham has suggested that it was a current saying in the church in connection with the delay of the parousia, asserting that Jesus had never claimed to know exactly when it would happen. But once more, if this is the best explanation, it seems unnecessary to ascribe it to someone other than Mark himself. The verse does not fit well with the preceding programme, it is true, but neither does the parable on watchfulness which follows in verses 33–6. Thus it serves an editorial function, making a bridge between the well articulated apocalyptic plan and the practical need to exhort the readers to be watchful. The fact that no one knows the time of the end is a commonplace of Jewish apocalyptic. The unique feature of the saying in this connection is the specification of angels, Son and Father. There is only one other place in Mark where all three are mentioned together, and that is 8.38! If Mark is himself responsible for this redactional verse, then it is not difficult to see how he has thought of the situation in the light of his own description in 8.38. The question *when* it shall be that 'the Son of Man comes in the glory of his Father with the holy angels' cannot be answered more precisely than has been done in the programme of 13.5–31, because the answer is not known to any of the participants other than the Father himself. On this showing, 'the Son' in this verse is certainly to be regarded as an unparalleled abbreviation for the Son of Man. This and 'the Father', which is an equally unusual departure from Mark's normal practice, nevertheless belong to Mark's editorial writing.[22] His language here reflects the Father/Son correlation of the contemporary Christology, which is already apparent in the Q material (Matt. 11.27=Luke 10.22), and will be exploited fully in the Gospel of John. Mark has slipped into it for the simple reason that he is *not* here reproducing a source.

Mark's use of the Son of Man thus confirms the picture which has been gained from study of Q. The Son of Man is accepted as a feature of the sayings tradition. It is understood by the editor as an exclusive self-designation of Jesus. It is easily and naturally applied to the christological interpretation of Dan. 7.13–14. Mark, however, goes beyond Q inasmuch as his overriding concern for Christology leads him to build on the sayings tradition in such a way as to bring home to the reader essential aspects of the confession of faith. Mark 2.10 gives a hint of the divine authority of Jesus, and this is enhanced by the introduction of a similar, but artificial, saying in 2.28. Peter's confession in 8.29 requires completion in two ways, first the necessity of the passion and secondly the parousia. These are supplied by the first passion prediction in 8.31 and the 'advocate' saying in 8.38. Mark has built up further sayings on both of these traditional elements, making the most of the passion sayings and also creating further sayings on the parousia, which are directly indebted to Dan. 7.13–14, in 13.26 and 14.62. In the latter case, the conflation of the Daniel text with Ps. 110.1 shows once more the influence of the kerygma on Mark's presentation. It has also been observed that his version of the 'advocate' saying shows Mark's familiarity with the Father/Son correlation, which belongs to the christological vocabulary of his time.[23] At 13.32 he employs this vocabulary in an editorial verse, with the result that 'the Son' is virtually an abbreviation of the Son of Man, though not in fact derived from it.

It is now clear from our study that the important place of the Son of Man in Mark is the result of Mark's literary activity. He has five authentic sayings from the tradition (2.10; 8.38, and the three passion sayings). These are exploited in relation to developments in Christology, which are also found to a lesser extent in Q. This literary exploitation of the Son of Man sayings is also a feature of Matthew, Luke and John. In the cases of Matthew and Luke at least this can be attributed to their use of Mark as a major source. But each evangelist has his own individual way of handling the material in accordance with his differing aims and outlook, and so makes his own contribution to the developed picture of Jesus as the Son of Man.

7

Matthew and the Parousia of the Son of Man

A new situation is presented to us, when we turn to Matthew. Here we have an author whose principal sources (Mark and Q) already include sayings which require the identification of the Son of Man with the Danielic figure. Because the Son of Man was not a current title for Jesus outside the sayings tradition, it must be assumed that Matthew derives his own idea of the Son of Man from these written sources. Considering his apocalyptic interests, it is not at all surprising that he tends mostly to take up and develop the apocalyptic sayings, thus increasing the stock of those which conflict with the genuine use of *bar enasha* by Jesus. It might be supposed that Matthew is so dominated by this element in the Son of Man sayings that he actually thinks of the phrase as an apocalyptic title. But we have a clear indication to the contrary in the one place where it can be shown indubitably that Matthew has removed the Son of Man from his source.[1]

In actual fact this is not so much an omission as a transference. In 16.13 Matthew begins the questioning which leads up to Peter's confession by *inserting* the Son of Man against Mark 8.27. Jesus asks, 'Who do men say that *the Son of Man* is?'[2] However Matthew leaves Mark unchanged when Jesus goes on to ask, 'But who do you say that I am?' (verse 15). The omission comes in the first passion prediction (Matt. 16.21 = Mark 8.31), where Matthew uses the third person pronoun, 'From that time Jesus began to show his disciples that *he* must go to Jerusalem and suffer many things . . . '

This apparently gratuitous change has its best explanation if the Son of Man was in Matthew's understanding a self-designation and not a messianic title in its own right. In verse 13 it *cannot* be such a title, because, if so, it would provide the answer to the very question of which it forms a part. But of course the answer is, 'You are the Christ,' not 'you are the Son of Man'.[3] Thus there was really no need for Matthew to bring in the Son of Man at this point at all, as it

115

adds nothing to the sense. It may be conjectured that he did so simply to compensate for the omission of it in the first passion prediction.[4] This also demands explanation. It seems likely that Matthew is anxious not to break continuity with the preceding confession that Jesus is the Christ, which has just been repeated at the end of verse 20. So it is *as Messiah* that Jesus is to suffer, and this explains the very stern rebuke which follows Peter's attempt to dissuade him (verse 23).[5] Precisely because the Son of Man was not a messianic title, it could not resume 'the Christ' of the preceding verse. Rather, being a self-designation, it would appear to introduce a new subject, so spoiling the close connection which Matthew wishes to maintain. Matthew has no objection to using the Son of Man as subject in the other passion predictions and related sayings (17.9, 12, 22; 20.18, 28; 26.2, 24ab, 45).

Thus Matthew does not think of the Son of Man as a title which automatically conveys the idea of the Danielic figure as its necessary content. That is so only in contexts referring to the future, when Jesus will fulfil that role. It follows that Matthew has no difficulty in retaining Son of Man sayings which do not refer to the future. This is how it comes about that he has preserved several of the authentic sayings which we have already considered, such as the 'foxes' and 'glutton' sayings (Matt. 8.20; 11.19) in Q and the passion predictions in Mark. It may be conjectured that, in using the Son of Man at these points, he had the future status of Jesus in mind, so that to his way of thinking Jesus was referring to himself as one destined for glory subsequently.[6] This would be quite possible, because he writes with the whole conspectus of the development of the Son of Man sayings in Mark and Q before him, so that the meaning of one is likely to be operative in his thought about another. But this does not lead him to alter the text so as to bring out the connection. Seeing that his use of the Son of Man in 16.13 shows that he understood perfectly well that the Son of Man was *not* a current messianic title, it is reasonable to conclude that he did not expect his readers to pick up a hint of Jesus' future destiny when he reproduced this range of sayings, whatever he may have thought privately.

1 *Matthew's use of Mark and Q*

a. The 'foxes' saying (8.20) is the first time that Matthew mentions the Son of Man, and there is nothing in the context to suggest that it means to him anything more than a self-reference on Jesus' part. The next occasion is 9.6, where he is reproducing the miracle of the paralytic from Mark. It is notable that, whereas he abbreviates the narrative drastically, the crucial verse (=Mark 2.10) is retained almost word for word. Thus Matthew agrees that Jesus has divine authority to forgive sins, but he does not feel the need to specify it as a future prerogative. Actually he has no need to do so, because to him Jesus is the Messiah from the start, so that the authority attaching to his future status already belongs to him, and there is no need to include a reference to the future.

The Son of Man is mentioned for the third time in Matthew in 10.23b, and here we have a different situation: 'Truly, I say to you, you will not have gone through all the towns of Israel, before the Son of Man comes.' This saying has been the subject of enormous discussion, but for the moment we shall pause only to note two points. First, it is a saying which is peculiar to Matthew, and secondly it belongs to the category of future sayings in which the identification with the Danielic Son of Man is presupposed. It will thus be appropriate to consider it in connection with other sayings peculiar to Matthew later.

Matthew happily accepts Mark's comment on the Son of Man's authority over the sabbath at Matt. 12.8=Mark 2.28. His only substantial change is his omission of the incompatible Mark 2.27. He also accepts the Q saying on blasphemy at Matt. 12.32=Luke 12.10. Here he does make some alterations, but that is only because he conflates the saying with the independent version of it in Mark 3.28–9.[7] He appears to be not in the least worried at the thought that blasphemy against the Son of Man may be forgiven. This again favours the supposition that he does not use the Son of Man as a status expression in this kind of context, but simply as a surrogate for the first person.

b. Changes begin to appear when Matthew handles sayings which refer to the future. He does not merely reproduce what is provided by his sources (both Mark and Q), but he brings them into line with his own ideas about Jesus as the exalted Messiah. This position of exaltation is Jesus' permanent state from the day of resurrection onwards, during the unspecified time when the faithful have to remain vigilant until the parousia, when he comes to claim his own.

117

Thus in 12.40, the Q saying on the sign of Jonah which is preserved in its original form in Luke 11.30, Matthew implicitly changes the verb ('will be') from a logical future to a real future, and the sign becomes the resurrection after three days and nights, like Jonah's sojourn in the belly of the whale. Even so, the Son of Man signifies no more than a substitute for the first person in this saying.

By the time that Matthew reaches Mark's first open identification of the Son of Man with Dan. 7.13–14, which is at Matt. 16.27 = Mark 8.38, he has already spoken of him in this way several times (i.e., at 10.23b and also in his special material at 13.37, 41). Here Matthew drops altogether the elements in Mark 8.38 which correspond with the 'advocate' saying, which he has already used in a first person form based on Q in 10.32–3. He reshapes the saying as an explicit statement of the coming judgement, and in doing so makes the Son of Man himself the judge, using words drawn from the Old Testament, which of course properly apply to God (Ps. 62.12; Prov. 24.12; Ecclus. 35.19). He thus continues the practice which we have already observed in connection with other apocalyptic sayings.

c. This explains what happens in the very next verse in Matt. 16.28 = Mark 9.1. Mark here has a solemn saying, introduced by the 'Amen' formula, which surely has a high claim to authenticity, seeing that it was rapidly becoming impossible of fulfilment at the time when the gospels were written: 'Truly, I say to you, there are some standing here, who will not taste death before they see *the kingdom of God come with power*'. Matthew changes the italicized words to ' . . . *the Son of Man coming in his kingdom*'. This has the effect of producing a very much smoother connection with the preceding verse. In both verses 27 and 28, Jesus speaks of himself as the Son of Man who will be coming on a future date. The second adds point to the first, because it suggests that this date will be very soon, within the lifetime of some of the audience. This suits Matthew's concern for vigilance. In Mark, on the other hand, the two sayings clearly belong to different strands of tradition. Mark 9.1 starts unnecessarily with 'and he said to them', which is an indication that he is joining together separate pieces. Moreover, there is no explanation of the precise relationship between the coming of the Son of Man in the glory of his Father (8.38) and the

118

coming of the kingdom of God with power (9.1). Presumably both refer to the same event. This is how Matthew understands it, and he has adjusted the text to make it plain.

There is, however, another consideration which is likely to have influenced Matthew in his alteration of this saying. Matthew follows the Jewish reverential custom of using expressions which keep God, so to speak, at arm's length. The best known example of this is the frequent substitution of 'the kingdom of heaven' for 'the kingdom of God'. It is also a feature of the Lord's Prayer, in which Luke's simple 'Father' is likely to be original against Matthew's 'Our Father, who art in heaven' (Matt. 6.9=Luke 11.2). With this mind and outlook, Matthew would certainly recognize that this same Jewish characteristic is present in the saying as it appears in Mark 9.1. To say that people will 'see the kingdom of God come in power' is a reverent way of saying that they will see God himself. Indeed the saying as given in Mark bears a remarkable similarity to the Targum of Isa. 40.9–10, where the words 'Behold your God! Behold, the Lord God comes with might' are rendered 'The kingdom of your God is revealed! Behold, the Lord God is revealed in might'.[8] We do not have to suppose that Matthew was conscious of this allusion, however. It is sufficient that the Targum reinforces what we already know from Matthew, that 'the kingdom' is one of the ways of avoiding direct reference to God. Thus there need be no doubt that he would understand the quasi-personification of the kingdom in Mark 9.1 as a way of speaking of the coming of God in person. For the saying does not refer to the coming of the kingdom in the sense of 'coming to pass', but carries with it the metaphor of the arrival of a mighty warrior. For this reason it obviously suits Matthew's presuppositions best to substitute the coming of the Son of Man in his kingdom (i.e., in royal state) for the coming of the kingdom with power. Thus his alteration is not made to introduce a reverential periphrasis, but depends upon his recognition that such a periphrasis is already there. And the motive is exactly the same as in previous apocalyptic passages, to substitute the coming of Jesus as the Son of Man for the coming of God.

Even this does not exhaust the reasons that can be assigned for this change. For if Matthew was writing later than Mark, the problem of fulfilment in the lifetime of the first generation of believers was becoming more acute. But by interpreting the saying in the light of his ideas about the Son of Man he could take advantage of the double polarity of the coming of Jesus. Jesus 'comes in his kindom' already in the resurrection. From that day onwards he can claim, 'All authority in heaven and on earth has been given to me' (Matt. 28.18, possibly alluding to Dan 7.14).[9] The fact that the resurrection/exaltation is intended by Matthew here is suggested by the avoidance of the judgement motive, just used in verse 27, in favour of the idea of 'coming in his kingdom', which can be taken to mean the assumption of kingly rule, which for Matthew begins at the resurrection. This, however, does not necessarily mean that two different forms of coming are meant—in verse 27 coming to earth for judgement at the parousia, and in verse 28 coming to heaven (like the Danielic Son of Man) to receive the kingdom. For the coming in verse 28 is also a coming to earth, inasmuch as the risen Lord is seen on earth as one who possesses heavenly glory. Thus verse 28, on this view, refers to the resurrection as a pledge or preview of the parousia, rather than as a separate event which must occur before Jesus can come in judgement.[10]

d. This view receives confirmation from other texts in Matthew. In Matt. 23.29 = Luke 13.35 a Q passage has Jesus say, 'I tell you, you will not see me until you say, "Blessed is he who comes in the name of the Lord" '. Matthew has inserted *ap' arti*, 'you will not see me *from now on*'. This does not affect the immediate issue, but its relevance will appear in a moment. The important thing is the future time referred to, when the messianic welcome of Ps. 118.26 here quoted will be spoken by the people. The only indication is Matthew's position for this material. It comes *after* the triumphal entry, in which Ps. 118.26 has already been used (Matt. 21.9). Thus it must refer to the next occasion when Jesus will be seen by the people as Messiah. If Matthew thinks of the *same* people as are now told that they will see him no more, then the occasion must be the resurrection rather than the parousia. The risen Jesus is acclaimed as the Messiah visibly in the life of the Easter community.

Matthew inserts *ap' arti* twice more into his sources, and the second of these additions comes in the answer of Jesus to the high priest. But in his account of the Last Supper Matthew has already inserted the phrase into Jesus' oath of abstention from wine.

This strengthens the connection between the Last Supper and the Messianic Banquet of the future, because these form the boundaries of the period of abstention (Matt. 26.29 = Mark 14.25; cf. Luke 22.18, where Luke has added *apo tou nun* with the same effect). The insertion into the answer to the high priest is similar (Matt. 26.64 = Mark 14.62; cf. Luke 22.69), 'You have said so. But I tell you, *from now on* you will see the Son of Man sitting at the right hand of Power, and coming on the clouds of heaven'. Thus the heavenly session is to start immediately. Obviously the death of Jesus has to come first, and so the reference must be to the resurrection as its consequence. This begins the period of the Son of Man's reign, and presumably the parousia marks the end of it in the sense that a further fulfilment is awaited. Here again Luke attests the same interpretation, using his own phrase *apo tou nun* for 'from now on'.[11] But he has also made the reference to the resurrection clearer by removing the parousia from the saying altogether. The answer of Jesus has thus become simply a statement of his heavenly session, which will shortly begin.[12]

Matthew has other changes which help to elucidate his understanding of the saying. Thus the high priest's question begins with a preliminary adjuration, and then the actual wording is conformed to Matthew's standard confession of faith (verse 63), 'I adjure you by the living God that you tell us if you are the Christ, the Son of God'.[13] The reply of Jesus begins 'You have said so' (*su eipas*). This is generally recognized to be a way of dissociating oneself from the form of words used without denying their truth (hence NEB, 'the words are yours').[14] The reason for this is explained by the next change. Matthew has inserted 'But I tell you, from now on . . . ' before continuing with the Son of Man saying. The strong adversative (*plen*) is misunderstood if it is taken to mean that, according to Matthew, Jesus repudiates the confession implied by the high priest's question in favour of a different confession, built around the idea of the Son of Man.[15] The Son of Man and the Messiah in Matthew are not opposed titles, corresponding with different concepts. The difference is merely temporal. *At present*, on trial before the Sanhedrin, Jesus cannot be seen to be Messiah, so that his power connot be demonstrated at this moment. But *from now on* his status will be visible, and the proof of his power to judge and to save will be available. Thus the resurrection, as proof of the heavenly session, guarantees the parousia.

2 *Sayings peculiar to Matthew*

a. When we turn to the Son of Man sayings peculiar to Matthew, the value of the above observations becomes evident. This is true especially in the case of 10.23b, 'For truly, I say to you, you will not have gone through all the towns of Israel, before the Son of Man comes'. The saying is placed by Matthew in the midst of his version of the mission charge of Jesus to the disciples. Characteristically Matthew has composed this sequence by conflating Mark and Q. The present verse, including 23a on fleeing to another town, forms the bridge between Marcan material on persecution (Matt. 10.17–22 = Mark 13.9–13) and Q material on discipleship, which includes the 'advocate' saying (Matt. 10.24, 26–33 = Luke 6.40; 12.2–9). But there is another conflation of Mark and Q earlier in the chapter, for Matt. 10.7–16 combines the sending out of the Twelve in Mark 6.8–11 with the sending out of the Seventy in Luke 10.1–12. When this conflate material is removed, a close connection between Matt. 10.5–6 and verse 23b is revealed (the affinities of 23a are less clear): the disciples are instructed to confine their mission to 'the lost sheep of the house of Israel', and the reason is that the time available is very short, because they will scarcely be able to complete the round of the towns of Israel, before the arrival of the Son of Man.[16] It seems, therefore, that Matthew has had a third source in composing the chapter, which he has combined with Mark and Q.

On these grounds it seems unlikely that the saying of 10.23b has been created by Matthew without the authority of an underlying tradition. This at once raises the expectation that it may be possible to take it back to Jesus himself. The chief argument in favour of authenticity is that it is unlikely to be pure invention within the post-resurrection church, because it was manifestly not fulfilled in the time to which it refers.[17] On the other side it must be said that the titular use of the Son of Man makes authenticity impossible.[18] As it stands, the saying cannot be construed as an example of the *bar enasha* idiom. It takes its place alongside the sayings in Mark and Q which have been formed within a Greek-language milieu, and presuppose the identification of Jesus with the Danielic Son of Man. There are thus good arguments on both sides.

A solution to the problem can be suggested which does justice to both these arguments. Matthew is not likely to have created a saying impossible of fulfilment, though he is, as we have seen, capable of accepting one from the tradition by presupposing a proleptic fulfilment in the resurrection. On the other hand, it is unlikely that the Son of Man was a feature of the present saying in its original form. It has often been noticed that the verse has its nearest parallel in a Marcan saying which we have already considered, Matt. 16.28 = Mark 9.1 Here we saw that Matthew himself has substituted the coming of the Son of Man for the coming of the kingdom of God. It is characteristic of Matthew's editing that he repeats his ideas, as we shall see again in a moment. There are thus good grounds to suggest that in 10.23b also Matthew is dependent upon an older tradition, but has altered it in the same way. Thus the tradition which Matthew received was, 'You will not have gone through the towns of Israel, before the kingdom of God comes.' As before, Matthew has understood the kingdom of God to be a periphrasis for God himself. In agreement with the christological interpretation of eschatological sayings, he has identified the coming of God with the parousia of Jesus. It is normal and natural for him to express this by means of the titular Son of Man.

The underlying saying, with 'kingdom of God' for the Son of Man, fits perfectly what we know of the eschatological teaching of Jesus. Jesus did not preach his own coming, but the coming of God himself to claim his own. His message of the kingdom certainly entailed the expectation of a particular event, not just a gradual transformation of society. That event would be the coming of God in mercy and judgement. It is attested in Mark 9.1, where Jesus speaks of the kingdom of God coming with power, and in the 'advocate' saying, where Jesus expects to participate in an advisory capacity at the judgement of God. On these grounds we can reaffirm the contention that Matt. 10.23b preserves an authentic saying of Jesus, and at the same time we can see how Matthew has brought it into line with the church's reinterpretation of the apocalyptic sayings.

b. This reinterpretation is responsible also for the other sayings peculiar to Matthew. In 13.24–30 he gives the parable of the tares, which is not found in the other gospels, but has a close parallel in the Gospel of Thomas 57. The Thomas version begins, 'The kingdom of the Father is like a man who had [good] seed'. It continues along the same lines as Matthew, but it is pared down to the minimum required to make the point, and there is nothing corresponding with the interpretation which Matthew provides in 13.36–43. Almost all editors ascribe the composition of the latter to Matthew himself. In so far as the original parable permits a modicum of allegory, it would seem obvious that the man who sowed the seed, and eventually instructed the reapers at harvest time to separate out the tares, is intended to be God himself.[19] In verses 37 and 41 Matthew identifies him with the Son of Man. Other features of this allegorical interpretation (the angels, the furnace, 'the kingdom of their Father') can be taken as typical of Matthew's apocalyptic ideas.

c. Matthew thus has a well defined picture of Jesus as the Danielic Son of Man, who performs the coming judgement. He introduces it twice more, at 19.28 and 25.31–46. The first of these is a Q saying, which Matthew has adapted in order to make it fit into a Marcan passage on the rewards of discipleship (Mark 10.28–31). As usual, Luke does not conflate the two strands of material, and so is likely to preserve the Q saying better. But his setting (the Last Supper) is probably just as artificial. In this case it is natural to suppose that Matthew has introduced the Son of Man into a saying which did not have the title in its Q form, as will be seen by comparing Matthew and Luke:

Matt 19.28	*Luke 22.28–30*
. . . You who have followed me,	28 You are those who have continued with me in my trials; 29 and I appoint to you, as my Father appointed to me, a kingdom,
in the regeneration, when the Son of Man will sit on his glorious throne, you also yourselves will sit on twelve thrones judging the twelve tribes of Israel.	30 that you may eat and drink at my table in my kingdom, and you will sit on thrones judging the twelve tribes of Israel.

Luke's form is not without difficulties.[20] There are features which tie it closely to the context of the Last Supper, and so suggest that Luke has not retained the Q form unaltered. The 'trials' anticipates the Gethsemane narrative (Luke 22.40, 46). Apart from this connection, it is a strange way of introducing the idea of places of honour and responsibility in the coming kingdom. But this idea itself is a further difficulty, because the promise contradicts the point of the preceding paragraph on greatness (22.24–7). The verb to 'appoint' (*diatithenai*) may allude to the new covenant (*diatheke*) in the blessing of the cup (verse 20, unless this is an addition to Luke's text). The final clause on eating and drinking may also be occasioned by the eucharistic setting. These verbs are subjunctive, and so are not well co-ordinated with the future indicative 'will sit'. Hence all the points which differentiate Luke from Matthew are problematical. Thus the first impression, that Luke preserves the saying better than Matthew, may have to be revised. If so, it may still be argued that the Son of Man belongs to the saying in its original form.

This, however, is unlikely in view of the affinities of Matthew's opening phrases. 'You who have followed me' is best understood as an artificial link with Matt. 19.27, where Peter has referred to himself and the other disciples in this way. It is a necessary insertion, because the relationship between verses 27 and 29 has been interrupted by the inclusion of the Q saying. The next phrase, 'in the regeneration', or 'new age' (*palingenesia*), is not found elsewhere in Matthew, but corresponds in meaning with 'in the age to come' in Mark 10.30, which is the parallel to the very next verse, Matt. 19.29.[21] But Matthew has altered Mark 10.30, describing the rewards for discipleship, in such a way as to exclude the notion that there will be material wealth 'now in this time', no doubt because it creates a contradiction with what Jesus has said earlier on the impossibility of entering the kingdom for those who have riches (Matt. 19.23-6 = Mark 10.23-7). Thus verse 29 is concerned only with heavenly rewards. This means that 'in the regeneration' is part of the rubric which covers both verses 28 and 29, and should be regarded as the product of Matthew's editorial work.[22]

Next there are affinities with the parable of the great assize, Matt. 25.31-46. The words 'when the Son of Man will sit on his glorious throne' are identical with the opening (Matt. 25.31): '*When the Son of Man* comes in his glory, and all the angels with him, then he *will sit on his glorious throne*.' But the parable yields further comparative material. In 25.34 the Son of Man is referred to as 'the King', and he says to the people at his right hand, 'Come, O blessed of my Father, inherit the kingdom prepared for you from the foundation of the world'. The word 'inherit' (*kleronomein*) is used by Matthew in 19.29 ('and inherit eternal life'), where there is no corresponding verb in Mark 10.30. The close link between the two passages in Matthew is maintained by 'eternal life' in the conclusion to the parable (25.46), as a shorter way of referring to 'the kingdom prepared for you from the foundation of the world'. This 'prepared (i.e., predetermined) kingdom' is comparable to the 'appointed kingdom' in Luke's version of the saying (Luke 22.29), though it does not appear in Matt. 19.28.

These comparisons furnish a fuller picture of Matthew's apocalyptic expectations, and so help us to understand the relationship between Matt. 19.28 and Luke 22.28–30. Matthew thinks of the messianic kingdom as a state that follows the parousia and judgement. The kingdom follows 'the close of the age' (*he sunteleia tou aionos*, Matt. 13.39, 49; 24.3; 28.20), and so constitutes the regeneration referred to in this passage. The kingdom is predetermined, and begins when Jesus comes and sits on his throne. Luke's idea, that the kingdom is 'appointed to' Jesus, just as it is 'appointed to' the disciples, does not suit Matthew's static view of it. Wishing only to concentrate on the twelve thrones in the context of rewards for discipleship, Matthew abbreviates the opening of the saying drastically, substituting his own conventional phrases. But it should now be clear that, even if Luke's version is influenced by the context of the Last Supper, it is probable that 'kingdom' (*basileia*) belongs to the original Q form. Finally, Matthew's choice of phrase for the opening includes the 'glorious throne' of the Son of Man because of the thrones in the saying, and thereby he achieves an excellent balance. It is very likely that he was conscious of the allusion to the thrones placed for the Ancient of Days and his entourage in Dan. 7.9.[23]

d. With regard to the parable of the great assize itself, it is worth noting that the fuller opening in Matt. 25.31 pictures the coming in terms reminiscent of Zech. 14.5.[24] The gathering of the nations and separating of them into two groups recalls the interpretation of the parable of the tares (13.41f) and the parable of the net, which is peculiar to Matthew (13.49f). In verse 34 the Son of Man is referred to as 'the king'. This may be a trace of an earlier state of the parable, in which the reference was to God himself.[25] If so, the address to those on the right hand as 'blessed of my Father' must be regarded as a Matthean adjustment (cf. the description of the righteous as shining 'in the kingdom of their Father' in 13.43). The same adjustment is not made in the case of those on the left hand, who are simply called 'accursed' in verse 41.

The common theme which binds Matthew's future references

together is not the Son of Man, but the apocalyptic picture as a whole. Matthew thinks of the close of the present age, the mission of the angels to gather in the nations, the great assize, with the King on his glorious throne, and the separation of good and bad for the kingdom or for the furnace respectively. This picture is given in the parable of the net (Matt. 13.47–50), where the last two verses are a Matthean interpretation comparable to that of the parable of the tares. The parable, adapted for gnostic use, is included in the Gospel of Thomas 8, and once more Matthew's special interpretation is omitted. It is altogether probable that this is Matthew's own work, and had no basis in his source. For our present purpose it is significant that he gives his conventional apocalyptic picture, except that he omits the coming of the Son of Man to take his throne for judgement. This did not need to be mentioned, because there was no corresponding detail in the parable.

Matthew's picture has a closely similar predecessor in 1 Cor. 15.23–4. Here Paul speaks of the parousia of Christ, the general resurrection (ushered in by the last trumpet, 1 Cor. 15.52), and 'the end'.[26] The 'end' evidently corresponds with the judgement, including separation of good and bad as in Matthew's parables, because it marks the point where Christ hands over the kingdom to the Father (cf. Matt. 13.43; 25.34), and the final enemy, death, is destroyed after the destruction of all other hostile powers. This last point is made by means of a midrash on Ps. 8.6, itself a commentary on the exaltation text, Ps. 110.1.[27] Ps. 8.4 has 'the son of man' (*ben adam*) in parallel with 'man' (*enosh*), and it is significant that Paul is completely unaware of it as a messianic title, and conducts his argument on Adam and Christ in the surrounding context without mentioning it.[28]

Matthew might similarly have used 'the Christ' as the subject of the parousia and judgement, but he uses the Son of Man because Jesus is himself the speaker in all these passages, and the Son of Man is his usual self-designation. The correlation of the Son of Man as an exclusive self-reference, the apocalyptic function of Jesus as Messiah, and direct application of Dan. 7.13–14, had already been made in both Mark and Q. Much of Matthew's apocalyptic picture is also present in them, especially in the Little Apocalypse of Mark 13. Here Matthew had ready to hand a good description of the mission of the angels to gather in the elect (Mark

13.27 = Matt. 24.31). As we have seen, he took this over with very little change, but added in the trumpet, like Paul.

e. This brings us to the context of the last of the Son of Man sayings peculiar to Matthew, which is the first of two additions to Mark's description of the parousia:

Matt. 24.30	Mark 13.26
[a]And then will appear the sign of the Son of Man in heaven, [b]and then all the tribes of the earth will mourn, [c]and they will see the Son of Man coming on the clouds of heaven with power and great glory.	And then they will see the Son of Man coming in clouds with power and great glory.

What is the sign of the Son of Man which will appear in heaven? It has been customary to connect this with the lightning-flash from the Q material, which has just been used by Matthew a couple of verses earlier (Matt. 24.27): 'For as the lightning comes from the east and shines as far as the west, so will be the parousia of the Son of Man.' The Church Fathers interpreted this to mean the sign of the cross as the final portent, causing the enemies of Christ to mourn (verse 30b; cf. Rev. 1.7), and heralding the appearance of Christ himself.[29] T. F. Glasson, wishing to argue that the Son of Man's exaltation *to God* is the proper interpretation of the saying as a whole, as in Dan 7.13, suggested that 'sign' (*semeion*) here has nothing to do with heavenly portents, but goes with the trumpet as the first stage in the gathering of the elect. It is the 'ensign', or rallying-point, for the dispersed people, as in Isa. 11.12, where the Septuagint uses the same Greek word.[30] The difficulty of this interpretation is that the idea of the ensign is out of place at this point. If it belongs with the trumpet, it ought to be mentioned in close connection with it. A further problem is that *semeion* has been used by Matthew at the beginning of the Little Apocalypse in quite a different sense. In 24.3 the disciples have asked, 'What will be the sign (*semeion*) of your parousia and of the close of the age?' Matthew here is adapting Mark, who has 'the sign when all these things are to be accomplished' (Mark 13.4). Mark clearly means an observable phenomenon which can be used to identify that the end has been reached. He then proceeds to show what this is by a series of steps (Mark 13.7,14, 24), ending up 'And then . . .' (*kai tote*, Mark 13.26). Thus the *semeion* is the actual appearance of the Son of Man, followed by the gathering of the elect. Matthew's alterations and conflations with Q tend to obscure the progression, so that Mark's *kai tote* (reproduced twice in Matt. 24.30) is not enough to show that the point referred to in the question of verse 3 has at last been reached. Hence the primary purpose of verse 30a is to signal to the reader that the answer to the question has now come. The link with verse 4 has already been re-established by 'the parousia of the Son of Man' in verse 27. This leads to the conclusion that 'the sign of the Son of Man' is to be taken as 'the sign consisting in the Son of Man', in spite of all arguments to the contrary.[31] The mourning of the tribes and their sight of the parousia appear to be in the wrong order, if this is the case, it is true.[32] But they are not necessarily to be taken as successive (*kai tote* introduces both verbs, which are closely co-ordinate), and the mourning may have been mentioned first so as to avoid any break of continuity between the arrival of the Son of Man and the gathering of the elect, which is the proper climax of the composition.

It seems, then, that Matthew does not refer to a 'sign of the Son of Man' as an additional portent which his readers are expected to understand without explanation. This would be possible only if the Son of Man was the title of a known personality already provided with a commonly accepted array of conventional symbols. But that is not the case. Matthew has listed an impressive catalogue of portents, and it is unlikely that he should then refer to one more—and that the crucial one for those who try to discern the divine plan—without explaining what it is. In fact the whole sentence (30a) is based upon verse 27, where the same verb (*phainesthai*) is used. The word *semeion* comes from verse 4, and there Matthew took it over from Mark. Unfortunately his way of using it here inevitably causes some confusion, which would not arise if he had said 'the parousia of the Son of Man', as in verse 27. Presumably he avoided this so as not to anticipate 'coming' (*erchomenon*) in verse 30c.

3 Conclusion

Our examination of Matthew has shown that the special features of the Son of Man in this gospel can be accounted for without postulating a well developed concept of the apocalyptic Son of Man outside the sayings tradition. Matthew contributes no further authentic sayings containing the expression besides those which he has incorporated from Mark and Q. But he has seized the phrase as a characteristic feature of the sayings tradition. He understands it as an exclusive self-reference. He is particularly delighted to find that Jesus is represented as referring to himself in this way in contexts which deal with the parousia. He builds on this feature, provided by both Mark and Q, in order to include the apocalyptic details which accord with his own expectations, and which he confidently believes stem from Jesus himself. The proliferation of sayings in which Jesus speaks of himself as the apocalyptic Son of Man is thus due to Matthew's interest in apocalyptic, not to general currency of a Son of Man title. Because Jesus always refers to himself as the Son of Man in sayings concerning the future (none of them authentic, apart from the 'advocate' saying), Matthew tends to use the Son of Man as a title for Jesus in his future role. Being aware of the connection with Dan. 7.13–14, he even makes the Son of Man the title of God's future agent without specifying that Jesus alone is intended, so that consciousness that the phrase is a self-designation falls into the background, and Jesus appears to be speaking about someone else. Of course that was not Matthew's intention, but it is a pardonable mistake to make on the basis of the sayings which are peculiar to Matthew.

It must be stressed that the development of the apocalyptic Son of Man in Matthew is a *literary* process, and does not reflect wider usage. A straight transposition is the best explanation of Matthew's *addition* of the Son of Man in 16.13 and *omission* in 16.21. Matthew's alteration of the Q saying on the sign of Jonah (Matt. 12.40 = Luke 11.30) is due to dissatisfaction with the failure of the saying to specify *how* Jonah was a sign to the Ninevites. As a biblical scholar, he has supplied the answer from his own knowledge of scripture.[33] In Matt. 16.28 = Mark 9.1 he has crossed out Mark's 'kingdom of God' and replaced it by 'the Son of Man', in much the same way as 'the Lord' (= God) in eschatological texts is regularly applied to the exalted Jesus in other parts of the New Testament. It is very likely that he has done the same thing in Matt. 10.23. In 13.36–43 he has composed what he considers to be the true interpretation of the parable of the tares, in which the Son of Man corresponds with the farmer of the parable, though God himself may have been the original intention. Matthew's work here has a very close relationship with the interpretation of the parable of the net (13.47–50), where, however, the Son of Man does not happen to be mentioned. In 19.28 Matthew has abbreviated and adapted a Q saying on the position of the disciples in the coming kingdom (Luke 22.28–30), using a form of words which he will use again in the opening of the parable of the great assize (Matt. 25.31). In the latter case the unusual designation 'king ' (verse 34) suggests that this is another instance of substitution of the Son of Man for God himself, which Matthew has failed to carry through completely. The overall effect of this literary activity is to give the impression that the Son of Man was far more frequent in the tradition than was actually the case, and to shift the balance of application to the apocalyptic expectations of the parousia of Jesus current at the time when the gospel was written.

8

The Son of Man in Luke and Acts

Luke is beyond any question the most accomplished writer in the New Testament. He has an excellent feeling for style and occasion. From the sources at his disposal he has created a picture which is both rational and sensitive, suitable for an educated Greek reader. The main part of the Gospel is based on Mark and Q, like Matthew, though Luke has produced a very different mix. In the infancy narratives (Luke 1—2) and resurrection account (Luke 24) he is in a position to exercise greater freedom, and here his personal qualities as a writer stand out more clearly. These qualities are displayed in Acts, where he has created a superb evocation of the beginnings of the Church out of very limited material of varying historical worth. Though it cannot be claimed that Luke is altogether free from tendentiousness in his writing (e.g., in his presentation of Paul in relation to the Jews on the one hand and the Romans on the other), his work bears the stamp of an honest historian, who is doing his best to make sense of the material at his disposal and to present it in a readable and acceptable manner.[1]

It is often asserted that Luke is more faithful to his sources than Matthew. This is true in the sense that he is less inclined to conflate them and therefore has less need to alter them in order to make them fit together. But he does frequently make stylistic improvements. This can be attributed not merely to an author's licence, but to positive necessity in view of the literary expectations of his readership.[2] It is also true that he tends to introduce details which reinforce the emotional impact of his material.[3] On the other hand it is a mistake to suppose that he freely invented the gospel material which is not found in Mark or Q, either by evolving stories out of Old Testament prototypes or by concocting further items from the sayings tradition.[4] Luke is more than a redactor of written sources, but he does not indulge in creation *ex nihilo*.[5]

These considerations need to be kept in mind as we approach the

Son of Man sayings which are peculiar to Luke. Luke begins his work with a large stock of such sayings already provided in the two major sources, Mark and Q. From Mark he has the two 'authority' sayings (Luke 5.24 and 6.5 = Mark 2.10, 28), the passion sayings (Luke 9.22, 44; 18.31; 22.22), and the future sayings (Luke 21.27 = Mark. 13.26; Luke. 22.69 = Mark 14.62; cf. Acts 7.56). The last class should also include the 'advocate' saying, which Luke has both in its Marcan form (Luke 9.26 = Mark 8.38) and in its Q form (Luke 12.8f = Matt. 10.32f), both with the Son of Man (against Matt. 10.32f). Besides these he has eight other sayings from Q (Luke 7.34; 9.58; 11.30; 12.10, 40; 17.24, 26, 30).

There remain seven more sayings in the gospel and one saying in Acts. These can be divided into four groups: (i). Two of them (Luke 22.48; 24.7) belong to the class of passion sayings, and are clearly the work of Luke himself. (ii). Two others (Luke 6.22; 17.22) are found in Q material, and should probably be attributed to Luke's editing, though it is possible that they belong to the source. (iii). The three others (Luke. 18.8; 19.10; 21.36) have a distinctive character, and must either be reckoned as further examples of Luke's editorial work or assigned to his special sources of material. Obviously the decision on these three sayings will have an important bearing on our understanding of the development of Son of Man sayings in the Jesus tradition. (iv). There is also the saying of Stephen in Acts 7.56, which might be derived from Luke's source.

1 *The passion sayings*

The first of the two passion sayings can be regarded as the result of transposition, comparable to Matthew's transference in Matt. 16.13, 21. Luke has considerably shortened the Gethsemane narrative, omitting the reference to the betrayal of the Son of Man in Mark 14.41. Instead he has introduced it with great effect into the actual moment of betrayal (Luke 22.48): 'Jesus said to him, "Judas, would you betray the Son of Man with a kiss?" ' Two things about this are significant for our study. First, it is clear that Luke here treats the Son of Man as an exclusive self-designation of Jesus. He is not aware of the *bar enasha* idiom which belongs to the original passion saying in the the pre-Marcan tradition. Secondly, this is an excellent example of Luke's capacity to add a touch of pathos to his narrative, comparable to the addition to the story of Peter's denials (Luke 22.61a), 'And the Lord turned and looked at Peter'. The saying does not in any way emphasize the Son of Man. It is simply a substitute for the first person, though it is perhaps a little stronger than the pronoun 'me' would have been. But the real point is the irony of betrayal by means of a kiss. The mark of friendship is the means whereby friendship is destroyed. Thus it is possible that Luke thinks of the Son of Man here as a way of saying, 'I, being the man who I am, i.e., (in this context) your friend'. There is no indication that the future status of Jesus is in his mind.

The other passion saying is Luke 24.7. Here the text is manifestly composed from the three passion predictions which Luke shares with Mark. Luke has incorporated this into the words of the angels to the women in the empty tomb, with an actual cross reference to the passion predictions ('Remember how he told you, while he was still in Galilee . . .', verse 6). This is, of course, a favourite theme of Luke (cf. 24.20, 26, 44–6), and he has used it here to soften the stark Marcan ending, where the women appear not to believe the message that Jesus is risen and run away in terror.

2 *The Q Sayings*

The two examples just considered are sufficient to prove that the claim, put forward by some scholars, that Luke does not create Son of Man sayings cannot be upheld.[6] This argument, therefore, cannot be used to support the originality of the Son of Man in the two passages from Q which must now occupy our attention.

For the first one this argument is almost the only criterion. The last of the series of beatitudes in Luke 6.22 reads, 'Blessed are you when men . . . cast out your name as evil for the sake of the Son of Man'. But Matthew has it in the 'I' form (Matt. 5.11): '. . . speak all kinds of evil against you falsely for my sake'. We had the same problem in the 'advocate' saying, where Luke has the Son of Man against the first person in Matthew (Matt. 10.32=Luke 12.8).[7] There it was suggested that Matthew was following Q, in which the *bar enasha* idiom had in this case been paraphrased with *ego*, while Luke conformed the text to the Marcan parallel, which he retains in the context elsewhere (Mark 8.38=Luke 9.26). However, it was not possible to reach a firm conclusion, and the possibility had to be left open that in this case Matthew himself was responsible for substituting *ego* for the Son of Man in the text of Q which he had received.

In the present instance it is necessary to insist that the decision in the one case should not be allowed to dictate the decision in the other. Matthew *may* have changed the Son of Man to 'I' in Matt. 10.32–3, but it does not follow that he has done so here. So also Luke *may* have introduced the Son of Man in Luke 12.8, but it does not follow that he is responsible for it in this verse. There is one factor which makes the two cases completely different. In the 'advocate' saying the evidence strongly points to the originality of the Son of Man in the underlying tradition, and its authenticity is vouched for by the fact that it makes an excellent example of the idiomatic use of *bar enasha*, which is lost in the Greek translation. But this is not so in the case of the present saying. The Son of Man here can only be an exclusive self-reference (unless we choose the wholly erroneous explanation that Jesus is referring to a particular personality other than himself), and therefore it cannot go back to Jesus himself. Seeing that it is found only in Luke, it is *a priori* more probable that Luke has introduced it than that it had entered the common tradition, but was subsequently removed by Matthew.[8]

If Luke is responsible for it, why has he suddenly decided to put it in here? Though the precise reason may be impossible to guess, it is clear that Luke has a tendency to avoid 'for my sake' (*heneken emou*) where it occurs elsewhere in parallel passages. He retains it only once (Matt. 16.25 = Mark 8.35 = Luke 9.24), where all three gospels are almost identical.[9] But in the Q version of this saying (Luke 17.33 = Matt. 10.39) he omits the phrase against Matthew (but this may be a Matthean insertion from the Marcan form). In another Marcan passage (Matt. 19.29 = Mark 10.29 = Luke 18.29) the three gospels go separate ways (Matthew: 'for my name's sake'; Mark: 'for my sake and for the sake of the gospel'; Luke: 'for the sake of the kingdom of God'). Finally, it is Luke's turn to have 'for my name's sake', against 'for my sake' in both Matthew and Mark, in a passage on persecution in the Little Apocalypse (Matt. 10.18 = Mark 13.9 = Luke 21.12). Evidently Luke feels the need for a slightly fuller, and therefore more solemn, expression in this kind of context. The fact that, following Mark, he has just used the Son of Man in connection with Jesus' authority in 5.24 and 6.5 is surely sufficient to explain why in this instance he brings in the expression again, whereas elsewhere he achieves the same object by different means.

This example has given us a further factor with regard to Luke's editorial work, influence from the larger context. This is the obvious explanation of the other Lucan addition to Q material in Luke 17.22, 'The days are coming when you will desire to see one of the days of the Son of Man, and you will not see it'. This saying begins the sequence on the day of the Son of Man, which we have previously considered.[10] The arguments for regarding it as Luke's own work need not be repeated here.

3 *Sayings peculiar to Luke*

a. The first of the three remaining sayings which are peculiar to Luke has a close connection with this Q passage, and again the influence of the larger context is an important factor. At the conclusion of the sequence Luke has inserted the parable of the unjust judge (Luke 18.1–8a). It is aimed at recommending persistent prayer in view of the fact that the time of vindication of the elect cannot be determined in advance. Then comes the final comment (18.8b), 'Nevertheless, when the Son of Man comes, will he find faith on earth?' It has been pointed out by several scholars that this is more than a comment on the parable. It gathers up the moral of the whole preceding Q sequence, and makes an inclusion with 17.22. The reference to the coming of the Son of Man places it firmly in the context of the future (cf. 12.40).

Is this saying Luke's own composition, or has he received it from earlier tradition?[11] In any case it cannot be considered genuine, because the Son of Man operates as an exclusive self-designation. There is no close connection with the preceding parable, because the elucidation of it in verses 6–8a has identified God as the true judge who vindicates his chosen ones.[12] The change to an implied reference to Jesus himself thus breaks in harshly, and would not have been necessary, if Luke had not wished to relate the parable to the larger context. The saying also changes the point of interest from the promise of speedy vindication (in spite of delay) to the exhortation to persistent prayer, as in the editorial verse 1. This suits the moral lesson of the preceding passage on the day of the Son of Man, which is concerned with the peril of heedlessness. Thus the saying does relate to Luke's overall purpose here. But it is more difficult to think of it as a detached saying. The observation that the definite article with 'faith' may be a Semitism[13] is not compelling. Much more to the point is the literary style. This is a rare example of the rhetorical question as a means of bringing a discussion to a point, and it includes the less common particle *ara*, which is a mark of educated writing.[14] The use of this device also has a pathetic effect, as it suggests that people who have the virtue of perseverance are sadly hard to find. These are positive indications that the saying is the work of Luke himself.

b. The second of these sayings is also a summarizing conclusion (19.10) 'For the Son of Man came to seek and to save the lost'.[15] It comes at the end of the story of Zacchaeus, but it does not belong to the story, which has its own conclusion in verse 9. Thus the *situation* is closely parallel to that of Luke 18.8 which we have just considered. The *content* of the saying, however, takes us to Mark 2.13–17=Luke 5.27–32, the call of the tax-collector Levi (=Matthew, Matt. 9.9–13). This concludes, 'I came not to call the righteous but sinners (Luke adds: to repentance)'. The fact that Zacchaeus is also a tax-collector suggests that Luke is well aware of the thematic connection between the two traditions. But the important point is that, whereas the conclusion to the Levi story is indispensable, here the similar conclusion is an optional extra. Moreover the *language* of the saying is that of the parable of the lost sheep, used by Luke in 15.1–7 specifically in connection with Jesus' ministry to the tax-collectors and sinners.

There is thus every reason to believe that Luke has created the saying out of genuine material which he has used elsewhere in the gospel. But the use of the Son of Man betrays the artificial character of the saying, for once again it is an exclusive self-reference, replacing the first person of the original in Luke 5.32. There is no particular reason why it should be used here. It is best explained by Luke's feel for style. He has seized a characteristic of the sayings tradition, but in fact he has used it wrongly. Nevertheless the saying as a whole splendidly conveys the impression of Jesus' teaching about himself, and makes its own special emotional impact upon the reader.

c. The last of our three sayings is yet another summarizing conclusion, this time rounding off Luke's version of the Little Apocalypse (Luke 21.36): 'But watch at all times, praying that you may have strength to escape all these things that will take place, and to stand before the Son of Man'. Luke has followed Mark fairly closely in the immediately preceding section,[16] but he is evidently embarrassed by the thought that no one, not even the Son, knows the hour of the parousia (Mark 13.32). Instead, he has a short section on heedlessness (Luke 21.34f), which has no synoptic parallels, followed by the present verse. This agrees with Mark 13.33 in its opening phrase, but the emphasis on prayer in the interval before the parousia takes us back to Luke. 18.1–8. The disciples are thus exhorted to show precisely that 'faith' which 18.8b suggested might be lacking at the coming of the Son of Man. Naturally, if they possess it, they will 'have strength . . . to stand before' him. The saying thus has a close thematic connection with 18.8b, and this already suggests that Luke again is responsible for its composition. This is supported by details of vocabulary. The verb for 'pray' (*deomai*) is used fifteen times in Luke/Acts, against seven times in the rest of the New Testament. To 'have strength' (i.e., 'be able', *katischuo*) occurs again at Luke 23.23, but elsewhere only in Matt. 16.18. The word for 'stand' (*stathenai*) is a technical term for a person on trial (e.g., Jesus before Pilate, Matt. 27.11), and is used in the Little Apocalypse in connection with the tribulations of the disciples (Mark 13.9: 'stand before governors and kings for my sake', changed in Luke 21.12 to '*brought* before kings and governors *for my name's sake*', as noted above in connection with Luke 6.22). It is characteristic of Luke to use a word which he has altered or omitted from Mark in another context.[17] Here, however, it has the added nuance of 'stand fast', i.e., be acquitted in the judgement, which can be attributed to Luke's familiarity with the language of the Septuagint.[18] This gives to the saying a certain stirring quality, which agrees with Luke's capacity for emotional effect. A final consideration is that the saying cannot be detached from its context, because it refers directly to the coming events which have just been described. For all these reasons the attribution of the verse to Luke himself is highly probable to say the least, if not completely certain.

d. It seems, then, that Luke *does* create Son of Man sayings. This is very largely a matter of his sense of style. He uses it as a self-reference on the part of Jesus, because that appears to him, from his knowledge of Mark and Q, to be characteristic of Jesus' way of speaking about himself. Moreover the titular usage of the phrase in sayings with a future reference made him think of it as having at least the nuance of 'the appointed person', who acts either with or for God in the coming judgement. Luke is well aware of the Semitic flavour of the expression. With his vivid concept of Jesus as the exalted Lord he undoubtedly saw the connection with the figure of Dan. 7.13–14. These factors need to be borne in mind as we now turn our attention to Acts 7.56, the only place in the New Testament outside the gospels where the Son of Man title is used.

4 *The Son of Man in Acts 7.56*

Of course this is not a saying of Jesus, but a saying of Stephen. It comes at the climax of his trial before the council, immediately before he is dragged out of the city and stoned to death.[19] Luke describes how, at this crucial moment, Stephen was able to see into heaven, where Jesus is standing at God's side, presumably as his advocate before the divine tribunal, where *real* justice will be done. Thus the situation presents a splendid example of what is asserted in the 'advocate' saying, and it will not be forgotten that Luke's version of it includes the Son of Man self-designation (Luke 12.8). Whether Q included the Son of Man in this saying or not, we have seen that Q certainly did have some sayings referring to Jesus' future role. It seems likely that Q was originally an Aramaic document, and that it was translated into Greek by the Hellenist converts in Jerusalem, of whom Stephen was a prominent member. So at first sight there seems to be no difficulty in the view that Acts 7.56 could be an authentic saying of Stephen, spoken at this crucial moment, and remembered by his friends.

However, there is a world of difference between a feature of the tradition of Jesus' sayings and the titles for Jesus which became current in the early church. There is no evidence that the Son of Man was one of the early church's titles of Jesus anywhere in the New Testament apart from this verse. Thus, even though the evangelists, following the lead of Q, tended to use it in a titular way, it would not have been recognized as a title by the Jewish audience, and it is most improbable that Stephen would have seized it from the sayings tradition instead of using a title in closer accord with the confession faith, e.g., the Christ.[20]

A further factor is Luke's use of the trial and death of Jesus as the

139

model for his description here. This includes both material which he has omitted in the trial scene of the Gospel and echoes of the special features of his crucifixion narrative. Thus Acts 6.11 refers to blasphemy. This is applied to Jesus in Mark 14.64, but the word is dropped from the parallel in Luke 22.71. Acts 6.12, on the arrest of Stephen, reflects the vocabulary of Luke 22.66, where Jesus is brought to the Sanhedrin. Acts 6.13–14 describe how false witnesses accuse Stephen of saying that Jesus would destroy the temple. This is an unmistakable allusion to the false witness at the trial of Jesus (Mark 14.57f), which Luke has omitted. At the end of the story we find that Stephen prays Jesus to accept his spirit and intercedes on behalf of the murderers (Acts 7.59f). These features echo Jesus' self-commendation (Luke 23.46) and prayer for the executioners (Luke 23.34).[21] These parallels obviously raise the question whether the saying of Stephen has been modelled on Jesus' answer to the high priest (Mark 14.62=Luke 22.69). Moreover, as Stephen's words are anticipated by Luke in his description in the preceding verse, it will be desirable to make a fourfold comparison of these very similar texts:

Acts 7.55	*Acts 7.56*
But he, full of the Holy Spirit, gazed into heaven and saw the glory of God, and Jesus standing at the right hand of God.	And he said, 'Behold, I see the heavens opened, and the Son of Man standing at the right hand of God.'
Mark 14.62	*Luke 22.69*
And Jesus said, 'I am; and you will see the Son of Man sitting at the right hand of Power, and coming with the clouds of heaven.'	'But from now the Son of Man will be sitting at the right hand of the power of God.'

There is a further point of comparison to be taken into account, in that 'gazed . . . and saw' in Acts 7.55 repeats the idea of Acts 6.15, using the same verbs: 'And *gazing* at him [Stephen] all who sat in the council *saw* that his face was like the face of an angel.' If Luke planned the account of Stephen without the speech of Acts 7.1–53 in the first instance, then verses 54 and 55 can be regarded as redactional links, 54 being an anticipation of the reaction of the audience in 57, and 55 being the introduction of 56. In this case verse 56 would have followed directly on 6.15 in Luke's original plan, and 55 would have been created out of 6.15 and 7.56 after they were separated.[22] This means that priority must be given to the actual saying in 7.56 over verse 55, which may be secondary to it.

Taking 7.56 first, then, we can see that it agrees with Luke 22.69 against Mark 14.62 in omitting the coming with the clouds. Thus Luke has reduced the answer to the high priest to a statement of Jesus' exaltation in the immediate future, which (like Matthew in Matt. 26.64) he can regard as already fulfilled ('from now') in the resurrection of Jesus. So now he uses the same idea to represent Jesus as available in the period following the resurrection on this basis.

Secondly, the saying begins with a conventional formula for a theophany, which of course has no counterpart in the saying of Jesus. But it is possible that 'I see the heavens opened' owes something to Mark 14.62 ('you will see'), though a different verb is used. But the expression shows signs of Luke's own editorial work, inasmuch as the word for 'opened' (*dianoigo*) is characteristic of Luke (seven times in Luke/Acts), and occurs only once elsewhere (Mark 7.34).[23] Luke has an almost identical expression again in Luke 3.21; Acts 10.11.

Thirdly, the Son of Man is uniquely said to be standing rather than sitting. Dodd denies that there is any difference of meaning, as both verbs refer to the place of Jesus at God's right hand rather than his posture.[24] Most editors, however, follow Bengel in supposing that Jesus stands to give to Stephen a martyr's welcome.[25] But it seems better to take the choice of word seriously in relation to the implied forensic character of the heavenly court. The sitting position denotes kingly rule, and is adopted for giving sentence in a trial (cf. John 19.13). Luke knows perfectly well that it belongs to the conventional way of speaking of the exaltation of Jesus, derived from Ps. 110.1, alluded to in Luke 22.69 in dependence on Mark 14.62, and quoted in full by Luke himself in Acts 2.34. The standing position belongs not only to the defendants on trial (cf. Luke 21.36, where the disciples 'stand before the Son of Man' in this sense), but also to the attendants at the court. Thus Gabriel 'stands before God' in the heavenly court in Luke 1.19, and indeed when he is first introduced as 'standing at the right hand of the altar of incense' (Luke 1.11) precisely the same Greek words are used as in Acts 7.56. Along with Raphael, he is 'one of the seven holy angels who present the prayers of the saints and enter into the presence of the glory of the Holy One' (Tobit 12.15). Another function of the angels is to maintain before God the cause of those who cannot speak for themselves (Matt. 18.10). This provides a good parallel to the situation of Stephen, who has been made to stand before the council as a defendant (Acts 6.13), but whose face appears to be like the face of an angel (6.15). This is because in heaven his case is safely in the hands of the Son of Man before the throne of God. His angelic countenance is the reflection of the glory of the theophany before his eyes. His defence (7.56) is not a reasoned argument for his position (supplied by Luke in the speech of 7.1–53), but a statement which implies that the heavenly judgement is on his side. Thus the close connection between 6.15 and 7.56 confirms the primarily forensic character of the saying, and the Son of Man is said to be standing because he is Stephen's advocate before God.

Finally, the saying speaks of the right hand of God, where Mark 14.62 has the right hand of Power. Luke has already elucidated this in Luke 22.69 by his 'the power of God'. The omission of 'power' here cannot be regarded as sufficient grounds to deny that the answer to the high priest is the model of the saying.

There is thus a good case for the dependence of the saying on the tradition of the trial of Jesus, in agreement with other features of the context. Luke has introduced the theophanic opening precisely because Stephen is the speaker and not Jesus himself. He has also represented Jesus as standing in heaven, because the trial of Stephen goes on at two levels, an earthly condemnation and a heavenly acquittal, and the theophany represents the heavenly side of it.

When we turn to the editorial verse 55, we can see how Luke says the same thing in his own words. The opening takes up the description of Stephen already given in 6.5 ('full of the Holy Spirit') and prepares for the theophany in terms reminiscent of Isa. 6.1 and Ezekiel. Here Luke has the singular 'heaven' rather than the Semitizing plural used in the following saying. The only other change in the verse is Jesus instead of the Son of Man. These two verbal differences are important, because they reveal Luke's method. 'The heavens' and 'the Son of Man' in verse 56 are both archaisms, which Luke has used as being suitable to the setting of the trial of Stephen before a Jewish audience in the early days of the church's history.[26] Luke has retained the Son of Man from the answer of Jesus, in spite of the fact that Jesus is not now the speaker, because it seems to him to be appropriate in this context. This is not because it was a recognized messianic title, but because to him it was a rather solemn way of referring to Jesus as the one appointed by God, as we have seen in the sayings peculiar to Luke in the gospel. On the other hand, when he uses his own words he drops the title and speaks of Jesus.

Our argument leads to the conclusion that the Son of Man in Acts 7.56 is a stylistic feature of Luke's writing rather than a feature of an independent saying which he has presented from an underlying source. This result is confirmed by the parallel in Paul's speech at Athens, Acts 17.31:

> He has fixed a day on which he will judge the world in righteousness by a man (*en andri*) whom he has appointed, and of this he has given assurance to all men by raising him from the dead.

Here again, Luke is not speaking in his own words, but is using language which he considers to be appropriate to the audience. But this time it is not a Jewish audience but Greek. So long as it was supposed that the Son of Man was a recognized apocalyptic title derived from Hellenistic usage, it was natural to suppose that the Son of Man was intended here.[27] But then why has Luke gone out of his way to use *aner*, a word meaning an individual, instead? The answer is that there was no such title. The Son of Man (7.56), Jesus (7.55) and an individual (17.31) are different ways of referring to the same person—the one who rose from the dead and will come as judge.

Luke, like Matthew, has enlarged the number of Son of Man sayings as part of his literary work as evangelist and historian. But, whereas Matthew's originality was expressed especially in relation to contemporary developments in apocalyptic expectations, Luke presents a more varied picture. To him the Son of Man is a self-designation which Jesus used when speaking of his ministry to the outcast and the tax-collectors as well as in apocalyptic contexts. He thinks of it as a special feature of Jesus' style—as indeed it was, though not quite in the way Luke thought. He thus employs it in comments which are designed to appeal to the reader's emotions. This is true of most of the sayings which are peculiar to his gospel. It is especially effective in the first of the two additional passion sayings (Luke 22.48). Luke 6.22; 17.22; 24.7 are less obviously emotive, but cohere with other aspects of Luke's literary craftsmanship. The three summarizing sayings in Luke 18.8; 19.10; 21.36 are all designed to affect the reader. In the saying of Stephen in Acts 7.56 Luke makes climactic use of this feature of the gospel tradition, supposing it to be appropriate to the occasion.

9

The Son of Man in the Theology of John

The use of the Son of Man in Matthew and Luke has been described above as a literary matter, and in Matthew at least it could be seen in relation to developments of apocalyptic thought. In the Fourth Gospel the Son of Man is more than a literary feature. The title has become the vehicle for a definite theological idea. This is sufficiently consistent and coherent to permit a general treatment of the Johannine sayings, instead of a complete analysis. But it will also be necessary to attempt to ascertain the literary sources of John's use of the phrase, and to decide whether it was a current title for Jesus in the Johannine community.[1]

1 *The lifting-up of the Son of Man*

In the first place, the Gospel of John contains no sayings which can be taken directly back to Jesus as examples of the *bar enasha* idiom. The nearest that we get to this is John 3.14, ' . . . So must *a man* be lifted up'. It is universally recognized that this is modelled on the passion predictions, especially Mark 8.31, which does go back ultimately to an authentic saying, as has been argued above. But John shows no awareness of the idiom, which is in any case impossible in the verse which immediately precedes this one, where reference is made to the Son of Man (3.13), 'No one has ascended into heaven, but he who descended from heaven, the Son of Man'.[2] Here the context requires a specific personality, and the same is true of all the other Son of Man sayings in the Fourth Gospel.

The connection between 3.14 and the passion saying is important, because it provides the link between John's use of the title and earlier tradition. The passion predictions were developed in relation to the primitive kerygma, so that in Mark they include not only the death of Jesus but also his resurrection. It was also noted that the various forms of the prediction have been influenced by the prophecy of the suffering servant in Isa. 53, whether Jesus himself made allusion to this prophecy or not. These two features of the synoptic forms of the prediction are combined in John 3.14. Here the Son of Man is not said to be delivered up or to die, but to be lifted up (*hupsothenai*). The natural interpretation of the word is exaltation. But John has begun by referring to the brazen serpent which Moses set on a stake in the course of the journey of the Israelites through the Wilderness (Num. 21.8f). Thus the point of comparison is lifting up on a stake, and the application can only be to the crucifixion. This, then, is the *primary* meaning here, even if it is not the most obvious meaning of the word. Just as the serpent was raised so that 'everyone who saw it might live' (Num. 21.8, LXX), so the crucifixion of Jesus will have the result that 'whoever believes in him may have eternal life' (John 3.15). There is thus inevitably a double meaning in the verb 'lifted up', and this may be confidently traced to the suffering servant prophecy, where the servant of the Lord 'will be lifted up and glorified' (Isa. 52.13, LXX: *hupsothesetai kai doxasthesetai*).

These facts are well known, but the importance of them is not always sufficiently realized. John is certainly indebted here to what one may justly claim is the mainstream of early Christian thought. The process of the transformation of the passion sayings into passion and resurrection predictions in the light of the kerygma, and the further work upon them in relation to the passion prophecy, lie behind John 3.14. But John continues the process in his own unique and brilliant way. First, he adduces a further Old Testament text (Num. 21.9), which had not been used in this connection before. Secondly, he adopts an unusual word for 'lifted up', which normally refers to exaltation in an honorific sense, and thereby contrives to combine the two notions of crucifixion and exaltation in a single ambiguous word. This word, as we have seen, is probably drawn from the passion prophecy. Thirdly, his new contribution to the biblical typology of the crucifixion includes also the idea of the healing effect of the passion, even supplying the notion of giving life, which is John's chief way of expressing it. Finally, just as the passion sayings in Mark spawned further sayings, so also John has a series of sayings which depend upon this one, and reveal the central importance of it for John's theology.

Put in a nutshell, John's point is that the crucifixion, which is the actual method of execution, is an outward sign of Jesus' exaltation.

This is because the exaltation of Jesus denotes his special relationship with God, which is visible already in the passion to those who understand its true meaning. For Jesus accepts death as an act of union with the Father's will.

This point is clarified and pressed home in further Son of Man sayings. The 'lifting up' theme reappears in 8.28 and 12.32–4. The latter passage includes the information that, for the saving purpose of Jesus' death to be achieved, death had to be by a specific means. Obviously this means crucifixion (cf. 18.32).

In two places John varies the verb by using 'glorified' (*doxasthenai*), 12.23 and 13.31. The context in the first case suggests that John is thinking of the crucifixion in terms of the cosmic moral victory over the power of evil (cf. 12.31). But this is also true of the other, as it immediately follows the entry of Satan into the heart of Judas Iscariot at the Last Supper, and his departure to betray Jesus. That we have here a variant of 'lifted up' is suggested by the juxtaposition of both these verbs in Isa. 52.13. But the use of *doxazo* allows John to draw out the meaning further. For the exaltation of the Son of Man is an act which redounds to the honour both of Jesus himself and of God for whose glory it is undertaken. This agrees with the theological use of *doxazo* elsewhere in John.

The two themes of the lifting up and the glorifying of the Son of Man account for six out of the thirteen occurrences of the title in John. Behind them all stands the passion prediction, shaped in the light of the kerygma of the death and resurrection of Jesus, but ultimately stemming from a saying of Jesus himself. Obviously John has derived the title from this tradition, so that there can be no doubt that he understood it as an exclusive self-designation of Jesus, like the other evangelists. But it is also inevitable that his creative use of the passion prediction should colour his idea of the Son of Man. On the strength of these Johannine sayings we can conclude that the Son of Man is to John the earthly revealer of a divine and saving relationship. This relationship is available to all through faith (3.15).

2 *The Son of Man and revelation: John 1.51.*

This preliminary conclusion must now be tested by comparison with the other seven Son of Man sayings. The first saying in the order of the gospel is 1.51, 'Amen, amen, I say to you, you will see the heaven opened, and the angels of God ascending and descending upon the Son of Man'. The Amen-formula is a feature of Jesus' style in the sayings tradition.[3] Very frequently in John it is an indication that John is drawing on this tradition, but this does not prevent him from freely adapting his sources at the same time.[4] The closest parallel to the present verse is the baptism of Jesus in Mark 1.10, 'and immediately, *ascending* from the water, he *saw the heavens opened* and the Spirit *descending on him* like a dove'.[5] John is clearly aware of the baptism story, though it is not described directly in John 1.29–34, and he has referred to this very verse obliquely in verse 33, 'Upon whomsoever you see the Spirit descending . . .'. There is thus good reason to suspect that John has modelled the saying of verse 51 upon this tradition. On the other hand, the similarity to Stephen's words in Acts 7.56 may be no more than coincidence.

Of course John is not actually referring to the baptism in this verse. He is concerned with something that is to take place in the future. But it may be surmised that the baptismal experience of Jesus is not irrelevant to this future event. For John agrees with Matthew that the experience was not confined to Jesus alone, but was perceived by John the Baptist too. Indeed, it was the sign to him of the identity of Jesus as the coming one of whom he had preached. Thus it was an earthly act which revealed the true status of Jesus, in much the same way as the lifting up of the Son of Man is a revelatory act on earth. It may thus be concluded that verse 51, modelled upon the baptism but referring to the future, is also intended to indicate a future act which will reveal something about Jesus. In the light of 3.14 it is likely that this event is the cross, which at this stage John does not wish to mention directly.

The meaning of 1.51 in its context must be deduced from the remaining words about the angels. There is widespread agreement today that John has composed the saying in such a way as to recall Jacob's dream (Gen. 28.12), 'And he dreamed that there was a ladder set up on the earth, and the top of it reached to heaven; and behold, *the angels of God were ascending and descending on it*'. It is also recognized that the movement of the angels 'upon the Son of Man' has a parallel in rabbinic exegesis, in which 'on it' (the ladder) is taken to mean 'on him' (Jacob). This is possible in the Hebrew, but not in the Greek. In the rabbinic exegesis the angels are familiar with the heavenly archetype of the righteous man, and are now delighted to discover the earthly reality in Jacob.[6] It may be conjectured that the 'greater things' (John 1.50) which Jesus' audience will see are something that belongs to a similar line of exegesis. They will see an act in which the Son of Man on earth reflects a heavenly reality. There is a sense in which this is true of all the acts of Jesus in the Fourth Gospel. But it is especially true of the passion, in which death and glorification are two sides of a single reality. Thus, just as the baptism of Jesus was an earthly act which revealed his heavenly identity, so the cross will be a supremely revelatory act.

This interpretation of 1.51 makes full allowance for its contextual position.[7] It confirms the connection between it and the reference to the baptism of Jesus earlier in the chapter. This connection is indicated in the actual words with which the saying begins, but extends to the theme which they have in common. There is thus a literary inclusion which encapsulates the paragraphs concerning the call of the disciples, with their preliminary confessions of faith, and so suggests that the disclosure of the full meaning of the confession of faith must wait until a further revelatory act has taken place. Thus 1.51 is a programmatic statement, pointing to the significance of the story that is to be unfolded.

Two further points should be observed. First, the saying shows no influence from Dan. 7.13–14, or such sayings as Mark 14.62 which are related to it. This is not to say that John is unaware of the connection, but only that it is not operative here, and therefore is not a controlling factor for the interpretation of the saying.[8] The scene is not the heavenly court, and there is no reference to the coming of the Son of Man. Secondly, John's choice of the Son of Man title is not dictated by the contents of the saying, which, as we have seen, have different literary affinities. Moreover it is not clear that he intends it to be an additional form of the confession of faith, surpassing the confession just made by Nathanael in verse 49. What Nathanael and the others will see is an act which surpasses the display of insight on the part of Jesus which evoked Nathanael's confession, and that act will evoke confession not of the Son of Man, but of 'the Christ, the Son of God' (20.31; cf. 20.28). Thus the Son of Man is not here a title in the same series as the rest. It appears to be no more than the third-person self-reference of Jesus, with which we are familiar from the synoptic sayings. But our study of the 'lifting up' and 'glorification' sayings entitles us to see a functional use of the Son of Man in John. This saying agrees with them in denoting Jesus as the earthly revealer of a divine and saving relationship. But for the present the nature of the act by which Jesus fulfils this function is not specified. It is merely alluded to as something more significant than the baptism, and more significant than the act of recognition which evoked Nathanael's confession of faith. The reader has to wait until 3.14 to discover that in fact it is the cross.

These two observations show that the Son of Man in John is not a title which he has adopted already laden with meaning apart from the tradition of the sayings of Jesus. The function of the Son of Man in 1.51 is no different from the function in 3.14, and there it is derived from the passion predictions, as developed in the light of the kerygma and incorporated into Mark.

3 *The Son of Man and revelation: other texts*

a. The next occurrence of the Son of Man title is in 3.13; 'No one has ascended into heaven but he who descended from heaven, the Son of Man.' This can be quickly dealt with. The phrase is carefully placed at the end of the verse to prepare the way for the important statement on the lifting up of the Son of Man which immediately follows. In view of what has just been said above about the function of the Son of Man in John, it can suitably be paraphrased 'the revealer' (not, of course, implying Bultmann's mythological use of this idea).[9] John has asserted that salvation requires birth 'from above', i.e., from the Spirit,[10] and now he is going to prove the christological consequence of this, that the bringer of salvation comes from above too (3.11–13). So the revealer comes from heaven, and he will reveal on earth the heavenly truth by means of the exaltation described in 3.14. Because John uses the Son of Man in this functional way, there is no question here whether the Son of Man was thought to be pre-existent or not.[11] John does believe that Jesus is pre-existent, in the sense that he has divine origination, and therefore the Son of Man is pre-existent, because the Son of Man is none other than Jesus. But John has no concept of the Son of Man apart from Jesus, and so the theoretical question of the pre-existence of the Son of Man, which has often been raised on the basis of this verse, simply does not arise.

b. This seems to be the best place to mention 9.35, where the Son of Man is used in connection with what appears to be a confession of faith: 'Jesus heard that they had cast him out, and having found him he said, "Do you believe in the Son of Man?"'[12] The person addressed is the man born blind. So the theme is the removal of the blindness which prevents perception of revelation. According to our functional understanding of the Son of Man the question can be paraphrased, 'Do you believe in the revealer?', i.e., that there is one who 'makes manifest the works of God' (9.3). On the other hand this cannot be reduced to a mere substitute for the first person ('Do you believe in me?'), because the man does not realize that the Son of Man is to be identified with Jesus himself (verse 36). We may well ask what the man thought the title meant. No indication of its content is given. It seems, then, that it must be regarded as having a meaning that can be taken for granted. Naturally, scholars have assumed that the meaning was provided by the current apocalyptic title, which was held to be a feature of the background to the New Testament. This solution is no longer open to us. Hence the meaning must be derived from John's use of the title elsewhere in the gospel, rather than from external sources. If John 9 is taken to be historical reporting, it is, of course, difficult to think of the man as capable of understanding the Son of Man in the specifically Johannine sense. As the chapter has much more probably been artificially constructed on the basis of a much simpler tradition, this difficulty ought not to be pressed. The functional meaning of the Son of Man as the revealer of God is sufficient to justify the form of the dialogue in verses 35–37, and admirably suits the theological purpose of the chapter as a whole.

c. The discourse on the bread of life in John 6 mentions the Son of Man three times (6.27, 53, 62). In the dialogue which leads into the discourse proper, Jesus says (6.27), 'Do not labour for the food which perishes, but for the food which endures to eternal life, which the Son of Man will give to you; for on him has God the Father set his seal'. It is natural to interpret this saying in relation to the Jewish expectation of the renewal of the manna miracle in the eschatological age.[13] This has led to the conclusion that the Son of Man is the apocalyptic title of the future Messiah, who here includes the provision of the bread as one of his eschatological functions. The study of the Son of Man in John which we have so far undertaken suggests, however, that this may be a false track. The interpretation turns on the question *when* the bread will be given. It transpires in the course of what follows that the bread is the true teaching from God (verse 45). From this point of view the bread is available already (hence the timeless present participles in verses 35, 40, 47 and indefinite clauses in 50b, 51b). Finally, the bread metaphor is explained by the fact that the teaching from God is not so much what Jesus teaches verbally as what he is in himself, the one who gives his life for the world (51c). It then comes as no surprise to discover that consumption of the bread in this sense is identified with eating and drinking the flesh and blood of the Son of Man (6.53), 'Amen, amen, I say to you, unless you eat the flesh of the Son of Man and drink his blood, you have no life in you'. The language is eucharistic, but the reference is certainly to the passion as the essential factor in Christology which must not be missed. The faith required to gain the bread (verse 28) is inadequate unless it includes the necessity of Jesus' sacrificial death. The revealer must die (or, as John said in 3.14, be lifted up), and this *fact* is 'the food which endures to eternal life, which the Son of Man will give you' (verse 27).

These two Son of Man sayings belong together, and enclose the whole discourse. The climax in verses 53–8 has been prepared for from the very beginning. The connection between verses 27 and 53 shows that the Son of Man has the same functional purpose here as in the other passages. The title stems from the passion predictions, and the passion is the supreme moment of revelation. The Son of Man will give the imperishable food when he is lifted up on the cross.

We still have to ask why John adds in verse 27, 'for on him has God the Father set his seal'. Here Moloney, following Barrett, is right in suggesting that the sentence refers to the exclusive position of Jesus as the authentic revelation of God. God's plan to reveal himself through the act of the Son of Man is like a document signed and sealed. This detail thus confirms the interpretation which we have already reached. It suits the exclusive character of the discourse, which emphasizes several times the unique position of Jesus as the agent of salvation (verses 37, 40, 44f, 49f, 53).

The third of these three Son of Man sayings stands outside the discourse as such, and belongs to the record of the reactions of the audience (6.62), 'Do you take offence at this? Then what if you were to see the Son of Man ascending where he was before?' (verses 61–2). It is not clear whether this would remove the offence or make it even worse.[14] The former seems best, because it accords with the spiritual understanding required by the next verse. To see the ascension of Jesus would be to have proof that, contrary to outward appearance, the death of Jesus is the truly saving act. But the spiritual person (6.63) should be able to perceive this without actually seeing the ascension (cf. 20.29). Once more, as in 3.13, it is implied that the Son of Man has descended first. As before, it is necessary to stress that pre-existence is not ascribed to Jesus as Son of Man, as if there were a ready-made concept of the pre-existent Son of Man. But it is essential to John's position that Jesus could not achieve his saving work without origination from God, and so in this sense the revealer has descended from God, and in accomplishing his appointed task by way of the cross he reaches his destination in God. Thus the whole plan, sealed by God (verse 27), is brought to its conclusion. John uses the notion of ascension rather than 'lifting up' precisely because he is not speaking of the cross in its outward aspect, but in terms of a demonstration of its inner meaning.[15] The death and exaltation of Jesus are for John the reverse sides of a single coin. But John is careful to keep them separate conceptually. We have already observed a similar distinction in the use of *hupsoun* and *doxazein*.

d. John has one more Son of Man saying, and this appears to break the pattern which has held together so well up to this point. All the references to the Son of Man hitherto have been amenable to interpretation in the light of John's use of the passion predictions in 3.14. In his death on the cross Jesus reveals God, and it is in this capacity, and in relation to this act, that he is referred to as the Son of Man. But when we turn to 5.26–7 we find a different picture, 'For as the Father has life in himself, so he has granted the Son also to have life in himself, and has given him authority to execute judgement, because he is the Son of Man (*hoti huios anthropou estin*)'.

As far as the Greek text goes, this verse has a unique feature. This is the only place in the gospels where the Son of Man is mentioned without the definite article (*huios anthropou*).[16] This brings it into line with the places outside the sayings tradition where the phrase is used (Heb. 2.6, in a quotation of Ps. 8.4; Rev. 1.13; 14.14, both

alluding to Dan. 7.13). This difference from the rest of the sayings
has never been satisfactorily explained. A considerable number of
scholars trace it to direct influence from Dan. 7.13f on account of
further allusions to Daniel in the immediate context.[17] Thus verses
28–9 seem to be inspired by Dan. 12.2. In verse 27 itself the words
'has given him authority' (subject: God) may well be an allusion to
Dan. 7.14, 'and to him was given dominion . . .' This is strenuously
denied by Casey, who insists that John means that the Son will have
this authority 'because he is a son of man', i.e. a human being.[18] But
this interpretation is open to the objection that John certainly
means *huios anthropou* to be definite, in spite of the omission of the
definite articles, because this is always the case in comparable
passages (cf. 1.1; 8.33; 10.36).

The really significant feature is that the Son of Man is the
predicate of a simple noun-sentence. This is what makes this verse
different from all the other Son of Man passages, and demands
explanation, whether it means 'because he is a man' or 'because he is
the Son of Man'. The word order, with predicate *before* the copula,
places the emphasis on *huios anthropou*. It is because the Son (verse
26) is *huios anthropou* that the Father has given him authority to
execute judgement. Grammar and syntax cannot tell us why this
should be so. The question has to be decided from the context as a
whole.

The discourse of John 5 is based upon the nature of the
relationship between father and son. As a son learns his craft from
his father (verse 19), so Jesus' acts are done under the instruction
and at the bidding of God. Two functions have been specified in
verses 21 and 22, giving life and executing judgement. These are
both eschatological acts. Jesus has asserted that they have been
delegated to the Son by the Father, and that those who believe in
him can experience them now (verse 24). Then in verse 25 there is
a change of perspective. The present moment is not merely an
anticipation of the general resurrection and judgement. It is in fact
the beginning of the whole process, which ultimately includes all
men (verse 28). The entire eschatological action will be performed
by the Son, not mere anticipations of it, because the Father has
granted him the power and authority to do it. Why, then, has the
Father delegated his prerogatives to the Son in this way? It is
because he is the proper person to receive them. But what makes
him the proper person? Surely not the bare fact that he is a man! He

is not simply interchangeable with any other human being. It is because he is who he is, the revealer of God to mankind. The reader can be expected to know this, even when expressed so very briefly in the three words *huios anthropou estin*, because the function of the Son of Man has already been introduced in 3.14–15, and it has already been shown that his coming inevitably leads to judgement (3.16–21).

On this view, which is substantially that of Moloney,[19] the Son of Man in 5.27 has to be accepted as titular, in spite of the syntactical position which requires the omission of the articles. A connection with Dan. 7.13–14 may be allowed, because the apocalyptic picture derived from that passage is the source of the scenario of these verses. John need not be supposed to be ignorant of Daniel. But this does not alter the fact that he uses the Son of Man title in his own way. To him it refers to the one whose crucifixion reveals God's glory. Precisely because the cross is the vital factor for faith, it is the judgement, the criterion, for all time. The lifting up of the Son of Man brings into operation faith in Jesus as the new criterion for salvation. This not only applies now (verse 24), but to the whole subsequent history of humanity, culminating in the general resurrection and final judgement (verses 25–27).

4 *Conclusion*

The saying of 5.27 does not break the pattern after all. When John says that the Son has authority to execute judgement because he is the Son of Man, he means that he has it because he is the one who must 'be lifted up, that whoever believes in him may have eternal life'. The Son of Man in this verse is consistent with the functional idea which we have already noted. *The Son of Man in John is the agent of the revelation which is disclosed in the cross.* In this way the expression is almost a technical term. It is not intended to refer specifically to the humanity of Jesus, though the act of revelation is the climax of his human life. But the Son of Man sayings in John never occur in discussions of the human-ness of Jesus. From this point of view it may be considered a rather misleading phrase to use. One might feel that John could have found a better and more precise expression for the agent of revelation.

This takes us to the question of the source of John's use of the title. The reason why he used this title is that it came to him in the sayings tradition. It is not possible to be sure how far his familiarity with the sayings tradition extended. It cannot be proved that he had direct access to any of the Synoptic Gospels. But it is certain that he was in a position to use material which is also contained in them.[20] On the whole he uses a surprisingly small number of traditional sayings of Jesus in constructing the discourses. Hence we have no means of telling the range of Son of Man sayings available to him. But there can be no doubt that he had a form of the passion prediction, which he exploited in his own unique way in 3.14. None of the other Son of Man sayings in John relate to any other Son of Man sayings known from the Synoptic Gospels. Moreover, it has transpired that 3.14 is fundamental to all the rest. It is the basis of John's use of the Son of Man in a functional way, as a sort of technical term. It thus becomes unnecessary to look for any other source for the sayings in John, because all relate to the one saying which is derived from the passion prediction.

It thus comes about that, whether John was familiar with other Son of Man sayings or not, it can be safely asserted that he has derived his own use of the title from the passion prediction. The reason for this is obvious. It made an admirable base for one of his central theological themes. John is selective in his use of material, because he has a burning sense of purpose. There is no point in using what is not suitable to promote his argument. Having found what he wants, he makes good use of it.

What, then, of the Son of Man in the Johannine church?[21] The above argument suggests that, however distinct this church may have been in the spectrum of early Christianity, it possessed or had access to traditions of the sayings of Jesus, and these included at least the passion prediction, and perhaps other Son of Man sayings too. The fact that John uses the title fairly frequently argues that he is familiar with it as a style-feature of the Jesus tradition, just like the other evangelists. But we can scarcely impose upon the Johannine community the quasi-technical sense which John has derived from the passion prediction. That belongs to the creative, theological thought of the gospel, but it is not a distinctive feature of Johannine Christianity. Hence it is not found in the Johannine epistles. It follows that the Son of Man is unlikely to have been a title in current use in the Johannine church at all. There was no Son of Man Christology there any more than in any of the other early Christian communities. The Son of Man remains a feature of the sayings tradition. Like the other evangelists, John has exploited it in his literary work. In fact his whole presentation of the gospel is done by building on the Jesus tradition, repeating and refining the same words and themes until his purpose is achieved. The Son of Man in John begins in a promise of revelation (1.51) and ends at the moment when it is fulfilled (13.31).

10

The Son of Man and Christology

1 *Daniel 7 and Christology*

The Son of Man is a feature of the sayings of Jesus. This investigation has started from the assumption that the Son of Man did not have a specialized use in New Testament times as the title of an eschatological or mythological figure in either Jewish or hellenistic thought. The Son of Man is an Aramaic phrase (*bar enasha*), corresponding with Hebrew *ben adam*, which means a man as a specimen of humanity or, collectively, mankind. Its significance in any given instance must be deduced from the context. There is no warrant to take its meaning in one context (e.g., as a designation for Ezekiel) and apply it without more ado to a quite different context (e.g., as a self-reference on the part of Jesus). It is even more indefensible to postulate a meaning and a context in Jewish or hellenistic circles which have left no literary traces at all.

There is only one Jewish book known to us which uses the Son of Man in a titular way, and that is the Similitudes of Enoch (1 Enoch 37–71). But even in this work the Son of Man (usually 'that Son of Man') operates in a non-technical way, as Casey has convincingly demonstrated.[1] The phrase refers to the person who has already been described in chapter 46, which is based on the vision of Dan. 7.9–14. It is thus an excellent example of the messianic interpretation of the Danielic figure. But it is not evidence for an independent use of the Son of Man phrase as a messianic title.

The date of the Similitudes of Enoch is uncertain. But there is much to be said for composition towards the end of the first century or beginning of the second century AD.[2] This suits the affinities with 2 Esd. 11–13 and the Apocalypse of Baruch and the book of Revelation, at the same time as accounting for the lack of direct literary connections with these books. It also suits the messianism associated with R. Akiba in connection with the hopes surrounding Bar Cochba's ill-fated bid for Jewish freedom.[3] The Danielic figure is the central character in 2 Esd. 13, identified with the Messiah. But here again there is no titular use of the Son of Man. If the phrase occurred in the original at all (assuming for the sake of argument that the original was in Aramaic rather than Hebrew), it operated according to normal Aramaic usage.

The use of Dan. 7 for Christology belongs to much the same period as these Jewish works. The New Testament references begin as early as the Q collection, and therefore antedate these particular Jewish books. But there is no sign of literary borrowing on either side. It may thus be concluded that both are dependent upon a messianic interpretation of Dan. 7 which is already current.[4] Outside the sayings tradition, however, there is no use of the Son of Man as a title in connection with this Christology in the New Testament. The Book of Revelation is especially striking from this point of view. The description of the risen Christ in the first chapter is largely based on Dan. 7.9–14, and even refers to him as 'one like a son of man' (*homoion huion anthropou*) in Rev. 1.13. The phrase operates entirely in the usual Aramaic way, and there is no hint that it might be a *title* for Jesus (or for anyone else). Precisely the same phrase is used for a person who is seen to be sitting on a cloud, with sickle in hand, ready to reap the harvest of humanity (Rev. 14.14). The context does not indicate clearly whether this person is an angel or Christ himself. But as he is seated and wears a golden crown, there is enough to distinguish him from the other angels mentioned in the chapter, and his appearance at this particular juncture corresponds with the appearance of the Son of Man to gather in the elect in Mark's Little Apocalypse (Mark 13.26f).[5] It is thus most probable that he is intended to be Christ, described in a fashion which is suitable for this function. This explains why the imagery of the Lamb is dropped at this point.[6] There can thus be no doubt that the Danielic figure lies behind this description, though the function is derived from the eschatological judgement scene of Joel 3.12–13 (Hebrew, 4.12–13). Here, as so often, the Old Testament idea is transferred from God to the exalted Jesus.

These two references in Revelation are particularly striking, because they actually embody the Son of Man phrase in descriptions of Christ derived from Dan. 7.13–14, and yet use it in the normal Aramaic manner without the slightest hint of the titular usage found in the gospels. This is one of the most telling items of evidence that there never was a Son of Man title outside the sayings tradition.

It is thus necessary to distinguish sharply between the messianic interpretation of Dan. 7 and the titular use of the Son of Man. The latter is not attested outside the gospels (and Acts 7.56), even though Jesus is identified with the Danielic figure in Christian apocalyptic eschatology.

It has been shown in the preceding chapters that the titular use of the Son of Man is a secondary development within the sayings tradition. This came about as a result of two factors. In the first place, the Son of Man was recognized to be a special characteristic of Jesus' style. The tradition contained a sufficient number of sayings in which Jesus referred to himself as the Son of Man, not using it as a title, but employing a special Aramaic idiom. Even when spoken in Aramaic the phrase, though properly generic, certainly included reference to Jesus himself, and so was capable of being understood primarily from this point of view. When turned into Greek it could scarcely be understood in any other way than as an exclusive self-reference. Thus, from a purely stylistic angle it was tempting to the evangelists to exploit it in their handling of the sayings tradition.

In the second place, the identification of Jesus with the Danielic figure becomes increasingly important in the Jewish strands of the New Testament (Matt.; Rev.; Luke when writing in a Jewish context). As such, Jesus could be described in Danielic terminology as 'one like a son of man' without any suggestion of a title. We have seen this in Rev. 1.13 and 14.14. The phrase here is indefinite in a third-personal context. This makes it entirely different from the generic usage, incorporating a first-personal reference, which is the special feature in the authentic sayings of Jesus. It is also distinct from the definite usage, in which it appears to be a substitute for the first person, which is the impression given by the Greek translation (*ho huios tou anthropou*). Nevertheless, the existence of sayings of Jesus containing the phrase was bound to lead to assimilation. The Son of Man, as an exclusive self-designation of Jesus, was naturally employed in contexts where Jesus was identified with the Danielic figure. By this means it became an apocalyptic title for him. It could even be used as a title for the eschatological agent of God without any stress on the identification with Jesus at all. This is characteristic of passages which are concerned with the apocalyptic programme, notably the Little Apocalypse of Mark and its parallels in Matthew and Luke, and the special usage of Matthew himself in Matt. 13.37, 47; 19.28; 25.31.

In this way the Son of Man became the title of the Danielic figure, understood to be God's agent in the coming judgement. Precisely because it is a third-personal usage, it is possible to lose sight of the fact that it is intended always to have a first-personal reference, i.e., to Jesus himself. In many of the passages, it is easy to assume that Jesus is speaking of someone other than himself. Alternatively, they may be read as implying that Jesus identifies himself with a figure of contemporary Jewish expectations designated the Son of Man. These are false impressions, but they have dominated modern studies of the Son of Man problem, and are responsible for the myths of the Son of Man in current scholarship. Nowadays we speak of the Danielic figure as the Son of Man just as if that was the natural and normal way of referring to him, and we very easily assume that Jesus did so too. It takes a considerable mental effort for us to realize that there was no such titular usage and application in New Testament times, and that Jesus never referred to himself, or to the Danielic figure, in this way. This usage is a peculiarity of secondary developments in the sayings tradition, which became possible only because the Greek translation of the Aramaic sayings turned the idiomatic *bar enasha* into an exclusive self-reference.

These developments spring from the church's proclamation of the heavenly lordship of Jesus, which goes back to the earliest days of Christianity, and indeed reflects the resurrection experience from which Christianity began. Thus, though we do have to make a clear distinction between the meaning of the authentic Son of Man sayings on the lips of Jesus and the post-resurrection understanding and development of them in a Greek-speaking milieu, we are not bound to think in terms of a linear or evolutionary progression of thought. Our study has shown that authentic sayings are confined to Mark and Q. Matthew, Luke and John each make their own distinctive contribution to the subsequent development, but none of them preserves any further authentic sayings. For this reason it has seemed best to assume that the Son of Man sayings which they contain are the result of the literary activity of these evangelists themselves. Seeing that their unparalleled sayings are secondary in every case, it is unnecessary to assume that they drew them from earlier sources which are now lost.

2 *The Christology of the Gospel Writers*

a. The multiplication of Son of Man sayings begins with Mark. He had in the traditions available to him five authentic sayings, which can be divided into three groups, each of which has spawned further sayings:

> The 'authority' saying (Mark 2.10): But that you may know that a man may have authority on earth to forgive sins . . .

> The 'advocate' saying (pre-Marcan form, Mark 8.38): Every one who is ashamed of me before men, of him will a man be ashamed before the angels of God.

> The passion prediction (Mark 9.31; 10.33; 14.21b, 41): A man may be delivered up . . .

> The 'ransom' saying (Mark 10.45): A man may give his life for many.

> The 'destiny' saying (Mark 14.21a): A man goes as it is written of him.

The 'authority' saying of Mark 2.10 provided him with the model for another in 2.28. The 'advocate' saying, in the reduced negative form of Mark 8.38, was the basis of the titular use of the Son of Man, explicitly identified with the Danielic figure, in 13.26 and 14.62. The passion sayings can be traced to three original forms, but may have already undergone some degree of development before they reached Mark. The basic form of the passion predictions seems to be 'The Son of Man will be delivered up'. This is reflected in Paul's writings. It appears to have been developed in relation to the kerygma of Jesus' death and resurrection. It has also been exploited in relation to the special problem of Judas Iscariot. The other two authentic passion sayings (Mark 10.45 and 14.21a) also have links with other parts of the New Testament. Mark has made good use of these sayings, because the necessity of the passion has christological importance for him. The result is that Mark's five authentic sayings have grown to a grand total of fourteen.

Mark's use of the Son of Man is the servant, but not the master, of his Christology. Mark presents Jesus as one destined to be crucified, and to rise again and be glorified. Before long he will return as God's agent to gather in the elect. This was God's plan from the beginning, though it was not visible to people in general during Jesus' earthly life. Nevertheless it was always the truth of the matter, a secret which was waiting to be disclosed. This is the messianic secret, identified in modern times as a special feature of Mark. The ambiguity of the Son of Man designation was a gift to Mark from this point of view. His two 'authority' sayings (2.10, 28) thus refer obscurely to the authority which Jesus has by right as the Messiah. In these sayings the Son of Man is not a messianic title, but a self-reference of Jesus as he enigmatically makes this claim. The same is really true of the passion sayings as well. The Son of Man is a self-designation in them, and has no special content over and above what is said in the sayings themselves. Once again, the ambiguity of this third-personal way of speaking suits Mark's purpose well. For it has the effect of detaching Jesus from what he is saying about himself, and so enhances the impression that he is speaking of the proper destiny of the Messiah, which is to be fulfilled in himself. This effect is taken a stage further in the future sayings (8.38; 13.26; 14.62), where the ambiguity is removed, and the Son of Man becomes the title of the Messiah in his future role as the agent of God. In particular, 13.26 and 14.62 both come at moments of grand climax in Mark's composition. Though Mark is aware that the Son of Man is not a formal title for the Messiah (hence in 15.39 the centurion's confession 'the Son of God' corresponds with the high priest's question in 14.61 rather than with Jesus' answer), the connection with Dan. 7.13 has been present in his mind all along. This shows the importance of the 'authority' saying in 2.10, which is not a verbal allusion to Dan. 7.14, but may well have been related to it in Mark's intention. There is thus a double inclusion, the confession of the unclean spirit in 1.24 ('the holy one of God') corresponding with the confession of the centurion in 15.39, and the statement of Jesus concerning himself in 2.10 corresponding with his final statement in 14.62. The Son of Man is Jesus' title for himself in connection with his eschatological function as the agent of God's kingdom, and this is the reality to which the other confessions (including Peter's 'Christ', 8.29) all point.

These considerations show that Mark's use of the Son of Man belongs to a coherent and well articulated christological interpretation of the gospel. He has been able to make positive use of each of the sayings which he found in the tradition. By repeating them and elaborating them he has given greater prominence to this feature of the Jesus tradition than it would otherwise have had. But he has

163

done this simply because this feature was so valuable for the overall purpose of the Gospel. All the sayings are geared to his Christology, and therefore they fit into a unified pattern.

b. The position of Q is quite different. Of course it is difficult to characterize Q, because it can be reconstructed only very tentatively. But it is mainly a collection of sayings, sometimes grouped in related sequences. The fact that it does not set out to be a biography may explain the absence of references to the passion. In any case, the failure of Q to produce parallels to the passion sayings preserved by Mark must be seen in relation to this larger question. On the other hand Q is the most valuable source for authentic Son of Man sayings, numbering four without parallels in Mark, besides the 'advocate' saying, which may have been in the 'I' form in Q:

The 'advocate' saying (original form, Matt. 10.32f=Luke 12.8f): Every one who confesses me before men, him will a man confess before the angels of God; every one who denies me before men, him will a man deny before the angels of God.

The 'foxes' saying (Matt. 8.20=Luke 9.58): Foxes have holes and birds of the air have their nests, but a man has nowhere to lay his head.

The 'glutton' saying (Matt. 11.8f=Luke 7.33f): For John the Baptist has come eating no bread and drinking no wine; and you say, 'He has a demon.' Someone else has come eating and drinking; and you say, 'Behold, a glutton and a drunkard, a friend of tax collectors and sinners!'

The 'blasphemy' saying (Matt. 12.32=Luke 12.10): Whoever speaks a word against a man may be forgiven; but whoever speaks against the Holy Spirit may not be forgiven.

The sign of Jonah (Luke 11.30): For as Jonah became a sign to the men of Nineveh, so a man may be to this generation.

These show a wider range than is indicated by Mark. They tend to relate to Jesus' understanding of his mission from God—whether it be in relation to the hardship which it involves (the 'foxes' saying), or to its authenticity as a divine commission (the 'glutton' saying and the 'blasphemy' saying), or its crucial importance to the present generation (the sign of Jonah). The fact that the 'advocate' saying is doubly attested in Mark and Q is a sign that we have here very old material, which has been transmitted through two channels of tradition. But this also applies to other items in this list, because the 'glutton' saying, on Jesus and John the Baptist, is reflected in the question of authority in Mark 11.27–33, the 'blasphemy' saying actually does have a parallel in Mark. 3.28–9, though the Son of Man in it is obscured, and the sign of Jonah is related to the request for a sign in Mark 8.11–12. It should also be pointed out that the 'advocate' saying can be classified with the rest as a saying concerned with Jesus' mission, because it is aimed at impressing upon his hearers the crucial importance of their response to the message of God.

Apart from these authentic sayings (which will be considered further below), it was not found possible to attribute any other Son of Man sayings to Q except for the three sayings on the day of the Son of Man, best preserved in Luke 17.24, 26, 30, and the parable of the returning master (Matt. 24.44 = Luke 12.40). These could not be considered authentic in their present form, because the titular Son of Man cannot correspond with the *bar enasha* idiom. As they are all concerned with the coming of the Son of Man, it is natural to suspect the influence of Dan. 7.13. This makes a parallel to the process which we found behind Mark. The Greek translation of Q appeared to make the Son of Man an exclusive self-reference, and this was correlated with the Danielic figure in eschatological contexts. On the other hand, there is an important difference between Mark and Q. Mark was primarily concerned with the kerygmatic aspect of this identification. He has brought it to the surface only in Mark 13.26; 14.62, where in each case there is explicit allusion to Daniel. In both cases there is very little likelihood that Mark is adapting an authentic saying. In Q, however, it is possible that the Son of Man has been inserted into what is otherwise genuine material. The most convincing explanation of this is the contemporary tendency to adapt eschatological statements of the coming of the Lord to the parousia of Jesus. Such statements were an essential element in Jesus' preaching of the kingdom. The way for the alteration in Q had been prepared both by the implications of the 'advocate' saying (even in its 'I' form) and by the composition of the short sequence which includes the sign of Jonah (Luke 11.29–32). The application of such sayings to the parousia of Jesus is attested outside the gospels as early as the writings of Paul. There is thus good reason to conclude that Q extended the use of the Son of Man in a way that is quite similar to what is found in Mark, but entirely independently. Both start with the Son of Man as a given form of self-reference in Jesus' speech, and both work from it under the influence of the christology of their own day. Thus the Son of Man picks up the harmonics of the current christological tendencies. These are very similar in Mark and Q, but not quite identical.

c. These developments are taken for granted in both Matthew and Luke. Both realize that the Son of Man is primarily a self-designation of Jesus rather than a particular title, so that they are content to preserve the variety of sayings, both authentic and inauthentic, provided for them by Mark and Q. They do not, of course, appreciate the underlying Aramaic idiom, which might have made them hesitate to extend still further the titular usage of the phrase.

Matthew has two special features which give to his treatment of the Son of Man its distinctive flavour. First, he extends the practice, already noticed in Q, of substituting the Son of Man for God in eschatological statements. His Jewishness makes him sensitive to the way in which Jesus' preaching of the coming of the kingdom is really a preaching of the coming of God. This is the reason why he has replaced the kingdom of God in Mark 9.1 with the Son of Man (Matt. 16.28). It has been suggested above that the Son of Man in Matt 10.23b is also Matthew's own alteration of the kingdom of God in a similar type of statement. Matthew also substitutes the Son of Man for God in his interpretation of the parable of the tares (Matt. 13.37, 41), and probably in that of the great assize too (Matt. 25.31). In these cases he is not altering a written text, but incorporating his own interpretation of what lies before him by means of editorial additions. Thus the coming is for Matthew identified with the coming of Jesus as God's agent, and for this purpose Jesus speaks of himself in terms of the Son of Man designation.

Secondly, Matthew has a clear and vivid mental picture of Jesus' future glory in this capacity. He thinks of the parousia in a concrete way, as a literal fulfilment of the picture provided by Dan. 7.9–14, as it was understood in contemporary apocalyptic. This brings him closer to other Jewish writers of the New Testament (Jude; Rev.) and to Jewish apocalyptic of the same period (2 Esd.; Similitudes of Enoch). It is possible to speak of a Son of Man Christology from this point of view, because it is a Christology in which Jesus is pictured as the Danielic figure and his future function is expressed in terms of apocalyptic eschatology. But this does not alter the fact that the Son of Man was not a recognized title of the Danielic figure, and the use of it in Matthew is never completely detached from the sayings tradition, in which it always operates as a reference to Jesus himself. Moreover the Danielic element in Matthew's Christology does not stand by itself, in opposition to other types of Christology. For Matthew the Davidic element is very important. He thinks of the Messiah primarily in terms of the popular Jewish expectation of the Son of David, the idealized king of the people of God, and indeed of all the nations.[7] This is the picture which he has in mind when he speaks of the Son of Man sitting on his glorious throne (Matt. 19.28; 25.31; cf. also 16.27). He does not have a mental image of the Son of Man which is somehow different from that of the Son of David. The two are completely fused. But the Son of Man is the preferred title when Jesus is speaking of himself in relation to his future role.

It is thus clear that Matthew builds upon the Son of Man sayings in such a way as to produce a definite and distinctive impression. Though the variety of the Son of Man sayings in the sources remains unaffected, Matthew's additions and adaptations all tend to enhance the apocalyptic picture of the ideal ruler which is central to Matthew's Christology. The impression of the Son of Man given by Matthew can be regarded as a powerful factor behind the erroneous claim of modern scholarship that the Son of Man was the title of an apocalyptic figure in the expectations of the New Testament world.

d. Luke's use of the Son of Man, on the other hand, tends to confuse the picture. It is not possible to abstract his additions to the stock of Son of Man sayings and draw from them a specifically Lucan doctrine or tendency. They reflect the variety of usage which exists in the sources. Luke rightly observes that the Son of Man is a stylistic feature of the sayings of Jesus, and he wrongly supposes that it is an exclusive self-designation. He takes advantage of this feature to enhance the effectiveness of his portrait of Jesus. But he does so, not by fastening upon one favourite item in his sources, but by using several different models. Thus he makes fresh use of the passion sayings in 22.48; 24.7. The first of these, on the betrayal of Jesus, is a splendid example of his skill in introducing a note of pathos which is calculated to appeal to the reader's emotions. The Q sequence on the day of the Son of Man is the basis for 17.22, which is part of Luke's own introduction to it. Of course Luke is not unaware of other apocalyptic texts which allude to the Danielic Son of Man (Mark 13.26; 14.62), and may well have understood the 'advocate' saying in this sense. So it is no surprise to find that he uses this application of the Son of Man title in the summarizing verses which he has added to his sources at 18.8 and 21.36. Both of them are designed to have emotional effect upon the reader. It is possible that Luke has introduced the Son of Man into the Q version of the 'advocate' saying (12.8), deriving it from the Marcan version, which he has already used at 9.26. The apocalyptic usage thus accounts for three (possibly four) of the special Lucan sayings. We can add to these the saying of Stephen in Acts 7.56. But Luke is indebted to a different range of Son of Man sayings in the two remaining references. These are 6.22 (persecution for the sake of the Son of Man, where Q has 'for my sake') and 19.10 ('The Son of Man came to seek and to save the lost'). There are no apocalyptic overtones here, but the Son of Man functions simply as a substitute for the first person. But the use of the phrase adds a touch of solemnity, which would be missing if the first person were used. Luke's models in these cases are the 'authority' sayings of Mark 2.10, 28, which he has used at 5.24; 6.5, and the Q 'glutton' saying, used by Luke at 7.34, which has a close thematic connection with 5.32 and 15.1–7 (already referred to above in connection with 19.10). Once more, the emotional appeal to the reader is the reason why Luke composed 19.10 on the basis of these items in his sources. This he did so successfully that it has strayed into other places in the manuscript tradition of the gospels where it seemed appropriate (Matt. 18.11; Luke 9.56).

As far as Luke's Christology is concerned, it would seem possible at first sight to claim that he supports two different positions. Luke retains all the authentic items considered in chapters 3 and 4, which are very easily (but improperly) interpreted in terms of Jesus' humanity. His further contribution in Luke 19.10 seems to enhance this impression. It can then be said that Luke has a particular interest in the humanity of Jesus, and uses the Son of Man title with this in mind. This could be true of Luke's own intention, even if it is a false interpretation of the original sayings. But in fact it is very unlikely, because Luke does not draw out the theological implications of the humanity of Jesus. His birth narrative is entirely directed towards the destiny of Jesus as God's Son, and makes no mention of the significance of incarnation in its own right, unlike the prologue of John. Luke nowhere brings to expression the necessity of the human nature of Christ, such as we find in Paul and Hebrews.[8]

On the other side, Luke's apocalyptic sayings in addition to his sources are sufficiently numerous, especially if we include Acts 7.56, to suggest a growth of interest in the future Son of Man parallel to what we have seen in Matthew. However, it is questionable whether one can rightly speak of a growth of interest, where Luke is concerned. Rather, it is something that he takes for granted. In Acts he makes his Christology plain. Jesus ascends to heaven in a cloud (Acts 1.9; verse 11 implies an allusion to Dan. 7.13), and thereafter occupies his seat at the right hand of God (Luke 22.69; Acts 2.34–36; 3.21) to be God's agent in the coming judgement (Luke 21.36; Acts 1.11; 10.42; 17.31). This is not dissimilar to the primitive confession of faith, in so far as it can be recovered. In spite of writing at a comparatively late date, Luke has retained the simple, concrete outlines of the primitive confession because of his practical and unspeculative approach. His expectation concerning the duration of the period between the ascension and the parousia is different, of course. But this does not affect the basic Christology.[9]

Consequently Luke is hospitable to the Son of Man sayings which represent this aspect of his beliefs, and it is only natural that his editorial additions should represent this interest. His views can be appreciated from the summarizing verses, Luke 18.8 and 21.36. But the Son of Man is not a title which he would normally use outside the sayings of Jesus. He expresses the same Christology in Acts without the title at all, except in Acts 7.56, where he is modelling his description on the synoptic narrative of the trial of Jesus.

e. John also fails to produce a specific Son of Man Christology, in spite of the importance of the title within his Christology as a whole. John derives the title from its use in the sayings tradition in general. But his own use of it is entirely based on the passion predictions. The idea that Jesus foretold his own death is used by John as one of the foundations of his Christology. For it enables him to view Jesus' death in terms of Jesus' relationship with the Father. The death of

Jesus reveals his unity with the Father. Thus, paradoxically, the worst humiliation of Jesus is the outward sign of his highest glory. This paradox, expressed with the double meaning of 'lifting up', shows why the death of Jesus has to be by means of crucifixion. It would have failed in its saving effect if it had been done by any other means. Hence it is fundamental to John's Christology that, in order to accomplish the revelatory act which is essential for faith for all time (5.27), 'the Son of Man must be lifted up' (3.14). All the Son of Man sayings in John are related to this central position. It is therefore fair to speak of the Son of Man in John as having functional significance, denoting Jesus as the agent of the revelation which is disclosed in the cross. It is an entirely independent handling of the possibilities provided by the passion predictions, and owes nothing to other people's ideas concerning the Son of Man. It is in line with John's use of other items from the sayings tradition, which he uses creatively and with characteristic repetitiveness. It is one facet of John's brilliant recasting of the Jesus tradition in such a way as to make it the vehicle of a more profound theological interpretation of Jesus than had ever been achieved before.

3 *The Christology of the Authentic Sayings*

The starting-point for the church's faith was the resurrection of Jesus, and the earliest proclamation took the form of asserting that he was the Christ. The Son of Man is an expression which played no part in the earliest confessions of faith. It assumed christological significance only in a secondary stage of the transmission of the sayings of Jesus. It thus disappears altogether from the list of Jewish messianic titles which Jesus might have applied to himself in order to express his role in the saving purpose of God. It is, then, a mistake to suppose that the ambiguity surrounding the evidence for Jesus' personal claim to be the Messiah can be bypassed by his well-attested practice of referring to himself as the Son of Man. When he used this phrase in reference to himself, he was not using it as a title, and it carried no christological meaning as such, and it bore no relationship to the visionary figure of Dan. 7 and its interpretation.

Such a negative statement sounds very bleak, but it is necessary in order to clear the ground. It is notoriously difficult to pierce through the gospels so as to find out what Jesus really thought about himself in relation to God. Even when this is done successfully—and most people would admit that Jesus' sense of intimacy with God as Father is at any rate one firm datum—the significance for Christology is not easily assessed.[10] After reviewing all the evidence for the origins of the Christian doctrine of the incarnation J.D.G. Dunn concludes:

> We cannot claim that Jesus believed himself to be the incarnate Son of God; but we can claim that the teaching to that effect as it came to expression in the later first-century Christian thought was, in the light of the whole Christ-event, an appropriate reflection on and elaboration of Jesus' own sense of sonship and eschatological mission.[11]

The Son of Man, as used idiomatically by Jesus, tells us nothing about his sense of sonship. But it does have some bearing on his sense of eschatological mission. It is from this rather limited, but nonetheless important, point of view that we can discover positive value in the few surviving authentic Son of Man sayings.

The key to a proper appreciation of these sayings is the fact that the *bar enasha* idiom is an ironical way of speaking. Jesus employs it when he wishes to make his audience think more deeply about their reactions to him. It thus has special relevance to his conflict with the scribes and Pharisees and to the demands of discipleship in his teaching.

There are four sayings which belong to the context of conflict with the religious leaders. The point at issue was no academic matter. It concerned Jesus' right to set himself up as a religious teacher.[12] The scribes were the official interpreters of the Law to the people. They were properly trained, and received ordination with the laying-on of hands (*semikah*) for their office. They were a distinctive element in society, because of their special style of dress. They fulfilled an indispensable function, because the Law touched people's lives at every point. So they provided rulings on the way in which the Law was to be observed in particular cases, and indeed had built up a large body of case-law (the oral law, or *halakah*) to assist in determining difficult or disputed issues. They acted as local lawyers or solicitors, and dealt with such matters as property, damages, marriage and divorce, and so forth. They also had important functions in the synagogues, and ran the synagogue school.

The Pharisees were a distinct party, aimed at promoting

holiness, purity and obedience to the Law among the common people. They were largely recruited from the scribes, and represent the more zealous element among them. They were organized in groups for mutual support (*ḥaburoth*). They tended to greater strictness than the scribes in general. They sought to 'put a hedge around the Law' by advocating habits and customs which would, as far as possible, make it impossible for people to transgress the Law even by accident. In spite of the strictures against them recorded in the gospels, they were for the most part responsible and humane in their attitudes, and worthy of the respect which was generally felt towards them.

Jesus had no such official standing. He was not, of course, unique as an itinerant religious teacher. There seem to have been a number of such teachers in Galilee at this time.[13] But it is not difficult to see why the scribes and Pharisees took it upon themselves to investigate his activities. They found him particularly troublesome, partly because he appears to have had considerable success in creating a public following, but chiefly because the reason for that success was his radical approach to the Law, which seemed to them to be undermining all their own efforts. The context of this apparently lax attitude was Jesus' mission to announce the imminent coming of the kingdom of God (which we have seen is not to be distinguished from the idea of the coming of God in person). Jesus shifted the centre of attention from the Law as the embodiment of the will of God to the idea of direct confrontation with God in the coming kingdom.[14] This makes his teaching at once more merciful and more strict. The coming of God is a matter of grace and blessing. It is therefore good news to those who 'hunger and thirst after righteousness'. When God comes, he takes people for what they are, and does not count up their successes in keeping the minutiae of the Law. On the other hand his coming makes evasion impossible. People are revealed for what they are. There can be no place for self-righteousness or mixed motives.

It is against this background that we can see the significance of the four Son of Man sayings which belong to the setting of conflict.

a. The Sign of Jonah (Luke 11.30): *For as Jonah became a sign to the men of Nineveh, so a man may be to this generation.*

This saying has been preserved in connection with the Pharisees' request for a sign. Even if the connection must be assigned to the literary process of the Q collection, it is clearly the proper context, because the saying is concerned with a sign. A sign must be a sign of something. Usually in the New Testament a sign is an indication of the truth of a statement of prediction (cf. Matt 24.3; Luke 2.12). Here, however, the content of the saying makes it clear that the Pharisees are demanding a sign of Jesus' authority to preach to the people. It is implied that Jesus is claiming the authority of God himself, which more than compensates for his lack of any official position within the establishment. His point is that his preaching requires no sign of divine authority, because its result in the splendid response of his audience provides ample testimony that it comes from God.[15]

To make this point, Jesus compares his situation with that of the prophet Jonah. Jonah was unique among the prophets, inasmuch as his call to the Ninevites to repent actually met with an enormous response. The whole population of that great city repented, from the king to the humblest citizen, and even the animals had to fast and wear sackcloth (Jonah 3.7f). Of course it is a moral tale, and we are not bound to take it as literal history. But Jesus is not concerned with the historicity of it, but with its implications. Jonah was a sign of God's wrath to the Ninevites, but they repented, and God called off the promised destruction. Jesus also bears witness to God by his preaching, and the fact that so many people are turning to God as a result of it is the surest sign of its divine origin.

By using the *bar enasha* idiom Jesus avoids making a direct claim. He is not willing to be compelled to say more about himself than is necessary. No doubt his reticence is to be explained by his determination to avoid falling into a trap. He is well aware of the hostile intentions of his critics. So he speaks of a man who gains a response in this generation comparable to that of Jonah in his day. He turns attention away from himself, and suggests that his critics should find the answer to their question by looking at the results and working out the implications for themselves. If there is someone in this generation whose effect as God's spokesman can be compared with Jonah's, then the only proper conclusion is that 'something greater than Jonah is here'. The doublet saying on the preaching of Jonah and the wisdom of Solomon (Matt. 12.41f=Luke 11.31f) makes much the same point, though in the form of a reproach rather than in reply to a question. It has the same irony, and the same refusal to be more explicit. The whole point of using the *bar enasha* idiom is to avoid making a brash claim and to persuade the critics to think again before pursuing their opposition further.

b. The 'glutton' saying (Matt. 11.18f=Luke 7.33f): *For John the Baptist has come eating no bread and drinking no wine; and you say, 'He has a demon'. Someone else has come eating and drinking; and you say, 'Behold, a glutton and a drunkard, a friend of tax collectors and sinners!'*

In the last case Jesus defended his position by drawing attention to the comparison with the situation of Jonah. Here he defends himself by comparison and contrast with John the Baptist. Their position is somewhat similar, because the Baptist was a free-lance, like Jesus, who worked outside the normal establishment, and therefore provoked conflicting reactions. Like Jesus, he had considerable success among the common people. And like Jesus, he fell under the suspicion of the authorities. There was, however, a fundamental difference between them. John preached repentance and a stern ethic, which he demonstrated in his own extremely ascetic form of life. Jesus preached the grace and mercy of the coming of God, and expressed his teaching with appropriate rejoicings. This contrast comes out very clearly in the Marcan sequence, Mark 2.18–22, a programmatic collection of sayings which characterizes the whole of Jesus' preaching mission. Here the followers of the Baptist are represented as observing the extra fasts promoted by the Pharisees. Jesus causes surprise by not doing so. His defence is that a wedding is no time for fasting. If the bridegroom is present, it is a time for feasting. Though it is inevitable that the bridegroom should have been supposed to be a reference to Jesus himself (hence the addition of verse 20, justifying the church's practice of fasting), it is much more likely that Jesus is alluding to the well known Old Testament idea of God as the husband of Israel. The response of the common people means that God is gaining his bride. Fasting is inappropriate in such circumstances. Jesus' refusal to follow the ascetic way marked out by the Baptist and by the Pharisees is justified by his success in winning people for God. Jesus makes this point by means of an irony which compels his critics to think again, exactly as in the sign of Jonah sayings.[16]

This contrast between Jesus and John is the basis of the present saying. John is (or was in his lifetime) ascetic, and Jesus is not. It might be supposed that Jesus repudiated John's teaching, seeing that his own was so very different. But we have other evidence that he regarded John as an authentic spokesman for God. The question of authority in Mark 11.27–33 turns on the fact that Jesus regards his own authority as comparable to that of the Baptist, in spite of the considerable difference between them.[17] Mark places this episode in the temple at Jerusalem, and it is natural to take it in close relation with the cleansing of the temple which has just been described (Mark 11.15–18). The question is a trap on the part of the 'high priests, scribes and elders'. Having taken such high-handed action, there is every likelihood that Jesus will incriminate himself by claiming too much. It is important that the question is put in terms of authority. Jesus has no formal authority for his preaching and his prophetic actions, but he acts under the pressure of an inward certainty that his message comes from God. His device of appealing to the situation of the Baptist implies that there is a wide general consensus that John was a prophet inspired by God, even though the official reaction was hostile. Thus he can uphold his claim to divine inspiration without having to say how it relates to the usual channels of spiritual authority. In this episode there is no Son of Man saying, and Jesus speaks of himself in the first person. But Jesus' characteristic irony is present in the way he uses the parallel case of the Baptist to alter the terms of reference of the question. There is then no need to answer it, for it has been answered already.

Both the contrast and the comparison between Jesus and John are operative in the present saying. Their methods and message are different, but their divine inspiration is the same. The saying ridicules those who try to take advantage of outward appearances to evade the real challenge which this implies. The critics are as bad as children who say they don't want to play at weddings, and then won't play at funerals either. They dismiss John as a madman and Jesus as a glutton. In both cases they excuse themselves from taking the message seriously by denigrating the spokesmen. And by using the *bar enasha* idiom, Jesus shows that it is not just a matter of John the Baptist and himself. Such perverse people would do this to anyone with a message from God, if they could find a similar excuse. As they refuse to heed John on such inadequate grounds, they will refuse to heed anyone else. It is thus not surprising that

they show the same attitude to Jesus himself. But they really ought
to think again! And, just as the bridegroom saying of Mark 2.19 has
a certain lightness of touch which is aimed at disarming criticism
and appealing to the finer feelings of his opponents, so the present
context, with its charming illustration of the children, carries no
trace of bitterness or hostility, but is rather a wistful comment on
the way people deceive themselves, and so constitutes an appeal to
face the truth of the matter.

c. The 'authority' saying (Mark 2.10): *But that you may know
that a man may have authority on earth to forgive sins* ...

Jesus regarded himself as a spokeman for God in his own
generation, comparable to the prophet Jonah or his own contemporary, John the Baptist. He asked to be judged by the effectiveness
of his message in bringing those who accepted it to God (the
implication of the Jonah saying). If it produced such a result, then
his claim to be speaking for God ought not to be questioned. He also
strongly resisted the suggestion that his behaviour in reaching out
to the common people could be held against his claim (the
implication of the 'glutton' saying). This was an attack on his
integrity. But it also touched a fundamental element of his teaching,
the fact that the grace of God is *not* to be regarded as contingent
upon the acceptance of the burden of extra rules of holiness. From
this point of view it constituted a direct attack on the characteristic
teaching of the scribes and Pharisees, and was bound to provoke
their opposition.

It is for this reason that the Jesus tradition includes a number of
incidents in which these opponents attempt to trap Jesus into
incriminating himself. They are trying to counteract his teaching
by undermining his authority. The sequence in Mark 2.1—3.6 is
largely a collection of incidents of this type. In each case Jesus
makes a circumspect answer, in which he defends himself without
falling into the trap (Mark 2.9–11, 17, 19, 25–7; 3.4). The first item
in the series (Mark 2.1–12), containing our present saying, may be
artificial in its construction, but there is no reason to doubt that
it preserves a genuine point of dispute between Jesus and the
recognized teachers. The story of the paralysed man who was let
down through the roof has been used as the setting for a dispute
over Jesus' claim to have authority to forgive sins in the name of
God. The crucial feature of this dispute is the Son of Man saying.

Jesus is asserting that a man may on occasions have the authority to act in God's name in this way. Therefore (it is implied) his own right to do so should not be ruled out *a priori*. On the contrary it ought to be accepted as evidence for his commission from God. In our previous analysis of this pericope it was shown that the Son of Man saying, understood in this way according to the *bar enasha* idiom, is the nucleus of the dialogue element in the story. The story itself may well have circulated in the first instance without this element, but proved to be a most suitable setting in which to incorporate the saying. The fact that the pericope is best regarded as an artificial construction on form-critical grounds, does not in any way reduce the value of it as evidence for Jesus' work, both as a healer and as a preacher of the forgiveness of God. For Jesus, as a free-lance, charismatic preacher, certainly included healing in his ministry, like any other preacher in his time. And the controversial character of his teaching is a matter of the ease with which he spoke to all about the grace of God's coming, representing it as virtually a general amnesty, if we may judge from the verses that follow (Mark 2.13–22). Thus the pericope as a whole can be accepted as evidence for a type of situation which was bound to arise in the course of Jesus' ministry.

The point at issue is the authority of Jesus to announce forgiveness in the name of God. This would be likely to be offensive to the scribes, because it constitutes a claim to a higher authority than is implied by Jesus' practice of setting aside the rules of holiness. They even go as far as to call it blasphemy. This is not blasphemy in the formal sense of misusing the name of God, but in the more general sense of defaming God by lightly claiming one of his prerogatives.[18] It is, of course, a debating point, because Jesus is not really claiming anything more than might be claimed by any other person with healing powers. He only acts as God's agent. It must be presumed that his opponents know this perfectly well. If so, then the object of their protest is not to dispute the use of a formula of absolution as such, but to raise the question of Jesus' authority to do so. The challenge to Jesus is to say *why* he claims this authority. His answer would be that it is an integral part of the commission which he has received from God. But he refuses to say so directly. He will not be trapped into saying that his commission can be distinguished from the message itself. His healing work is a living witness to his message. And that is to be accepted as the message of God, regardless of his lack of official authorization. By means of this *bar enasha* saying he shows that a genuine commission from God is a real possibility, which should not be brushed aside with abuse.

d. The 'blasphemy' saying (Matt. 12.32=Luke 12.10): *Whoever speaks a word against a man may be forgiven; but whoever speaks against the Holy Spirit may not be forgiven.*

The saying has been preserved in two different forms in Mark and Q, which can be traced back to independent Greek translations of a common Aramaic original. The Marcan version (Mark 3.28f) comes in the context of the Beelzebul controversy (Mark 3.22–7), which also has a parallel in Q (Matt. 12.22–30=Luke 11.14–23). The controversy consists of an accusation by Jesus' opponents to the effect that his success in casting out demons is due to a kind of private deal between him and Beelzebul, the chief demon. This is, of course, an utterly unscrupulous attack on Jesus' claim to commission from God, by making him out to be in league with Satan. It is nothing less than character assassination. It is therefore only to be expected that Jesus should make a very forceful reply, especially as it is not merely an attack upon his personal integrity, but also a means of evading the challenge of the message itself. The 'blasphemy' saying fits very well into this context.

The seriousness of the controversy is indicated by the variety of material which has been preserved in connection with it. It is characteristic of Q to bring together related sayings into a short sequence, as we saw in connection with the Sign of Jonah. The sequence in Mark may represent an earlier stage in the formation of such a short collection, whereas it has grown a little by the time that it is incorporated into Q. It is difficult to work out the relationship between them, because there is considerable overlapping of material. But it seems best to assume that Matthew, as so often, has conflated the two sources, whereas Luke has abandoned Mark and reproduced Q with very little editorial change.[19]

The first answer to the accusation, preserved in both Mark and Q in slightly different forms, is the twin parable of the divided kingdom and the divided household.[20] 'If Satan is divided against himself, how will his kingdom stand?' (Q). So Jesus points to the absurdity of the suggestion. The fact that he uses a parable, and leaves the audience to draw the obvious conclusion, is in line with the irony and lightness of touch which we have noticed previously in connection with issues touching his personal position.

A second answer, only found in Q, is to point out that the same accusation could be made against any other successful exorcist: 'By whom do your sons cast them out?' Then Jesus adds, 'But if I by the finger (Matthew: Spirit) of God cast out demons, then the kingdom of God has come upon you'.[21] We may object that surely this could be said in connection with the work of any other exorcist too. But perhaps Jesus would not wish to deny this. The point is that, if his acts of healing can be traced to the power of God, then his claim that signs of the kingdom are already visible must be taken seriously, and therefore his authority as God's spokesman to announce the kingdom should not be called in question. In this case, therefore, though the *bar enasha* idiom does not actually occur, and Jesus uses the first person, the argument is very similar to what we have found in the authentic sayings. Jesus speaks about himself in a non-exclusive way. It is at least theoretically possible that his words might apply to others. But he wishes the application to himself to be taken with due seriousness, because it affects the way people respond to the message which he brings from God.

Next, in both Mark and Q a parable is introduced, which in its briefer, probably more original, Marcan form speaks of the binding of a strong man before his house can be plundered.[22] Jeremias takes this to be a personal allusion on the part of Jesus to his victory over the devil in his temptations, alluded to by Mark in 1.12–13. But the Q parallel shows that its inclusion in the present context is not due to Mark's editing, and there is nothing in the Marcan form to suggest that Jesus is referring especially to himself. What he is saying is that the power of evil requires a stronger force to expel it. It is implied that only the power of God is sufficient. As a comment on the present issue it suggests that Jesus' exorcisms are achieved precisely by the exercise of such power. More generally, if Jesus is releasing people from the grip of evil of whatever kind, then the true source of his ability to do so ought to be recognized. This is followed by a detached saying in Q ('Whoever is not with me is against me, and whoever does not gather with me scatters'), which makes a suitable conclusion to the sequence, though Matthew then continues with the 'blasphemy' saying, following Mark, whereas Luke has preserved it in a different context.

The 'blasphemy' saying takes its place alongside the various items of the Beelzebul controversy, not necessarily as something spoken at the same time as any one of them, but as the strongest item which has come down to us in connection with same issue. It is a comment on the accusation rather than an answer to it. It looks like an entirely general statement, but is not really so. Jesus is not interested in making a theoretical distinction between slander against men and slander against the Spirit. On the contrary, he starts from this distinction and applies it to his own situation by means of the *bar enasha* idiom. To speak against a man—and therefore, it is implied, to speak against *me*—is forgivable. But to speak against the Spirit—i.e., the power through which I work—is nothing less than blasphemy against God, and cannot be so easily forgiven. Understood in this way, the saying affords a vivid impression of the total involvement of Jesus in his mission, which cannot be questioned without causing affront to God himself.

Thus the four sayings which belong to the setting of conflict give valuable information about Jesus' own understanding of his mission from God. In each case there are links with other items in the tradition which have a good claim to be considered authentic. The 'Jonah' saying places Jesus in the line of the prophets, and gives him a special position as the spokesman for God in his own generation. Though Jesus lacks an official position and has received no formal authorization, the response to his preaching, whereby people are turning to God in large numbers, is sufficient evidence that he has received his commission from God himself. The 'glutton' saying, with its contrast of the hostile attitudes towards John the Baptist and Jesus, puts the same point negatively: those who find excuses for refusing to accept the authority of Jesus are flying in the face of the evidence of this response, and thereby evading the conclusion that he has been sent by God. The 'authority' saying uses the evidence of the healing ministry of Jesus in a similar way: if he exercises spiritual authority, it is because it is an essential aspect of his divine message, and his right to do so should not be questioned. Finally, the 'blasphemy' saying virtually makes any attack upon Jesus an attack on the Spirit of God himself, though a proper distinction is maintained between Jesus as an individual and the Spirit with which he speaks and acts.

In so far as these glimpses into Jesus' self-understanding permit a conclusion about the nature of his relation to God, it would seem to be obvious that he would most likely style himself a prophet.

This is indicated by the comparisons with Jonah and John the Baptist, besides the prophetic character of his work as a spokesman for God. But of course there is not one single category of prophet. Prophets were in various kinds, and each one has to be considered as an individual. The thing which distinguishes Jesus, as far as can be seen from the admittedly limited range of this study, is the degree of his personal commitment to his message. Resistance to it is virtually equivalent to resistance to God himself. Moreover, and more importantly, he requires no authority other than the intrinsic authority of the message itself. He does not speak because he is a prophet. He is a prophet because he has a message which must be spoken. Further light on these matters may be gained from the remaining authentic sayings.

e. The 'foxes' saying (Matt. 8.20=Luke 9.58): *Foxes have holes, and birds of the air have nests, but a man has nowhere to lay his head.*

The generic idiom was found to be the clue to proper interpretation of this saying. It means Jesus himself, but it also means anyone else in his position, therefore the prospective disciple who stands before him. If we accept the setting of the saying as authentic, then it is Jesus' reply to one who wishes to commit himself wholly to Jesus' mission, 'Teacher, I will follow you wherever you may go'. In answer Jesus makes no secret of the hardship that that would entail. It thus fits into the pattern of Jesus' sayings on discipleship, which frequently emphasize the severity of the demand (e.g., Mark 8.34f; 10.23–31). The characteristic irony, and the use of a simile from nature, save the saying from sounding too stark and grim. This implies a certain reticence on Jesus' part, which conceals his own strength and resolve. Thus the saying enhances the impression of Jesus' total commitment to his vocation. He is fully aware of the difficulties and hardships which it involves.

f. The 'advocate' saying (Matt. 10.32f=Luke 12.8f): *Every one who confesses me before men, him will a man confess before the angels of God; everyone who denies me before men, him will a man deny before the angels of God.*

This is the reconstructed text, based mainly on Luke, which corresponds most closely with the Aramaic which seems to lie behind the independent Greek versions of Q and Mark 8.38. It is a saying which has played a crucial part in the development of the Son of Man sayings, because it is the only authentic one which refers to the future judgement. It has thus paved the way for the identification of the Son of Man with the figure of Dan. 7.13–14. It was argued above, however, that Jesus had no such idea in mind.

The correct interpretation turns on the *bar enasha* idiom. Using the metaphor of a court-room, Jesus suggests that the response to his teaching can be compared with confession or denial of him in a court of law. From this point of view the saying belongs to the class of sayings on discipleship, in which hardship is stressed, and it is not surprising to find Mark's version of it following immediately upon a series of such sayings (Mark 8.34–7). Luke's context, on the other hand, is a short Q sequence on fearless confession of Jesus' teaching, comprising both warnings of God's power to punish and, more prominently, assurances of his power to protect the disciples (Luke 12.2–7). This gives excellent comparative material for the present saying. For Jesus now goes on to give both an assurance and a warning. If the response to his teaching can be compared to confession or denial before an earthly tribunal, it corresponds with what will happen at the heavenly tribunal. Then each person will have his advocate or accuser before God. Someone will be there to remind God that this is how they have responded to the message of God's own kingdom, when it was delivered to them by Jesus. That 'someone' is Jesus' own words, and therefore in a sense it is Jesus himself. It is the fact that the message of the kingdom was duly conveyed to them which is decisive for the coming confrontation with God. Those who have accepted it need have no fears, in spite of their failure to conform to the standards set by the scribes and the Pharisees. What Jesus has announced on behalf of God will stand them in good stead. But those who have failed to respond to Jesus will find that their heedlessness reaps its reward. They will realize too late that Jesus is indeed the spokesman for God.

The ironic use of *bar enasha* turns attention away from the position of Jesus himself. The point at issue is the crucial connection between Jesus' proclamation of the kingdom and the divine verdict at the coming judgement. Jesus is not interested in defining his position further than this. He does not wish to claim a formal position at the judgement as advocate and accuser. It is the decisive importance of his message which (for the sake of a vivid metaphor) puts him in this position. He is preaching for a decision in the present which is decisive for the future, rather than preaching about the future as such. The future will be determined by the resolution of the present confrontation between himself as God's spokesman, his words as the message from God, and the hearers as they adjust their minds to what he says and choose their response. This will be brought before God at the coming tribunal. Jesus will not have a new function at that moment. It is because he is God's spokesman now, that he can speak of himself ironically as advocate and accuser then.

The 'advocate' saying, so understood, does not include any personal claim on the part of Jesus, other than the claim which is inherent in his vocation to speak on behalf of God. It confirms the impression which we have already gained of Jesus' total commitment to his task. There is nothing grim about this, because he is not primarily a prophet of doom. His preaching of the coming confrontation with God is first and foremost a declaration of grace. If the present is decisive for that future coming, then it is a time for rejoicing more then weeping. But Jesus' preaching has its sterner side, sterner even than the religion of the scribes and Pharisees. For Jesus insists that the intentions of the heart will be exposed. There can be no evasion or concealment of the truth. Consequently he did not always win a favourable response. In fact the places, such as Bethsaida and Capernaum, which are most closely associated with the success of his mission are the subject of an extraordinarily bitter comment on account of their failure to repent (Matt. 11.21–3 = Luke 10.13–15). Jesus experienced not only opposition from the scribes and Pharisees, because of his independence from their teaching, but also resistance to the message of the kingdom itself.

There remain the three passion sayings. These are most suitably interpreted in connection with Jesus' decision to go to Jerusalem and make a public demonstration of his message. This took the form of two actions which correspond with the two sides of his proclamation. The entry into Jerusalem on Palm Sunday reflects the joy and excitement of his days in Galilee, in which he preached the gospel of grace. The cleansing of the temple reflects the sterner side of his teaching on purity of heart. Jesus must have known from past experience that he ran the risk of arousing official opposition, as he had done in Galilee, and that there would certainly be resistance to the actual message. He could see that there was likely to be suffering in store for him (cf. Luke 13.32f). But his total commitment to his mission from God, which we have already observed in connection with the authentic Son of Man sayings, was evidently such that the thought of suffering could not deflect him from his purpose. We may guess that his disciples were worried and anxious about what might happen. The passion sayings give glimpses of the ways in which he dealt with their fears.

g. The passion prediction (Mark 9.31; 10.33; 14.21b, 41): *A man may be delivered up . . .*

The precise form of the prediction cannot be reconstructed because of the complex development of it in relation to the primitive confession of faith. It has been applied both to the betrayal of Jesus by Judas Iscariot and to the handing over of Jesus to Pontius Pilate for trial. Paul, at least, has understood it in the theological sense of the act of God in these events. But, on the basis of the very brief form which lies before us, nothing more can be said than that it expresses Jesus' conviction that he may have to face arrest as he carries through the mission which he conceives to be his duty. It thus expresses his unwavering resolve. He uses the *bar enasha* idiom to turn attention away from his personal position, and set it in the perspective of all who have to face such unnerving possibilities. Anyone else in the same position would make the same decision. For Jesus, to draw back from his mission in the face of such danger would be unthinkable. That is what the disciples must try to understand.

Further content might be gleaned, if Jesus were deliberately modelling his words on the passion prophecy, Isa. 53. For the saying, short as it is, would carry with it the whole burden of that chapter, that the Servant of the Lord died for the sins of the nations. Thus the saying would include the notion of sacrificial death. It is not, however, possible to read this idea out of the present saying, and the connection with Isa. 53 cannot be proved. The saying simply attests the fact that Jesus was well aware that his fidelity to his mission carried the risk of arrest and dire consequences.

h. The 'destiny' saying (Mark 14.21a): *A man goes as it is written of him.*

The Lucan version of this saying (Luke 22.22) correctly understands it to be not primarily a reference to what is written in scripture, but to the predetermined plan of God. The situation presupposed is pressure upon Jesus to try to evade what he conceives to be his destiny. Just as Jesus pursues his mission, whatever the cost, because it is God's will for him, so when suffering meets him he must accept it as God's will. This is what the agony in the garden of Gethsemane is about. And it shows that, in spite of the resolution which Jesus has shown, it is no easy matter when it comes to the point. The *bar enasha* idiom again has the effect of broadening the scope of the saying. The disciples also cannot evade what lies in store for them in the secret counsels of God.

Although this time there can be no question of verbal allusion to Isa. 53, the possibility of a general reference to it must be considered. The church was quick to seize it as the definitive expression of God's predetermined plan for the Messiah, so that on the basis of it the primitive kerygma could assert that 'the Messiah died according to the scriptures' (1 Cor. 15.3). There is really no objection to the idea that Jesus' ideas concerning his destiny might have been shaped by the prophecy. But the difficulty is to prove it. In this case the lack of any possible verbal allusion precludes a direct link, and the generic *bar enasha* forbids such a rendering as 'the Son of Man goes as written in prophecies concerning him', i.e., according to messianic scriptures. Thus it seems unlikely that any reference to it is intended in this saying. The most that can be said is that the saying reflects Jesus' sense of destiny, and in thinking about his destiny he may well have been influenced by this prophecy.

i. The 'ransom' saying (Mark 10.45): *A man may give his life for many.*

It was argued above that the sacrificial meaning of this saying is secured by the preposition 'for' (normally *huper*; in Mark 10.45 *anti*, on account of *lutron*). But at a very early stage it circulated with the addition of 'ransom' in order to bring out the meaning. Another version of the saying, possibly based on an independent translation of the same Aramaic, has been preserved in 1 Tim. 2.6. Elsewhere the phrase 'to give (lay down) one's life for' someone is applied to Jesus both in Paul and John, and in each case it refers to his sacrificial death. But it was pointed out that the underlying Aramaic expression is commonly used for 'to risk one's life'. If Jesus is prepared to risk his life 'for many', it is because his mission is for the benefit of many. Thus he goes in accordance with his destiny, taking the risk which this entails, not only because his vocation demands it, but because the salvation of the people to whom his message is addressed is at stake. The saying, understood in this way, receives support from the implications of the eucharistic words of Jesus in Mark 14.24 and 1 Cor. 11.24.

Though again it proved impossible to be sure that Jesus was referring to Isa. 53, in spite of the very close connection between his words and Isa. 53.12, the saying has cardinal importance for understanding Jesus' approach to his death. Still refusing to single himself out in a special way, still showing by the use of the *bar enasha* idiom that this is what any man in the same circumstances would be expected to do, he shows that his real concern is for the people—all people—to whom his message is addressed. It is because he was sent to proclaim God's kingdom to the people that he risks his life. The good shepherd allegory in John 10.1–18, which actually incorporates the saying as its major motif, is very apt (cf. John 15.13). But, if he had come to Jerusalem with a sense that time was running out, and undertook his public demonstrations precisely because of the need to reach the largest number of people in the shortest space of time, he must have known that his primary object of preaching to all the people of God was liable to fail. The threat to his life is a threat to the accomplishment of his mission. And if his life had been dedicated to the salvation of the people by bringing to them the message of the coming of God, his sacrificial attitude towards the prospect of death can be seen as a wish to serve, by the only way still open to him, those whom he has not been able to reach. And it is of the utmost importance, for the sake of those who have heard and have responded favourably, that he should not go back on what he has preached. For this reason he can take no step to avoid condemnation, if it means denying his message from God. If the suggestion mentioned above (p. 112) is correct, that the temple saying of Mark 14.58 actually secured Jesus' conviction for blasphemy, then this impression is confirmed. For the prophecy of destruction of the temple corresponds with the demand side of Jesus' message: nothing less than a radical reform of Jewish religion is sufficient for the coming of God. But at the same time the prophecy of rebuilding in three days reflects the grace side: it catches the exuberance of the triumphal entry and expresses the joy of renewal in God's kingdom, so soon to come to pass.

These suggestions are at least possible ways in which a rational account of Jesus' approach to death in a sacrificial way may be understood, keeping strictly within the limits of the implications of his vocation to herald God's kingdom. The authentic Son of Man sayings reveal Jesus as one who was wholly committed to this vocation. He regarded himself as certainly not less divinely inspired than John the Baptist (*a*). Indeed, he repudiated any attempt to deny the divine source of his ministry as nothing less than blasphemy against the Spirit of God (*b*). He held that he had a unique task to perform for his own generation, comparable to that of Jonah (*c*). This included the gospel of forgiveness of sins (*d*). Though the element of grace predominated in his preaching, he also demanded radical renewal, and his requirements of a prospective disciple could be stern (*e*). He required his teaching to be put into practice, so that it affected public attitudes; acceptance or rejection of him from this point of view had decisive importance, because it would be the criterion for judgement at the coming of God (*f*). When faced with danger to his life, he would not allow that to alter what he conceived to be his duty (*g*). He declared that he must fulfil his destiny, whatever happened (*h*). He was prepared to risk his life for the salvation of those to whom he had been sent (*i*).

In these ways we have gained from the authentic sayings some idea of the way in which Jesus thought about his eschatological mission. They do not include a claim to be the Messiah. Nevertheless, the suggestion was apparently made by Peter (Mark 8.27–30). Even if we regard the question on this issue at the trial of Jesus, with his answer, to be inauthentic (Mark 14.61b–2), it seems clear that he was crucified as a messianic claimant. And it was as Messiah that he was proclaimed to be the living Lord after the resurrection. It is clear from the gospels that Jesus was very reticent about making a messianic claim. It is possible—some would say probable—that he publicly repudiated such a suggestion (cf. Mark 12.35–7). Do the authentic Son of Man sayings give us any help in solving this problem?

At first sight they appear to be wholly negative. The Son of Man is not an expression which carries with it any messianic significance in the authentic sayings. In fact, it is not a title at all. The idiomatic use of generic *bar enasha* tends to deflect the thought from Jesus himself. It concentrates attention upon the particular issue, which often relates to Jesus' personal authority, but it evades the question of his identity. Jesus identifies himself with his eschatological mission, but he avoids identifying himself with a particular figure of popular eschatological expectation. He speaks of himself ironically, in such a way as to discourage further probing.

This reticence on Jesus' part has to be seen in conjunction with another facet of his teaching. Jesus proclaimed the kingdom of God, and we saw that that is properly to be understood as a proclamation of the coming of God himself. But he never spoke of the coming of the Messiah, except to score a debating point (Mark 12.35-7). Thus, if he refused to declare himself to be the Messiah, he did not apply the title to anyone else. His concept of the coming of God does not really make room for the coming of the Messiah. Thus, if there is to be a Messiah to usher in God's kingdom, it really can be only himself, even if he fails to fit the role as commonly understood. Thus there is a sense in which, as herald of God's kingdom, distinct from the line of prophets which ends with the Baptist (Luke 16.16), Jesus fulfils a messianic role. But, in so far as he accepted Peter's confession, it can be only according to his own valuation of the title. There is no difficulty in supposing that the disciples in general had come to the conclusion that he was the Messiah, even if they did not altogether understand him.

Similarly his reticence, and the teasing irony of the Son of Man sayings, would be likely to build up this conviction quite widely. Jesus refutes the objections of the scribes and Pharisees. But that leaves open the alternative possibility, that he is, after all, the Messiah. From this point of view Jesus' reticence is as much an affirmation as it is a denial. If he wanted to deny that he was Messiah in *any* sense, why have we no evidence that he did so? Is it entirely to be explained in terms of a cover-up by the church? But there are no *bar enasha* sayings which seek to persuade the people to form a lower opinion of him. Those that relate to the situation of conflict tend in the opposite direction.

It seems that Jesus' concern for his mission was far more important to him than any titles which might be applied to him. When we consider that he was popularly supposed to be a messianic claimant, that the disciples had formed the definite conviction that he was the Messiah, and that he was crucified on this charge, we can scarcely avoid the conclusion that this was the most widely accepted estimate of him. But Jesus eludes all definitions in terms of preconceived notions of messiahship. The church's proclamation of his messiahship after Easter is really a new definition. And it starts from the fact that his mission, so far from being falsified by his death, has been triumphantly achieved. This indeed is the proper conclusion to draw from the evidence of the authentic Son of Man sayings. Jesus has lived his own message of joy and renewal in the face of the coming of God, and preserved his integrity to the end. 'Therefore God has highly exalted him' (Phil. 2.9) as the leader of those who are ready for God at his coming. And though the coming of God did not follow in the way expected, the necessary readjustment was made, not by altering the position accorded to Jesus, nor by changing his essential message, but by the process whereby 'the proclaimer became the proclaimed'.[23]

In this way the early history of Christology consists in putting into relation with Jesus, now understood to be the exalted Messiah, more and more of the messianic concepts of the time. He absorbs, but also transforms, an ever increasing range of ideas connected with the Messiah and the new age. Part of this process is the application to him of the figure of the Danielic Son of Man. So the Son of Man, as traditionally understood, belongs to the development of Christology, which took place in the burst of creativity which accompanied the emergence of Christianity in the post-resurrection period. But the Son of Man starts simply as an idiomatic feature of Jesus' speech. And the authentic sayings convey something of the irony and saltiness of his references to himself. Jesus always wants his hearers to see beyond him and to be ready for the confrontation with God.

Notes

INTRODUCTION

1 The lecture was printed as Appendix E in M. Black, *An Aramaic Approach to the Gospels and Acts*, Oxford ³1967, pp. 310–28, and reprinted in G. Vermes, *Post-Biblical Jewish Studies*, Leiden 1975, pp. 147–65. See also id., *Jesus the Jew*, 1973, pp. 160–91.

2 *JJS* 29, 1978, pp. 123–34.

3 Printed in *BJRL* 63 (1981), pp. 437–62.

CHAPTER 1

1 cf. W.G. Kümmel, *The New Testament: the History of the Investigation of its Problems*, London 1973, pp. 245–308, especially on the work of Wellhausen, Wrede, Goguel and Loisy at this time.

2 e.g. R. Reitzenstein, *Die hellenistischen Mysterienreligionen*, Leipzig and Berlin 1910, ³1927; W. Bousset *Die Religion des Judentums im neutestamentlichen Zeitalter*, Berlin 1903.

3 G. Dalman, *The Words of Jesus*, Edinburgh 1902 (ET, *Die Worte Jesus*, Leipzig 1898); and in more recent times the works of J. Jeremias, especially *New Testament Theology I*, London 1971.

4 e.g. P. Vielhauer, 'Gottesreich und Menschensohn in der Verkündigung Jesu', *Aufsätze zum Neuen Testament*, Munich 1965, pp. 55–91; H. Conzelmann, 'Gegenwart und Zukunft in der synoptischer Tradition', *ZThK* 54 (1957), pp. 277–96; cf. his *An Outline of the Theology of the New Testament*, London 1969, pp. 131–7.

5 e.g. R. Bultmann, *Theology of the New Testament I*, London 1952, pp. 28–32; J. Knox, *The Death of Christ*, London 1959, pp. 52–109; H.E. Tödt, *The Son of Man in the Synoptic Tradition*, London 1965; F. Hahn, *The Titles of Jesus in Christology*, London 1969, pp. 15–53; R.H. Fuller, *The Foundations of New Testament Christology*, London 1965, pp. 119–25; W. Bousset, *Kyrios Christos*, Göttingen 1913.

6 P. Vielhauer, 'Gottesreich und Menschensohn' (as in n.4); also 'Jesus und der Menschensohn. Zur Diskussion mit H.E. Tödt und E. Schweizer' (*Aufsätze zum NT*, pp. 92–140). According to Casey (n. 24 below) the point had been made previously by H.B. Sharman, *Son of Man and Kingdom of God*, 1943, p. 89.

7 The only other possible source is 2 Esd. 13 (considered briefly below).

C. Colpe, 'Ho huios tou anthropou', *TDNT* VIII, 1972, pp. 400–77, has attempted to deduce a 'fourth source' (p. 429) for the Jewish tradition (alongside Daniel, 1 Enoch and 2 Esdras) from the Synoptic sayings themselves. The danger of arguing in a circle here is recognized by Colpe.

8 Translation from M.A. Knibb, *The Ethiopic Book of Enoch*, II, Oxford 1978, pp. 131f.

9 R.H. Charles, *The Book of Enoch*, Oxford [2]1912, p. 73. He held that an allusion to the overthrow of the Parthians and the Medes in 1 Enoch 56.5f compelled a date earlier than 63 BC, when Pompey took control of the Seleucid empire.

10 E. Sjöberg, *Der Menschensohn im Äthiopischen Henochbuch*, Lund 1946, p. 38, argues that the reference to the Parthians and Medes reflects the threat which recurred in 40–38 BC, and continued to be a factor thereafter, but the reference presupposes that Jerusalem is still standing.

11 C.L. Mearns, 'Dating the Similitudes of Enoch', *NTS* 25 (1978–9), pp. 360–9.

12 M.A. Knibb, 'The Date of the Parables of Enoch: a Critical Review', *NTS* 25 (1978–9), pp. 345–59.

13 J.C. Hindley, 'Towards a Date for the Similitudes of Enoch: an Historical Approach', *NTS* 14 (1967–8), pp. 551–65 (*c.* AD 120); J.T. Milik, *The Books of Enoch*, Oxford 1976, pp. 91–6 (*c.* AD 270). The latter assumes that the Similitudes are a Christian work, dependent upon the Sibylline Oracles, but the arguments adduced are not convincing.

14 1 Pet. 3.19f (cf. 1 Enoch 12–16); Jude 14f (= 1 Enoch 1.9). In fact the whole of Jude 4–16 is based on Enoch.

15 For an attempt to use the Similitudes in this way, but without regarding the Son of Man as an accepted title in Judaism, see my article 'Re-enter the Apocalyptic Son of Man', *NTS* 22 (1975–6), pp. 52–72, and the criticism of it by A.J.B. Higgins, *The Son of Man in the Teaching of Jesus* (SNTMS 39), Cambridge 1980, pp. 49–53.

16 cf. J. Bloch, 'The Ezra-Apocalypse, was it written in Hebrew, Greek or Aramaic?' *JQR* 48 (1957–8), pp. 279–84. A Hebrew original is postulated by Wellhausen, Charles, Gunkel, Violet, Box and Eissfeldt; Aramaic by Pfeiffer and Gry.

17 Philo, *De Opificio Mundi* §§ 69–71; 134; *Legum Allegoria* I §§ 31–42; 88.

18 For the teachings of the Valentinians see W. Foerster, *Gnosis* I, Oxford 1972, pp. 121–243.

19 cf. G. Widengren, *Mani and Manichaeism*, London 1965, pp. 49–56.

20 cf. E.S. Drower, *The Secret of Adam*, Oxford 1960.

21 cf. W. Bousset, *Hauptprobleme der Gnosis*, Göttingen 1907; R. Reitzenstein, *Das iranische Erlösungsmysterium: Religiongeschichtliche Untersuchungen*, Heidelberg 1921; C.H. Kraeling, *Anthropos and Son of Man: a Study in the Religious Syncretism of the Hellenistic Orient*, New York 1927.

22 J.R. Hinnells, 'Zoroastrian Saviour Imagery and its Influence on the New

Testament', *Numen* 16 (1969), pp. 161–85; id, 'Zoroastrian Influence on the Judaeo-Christian Tradition', *Journal of the K.R. Cama Oriental Institute* 45 (1976), pp. 1–23. R. Otto, *The Kingdom of God and the Son of Man*, London 1938, pp. 389ff, also denies the connection of the Son of Man in Enoch with the Primal Man, and suggests that the Son of Man is the 'fravashi' of Enoch.

23   In one gospel passage (John 5.27) it occurs without the articles, but this is due to the Greek idiom employed, and it should be regarded as defined in the same way as the other gospel passages (cf. p. 154 below).

24   cf. Maurice Casey, *Son of Man: the Interpretation and Influence of Daniel 7*, London 1979, pp. 99–112.

25   cf. Casey, pp. 122–9. The crucial phrase 'something like the figure of a man' (13.3) is missing from the Latin MSS, and has been supplied from the Syriac version, which reads *ak demutha de-barnasha*. The Greek from which this was taken is likely to have been *hos homoioma anthropou*, corresponding with Hebrew *ki-demuth adam*. Even if the original were in Aramaic, it would be likely to be *ki-demuth enash* rather than *ke-bar enash*; cf. p. 195 n. 4 below.

26   This point is expressed forcibly by G. Vermes, *Jesus the Jew*, London 1973, p. 170.

27   The position is specially associated with N. Schmidt, 'The Son of Man in the Book of Daniel', *JBL* 19 (1900), pp. 22–8. More recently it has been taken up by J.J. Collins, 'The Son of Man and the Saints of the Most High in the Book of Daniel', *JBL* 93 (1974), pp. 50–66.

28   Allusion to Daniel appears in Mark 8.38, and direct quotation in Mark 13.26; 14.62. In Q there is implicit identification with the Danielic Son of Man in Matt. 24.27, 37, 39, 44=Luke 17.24, 26, 30; 12.40. This is specially characteristic of Matthew, cf. 10.23; 13.37, 41; 16.28; 19.28; 25.31, and occurs also in Luke 18.8; 21.36.

29   The most plausible alternative is the theory that Jesus adopted the Son of Man title as a prophetic designation, following Ezekiel, who is frequently addressed by God as *ben adam* (so E.A. Abbott, *The Son of Man*, Cambridge 1910; P. Parker, 'The Meaning of "Son of Man"', *JBL* 60 (1941), pp. 151–7; G.S. Duncan, *Jesus, Son of Man*, London 1947, p. 145f). But this cannot be maintained to the exclusion of the Danielic reference in sayings which refer to the future. In no saying is there any literary allusion to Ezek. In any case it is most unlikely that *ben adam* in Ezek. has any relevance to Jesus' use of *bar enasha* as a self-designation. It has been noted (e.g., by Schweizer) that *ben adam* in Ezek. is always vocative (93 times), whereas Jesus is never addressed as Son of Man. This point is more important than is commonly realized. For *ben adam* is God's address to Ezekiel. There is nothing in the phrase as such which characterizes Ezekiel as a prophet or as a representative of the people. It is simply God's mode of address to a human being, the address of a superior to an inferior, the precise opposite of the address 'Lord'. This use of *ben adam* is not confined to Ezek. There is a striking parallel in Dan. 8.17, where Daniel the seer is addressed by the angel as *ben adam*. This is because Daniel is an inferior, whereas the angel belongs to the celestial orders. It should now be

clear that the attempt to derive Jesus' use of the Son of Man phrase from Ezek. rests on a misunderstanding of the meaning and function of the phrase in Ezek. itself; cf. W. Zimmerli, *A Commentary on the Book of the Prophet Ezekiel 1–24* (Hermeneia), Philadelphia 1979, p. 131b.

30 Righteousness is the special quality of Enoch, which explains his translation to heaven and his privileged status as a seer, cf. Ecclus. 44.16; Wisd. 4.7–15; Heb. 11.5; 1 Enoch 1.2; 12.4, etc. In the Similitudes there is a special development of this theme, as the Messiah is spoken of as 'the Righteous One' and 'the Chosen One', corresponding with his leadership of the 'righteous' and 'chosen' people of God (1 Enoch 38.2; 40.6). Eventually he is identified with Enoch himself, in a passage where righteousness is repeatedly stressed (1 Enoch 71.14–17).

31 cf. verse 51. This detail is derived from Dan 7.2f, but the description of the beasts which follows in Daniel forms the basis of the preceding vision in 2 Esd. 11–12. The two visions thus split the material of Dan. 7, and the Son of Man imagery is confined to chapter 13. For the hidden origin of the Messiah, cf. John 7.27; Justin, *Dial.* 8.

32 Zech. 14 is a collection of various eschatological prophecies, and is now generally assigned to the third century BC; cf. O. Kaiser, *Introduction to the Old Testament*, Oxford 1975, pp. 286–90.

33 Reading *'lhyk wkl* for *'lhy kl* and *ᶜmw* for *ᶜmk*, with partial support from LXX and versions.

34 cf. M.A. Knibb, *The Ethiopic Book of Enoch* II, pp. 59f; J.T. Milik, *The Books of Enoch*, pp. 184–6 and Pl. IX. For the interpretation of this passage in Jude, cf. C.D. Osburn, 'The Christological Use of 1 Enoch 1.9 in Jude 14, 15', NTS *23* (1976–7), pp. 334–41.

35 1 Enoch 89.61–64, 68, 76–77; 90.14, 17, 20.

36 1 Enoch 87.3f.

37 This can be no more than a very tentative suggestion. It is not considered by Charles (cf. n. 9).

38 A.S. van der Woude, 'Melchisedek als himmlischer Erlösergestalt in den neugefundenen eschatologischen Midraschim aus Qumran Höhle XI', *OS* 14 (1965), pp. 354–73; ET, G. Vermes, *The Dead Sea Scrolls in English*, Harmondsworth ²1975, pp. 265–8.

39 cf. F.L. Horton, *The Melchizedek Tradition* (SNTSMS 30) Cambridge 1976, pp. 64–82.

40 Hence Casey, *Son of Man*, pp. 154, 201, regards this as a post-Pauline development. He wishes to play down the influence of Daniel as a whole in the New Testament. It is, however, significant that the crucial text for the heavenly lordship of Jesus is not Dan. 7.13f but Ps. 110.1. In 1 Cor. 15.25 Paul alludes to Ps. 110.1 in this sense. He then elucidates this text by means of Ps. 8.6, referring to the subjection of all things to the exalted Lord, and no reference is made to *ben adam* in Ps. 8.4. It is very probable that Dan. 7.13f also first came into currency with reference to Jesus as a secondary development from Ps. 110.1. For the cardinal importance of Ps. 110.1 see M. Gourgues, *A la Droite de Dieu*, Paris 1978.

CHAPTER 2

1 F. Blass, A. Debrunner and R.W. Funk, *A Greek Grammar of the New Testament*, Chicago and London 1961, §§ 252,259.

2 According to G. Svedlund, *Aramaic Portions of the Pesiqta de Rab Kahana*, Uppsala 1974, pp. 21–2, this form is characteristic of Middle Aramaic (300 BC–AD 200), but during the first centuries AD the indistinct *e* of *enasha* disappeared, leading to omission of initial aleph, so that the expression was written as one word *barnash(a)*. This is the normal form from AD 200 onwards. This development has nothing to do with changes in the *usage* of the expression (to be explained below), and therefore the contention of J.A. Fitzmyer ('The New Testament Title "Son of Man" Philologically Considered', *A Wandering Aramean: collected Aramaic essays*, Missoula 1979, pp. 143–60) that passages in which this form is found cannot be used to elucidate the meaning of the phrase in the gospel sayings is incorrect. An entirely different reconstruction of the history of the word has been put forward recently by R. Kearns, *Vorfragen zur Christologie, I: Morphologische und semasiologische Studien zur Vorgeschichte eines christologischen Hoheitstitels*, Tübingen 1978. He takes the latest form *barnash* as closest to the original form, which was derived ultimately from a north Semitic root *bnsh*, which is found in Ugaritic and may mean 'lord'. The form *barnash* is derived by dissimulation from the intensive form *bnnsh* according to a well known feature of consonantal change. The separation into two words *bar (e)nash* is then explained as due to confusion with the indigenous Aramaic *bar enash*, from which it becomes indistinguishable. On this basis he can argue that *ke-bar enash* in Dan. 7.13 does not mean 'one like a son of man' but 'one like a king'. Though the theory is presented with immense learning, it suffers from fundamental weaknesses. *a.* The form *barnash* is not found in the earlier sources, so that it is most unlikely to preserve the more ancient form. *b.* The problem of homonyms is not faced, though the theory requires the existence of two entirely different words *barnash*. *c.* Kearns is guilty of the etymological fallacy in supposing that an original meaning necessarily persisted unchanged through different dialects and cultures centuries apart. *d.* He is also guilty of the semantic fallacy in attempting to prove that the meaning of lordship provided by a given context actually belongs to *barnash* in itself (in all the examples cited, including Dan. 7.13, 'man' is possible for the literal meaning, and the meaning 'lord' is not actually required). In a second volume (1980) he suggests that the word was in use in non-Jewish circles of Palestinian heathendom, and only entered Judaism late (p. 97). He suggests that this was helped by the identity of *barnash* = 'lord' with *mari* = 'lord', already applied to Yahweh. But he has no texts to prove the connection (p. 148, n. 217). It is obvious that, even if this far-fetched theory could be upheld, it could have no bearing on those Son of Man sayings in which the lordship of Jesus is not expressed.

3 The plural expression (*hoi huioi tou anthropou*) occurs in Mark 3.28, but there it probably represents a collective understanding of the singular in the original Aramaic (cf. p. 36 below). Elsewhere in the NT it is found only at Eph.

3.5. This Greek phrase, including the articles, is common in the LXX, e.g., Ps. 10 (11).4; 11 (12).2, 9; 13(14).2; 30 (31).20; 32 (33).13; 35 (36).8; 44 (45).3; 48 (49).3, etc. (without the articles in 4.3; 20 (21).11, etc.), translating the Hebrew *bene adam* in most cases. The Aramaic *bene anasha* in Dan 2.38 is rendered *hoi huioi tou anthropou* by Theodotion, but simply by *hoi anthropoi* at 5.21. The latter rendering also occurs in 1 Enoch 7.3; 14.2, where both Aramaic fragments and the Greek translation are preserved (Milik, pp. 342, 349). Thus there is a tendency to avoid the full expression in Greek translation of Aramaic, and this may explain its rarity in the NT.

4   Hence the simple *enash* can be used where the idiomatic *bar enash* might be expected. Thus an Aramaic fragment (Milik, p. 294) corresponding with I En. 78.17, 'like a man', has *ki-demuth enash* (=according to the likeness of a man). Though the context is completely different, the meaning is the same as *ke-bar enash* of Dan 7.13; cf. 8.15 (*ke-mar'eh geber*).

5   H. Lietzmann, *Der Menschensohn: ein Beitrag zur neutestamentlichen Theologie*, Freiburg i.Br. and Leipzig 1896, pp. 51ff.

6   G. Dalman, *The Words of Jesus*, pp. 234ff.

7   See n. 2 above. For the loss of the sound of initial aleph (represented by the *e* of *enash*), compare the name Lazarus (Luke 16.20, 25; John 11.1, etc.), which is equivalent to the Semitic Eleazar. These references prove that the tendency to drop the sound was already present in Galilean speech in NT times, even if aleph continued to be written until a later date (cf. G. Vermes, *Jesus the Jew*, London 1973, pp. 190f., where further evidence is given).

8   Especially Matt. 8.20=Luke 9.58; Matt. 11.19=Luke 7.34 (see next chapter).

9   G. Vermes, 'The use of *bar nash/bar nasha* in Jewish Aramaic', Appendix E in M. Black, *An Aramaic Approach to the Gospels and Acts*, Oxford [3]1967, pp. 310–28 (reprinted in G. Vermes, *Post-Biblical Jewish Studies*, Leiden 1975, pp. 147–65); *Jesus the Jew*, pp. 160–91.

10   J. Jeremias, 'Die älteste Schichte der Menschensohn-Logien', *ZNW* 58 (1967), pp. 159–72; id., *New Testament Theology I*, London 1971, p. 261, n. 1. A similar explanation of *ho huios tou anthropou* as an exclusive self-designation was put forward by J.Y. Campbell, 'The Origin and Meaning of the Term Son of Man', *JTS* 48 (1947), pp. 145–55 (reprinted in id., *Three New Testament Studies*, Leiden 1965, pp. 29–40), but without adequate basis in Aramaic usage. The same criticism applies to R.E.C. Formesyn, who wishes to claim the use of *bar nash*, or *hahu bar nasha*, in Palestinian Aramaic as an equivalent to the first person pronoun: 'Was there a pronominal connection for the "Bar Nasha" self-designation?', NT 8 (1966), pp. 1–35. Also on the same lines is J.P. Brown, 'The Son of Man: "This Fellow"', *Bib.* 58, (1977), pp. 361–87.

11   Casey, *Son of Man*, pp. 224–8.

12   The five examples are taken from G. Vermes, *Jesus the Jew*, pp. 164–7. It will be seen that only the last three are true examples of the idiom. The usual meaning of *bar nash(a)* in this literature is 'a certain man' or 'anyone', cf. example (b). Examples with a first-person reference are very rare, but cf. next note.

13   cf. Casey, pp. 227f., for the opinion that there is already by NT times a
      tendency to use the emphatic state where the absolute (anarthrous) form
      would be more correct. But it is a mistake to assume that this is the only reason
      for the use of the emphatic form in the case of *bar nasha*, particularly in an
      example like this, where the two forms are juxtaposed. A further case of *bar
      nash* with self-reference may be cited from Pesiqta de Rab Kahana (Svedlund,
      pp. 59f; text in the edition of B. Mandelbaum, 2 vols., New York 1962, I pp.
      64f). Here R. Ḥaggai is reported to object to the teaching of Jacob of
      Nebburaya. He summons him and commands him to submit to punishment
      on two similar occasions. In each case the response of Jacob is the same and he
      receives the same reply, 'A man (*bar nash*) who speaks a word of Scripture is to
      be punished? He (Ḥaggai) said to him: Because you did not teach well'. In this
      case *bar nash* is defined by the relative clause, and the anarthrous form is
      required to denote a single member of the class so specified.

14   The best example is the substitution of the first person for the Son of Man in
      Matt. 10.32f=Luke 12.8f; pp. 48ff below.

15   Casey, pp. 224–6. The story also occurs in Pesiqta de Rab Kahana (Sved-
      lund, p. 71; Mandelbaum I, pp. 192–4), but the crucial sentence with *bar
      nasha* is omitted in this version. The sentiment is thus simply taken for
      granted.

16   Literally 'javelin', but adopted into Aramaic as a loanword for judgement or
      sentence. This applies also to *dimissio*=pardon or release. God is not
      represented as speaking Latin intentionally!

17   Casey, pp. 228–31.

18   Contrary to the main thrust of scholarship in this century, which gives
      priority to the future, Danielic, sayings, cf. R. Bultmann, *Theology of the New
      Testament* I, p. 30; most recently A.J.B. Higgins, *The Son of Man in the
      Teaching of Jesus*, Cambridge 1980, p. 123.

19   This is also the rule in the inauthentic sayings. The apparent exception in
      John 5.27 will be discussed below, p. 154.

20   M. Hengel, 'Zwischen Jesus und Paulus', *ZThK* 72 (1975), pp. 202f.

21   This point is not invalidated by the doubtfulness of the authenticity of Acts
      7.56, because Luke clearly recognizes that the Greek form of the title belongs
      to the primitive community, and does not make the mistake of using it
      elsewhere in Acts; cf. pp. 139ff below.

22   C.F.D. Moule, 'Neglected Features in the Problem of "the Son of Man"', in
      Neues Testament und Kirche (für Rudolf Schnackenburg), ed. J. Gnilka,
      Freiburg 1974, pp. 413–28.

23   cf. C.F.D. Moule, *The Origin of Christology*, Cambridge 1977, pp. 11–16,
      who states that Hengel regards *bera d-enasha* as a possible underlying form (p.
      11, n. 1). There is a comparable expression for 'the son of God' (*ho huios tou
      theou*) in an Aramaic fragment from Qumran, i.e., *bereh di-El*, which has
      striking parallels with Luke 1.32–35; cf. J.A. Fitzmyer, 'The Contribution of
      Qumran Aramaic to the study of the New Testament', *NTS* 20 (1973–4), pp.
      382–407.

24   Casey, pp. 228–31.

25 For what follows, cf. B. Lindars, 'Jesus as Advocate: a Contribution to the Christology Debate', *BJRL* 62 (1980), pp. 480–4.

26 We have sure evidence for the rendering of the plural *bene anasha* by the simple *hoi anthropoi* in Dan. and 1 Enoch (see n. 3 above), but there is no instance of a Greek translation of Aramaic *bar enash(a)*, apart from Dan. 7.13, known to me.

27 This suggestion presupposes that verse 28, 'So the Son of Man (*ho huios tou anthropou*) is lord even of the sabbath', is an addition to the pericope, which originally ended with verse 27. Some commentators think that it is a pre-Marcan addition, but reason will be given below for believing that it is due to Mark himself (pp. 102–6). Another case where *ho anthropos* may translate *bar enasha* is Matt. 12.43 = Luke 11.24: 'When the unclean spirit has gone out of a man (*apo tou anthropou*) . . .'. Here both 'spirit' and 'man' have the generic article, which cannot be represented exactly in English. In the conclusion, 'the last state of that man (*tou anthropou ekeinou*)', the underlying Aramaic might have been *hahu gabra*; cf. Syriac Peshitta (Old Syriac in Matthew), or *hahu bar enasha* (Old Syriac in Luke).

28 On the other hand one example of *ho huios tou anthropou* may represent generic *bar enasha* without the self-reference, viz., Matt. 12.32 = Luke 12.10. However, it will be argued below that even in this case a self-reference on Jesus' part should not be excluded (pp. 34–8).

29 See below, pp. 48–53

30 cf. M. Hengel, 'Zwischen Jesus und Paulus' (n. 20 above), where a number of examples, including Son of Man, is given.

31 cf. Casey, p. 238 and n. 23.

CHAPTER 3

1 Translation by B.M. Metzger in K. Aland, *Synopsis quattuor Evangeliorum*, Stuttgart 1964, Appendix I. Square brackets denote a lacuna in the text, filled in by conjecture; round brackets enclose words added for the sake of the translation.

2 For the discussion of the problem, cf. R.M. Grant and D.N. Freedman, *The Secret Sayings of Jesus*, London 1960; R.McL. Wilson, *Studies in the Gospel of Thomas*, London 1960; G. Gärtner, *The Theology of the Gospel of Thomas*, London 1961; W. Schrage, *Das Verhältnis des Thomas-evangeliums zur synoptischen Tradition und zu den koptischen Evangelienübersetzungen* (BZNW 29), Berlin 1964.

3 Another Thomas version of a Son of Man saying (logion 44) has 'the Son' instead of the Son of Man, but here the saying had probably been expanded in a trinitarian direction before it was adopted by Thomas, so that the change may belong to his source, cf. A.J.B. Higgins, *The Son of Man in the Teaching of Jesus*, p. 150, n. 49. In logion 106 to 'become sons of man' probably refers to achieving the permanent spiritual condition, which is regarded as exclusively male (cf. logion 114: 'Simon Peter said to them: let Mary go away from us, for women are not worthy of life. Jesus said, I shall lead her, so that I may make

her a male, that she too may become a living spirit, resembling you males. For every woman who makes herself a male will enter the kingdom of heaven').

4   So I.H. Marshall, *The Gospel of Luke*, The New International Greek Testament Commentary, Exeter 1978, p. 410, against Bultmann, who held the second view.

5   This meaning is accepted here by C. Colpe, *TDNT*, VIII, pp. 432f. But this is then taken (along with Mark 2.10 and Matt. 11.19 = Luke 7.34) to be a case where the Greek *ho huios tou anthropou* is to be regarded as a mistake. Colpe distinguishes these three sayings from the other sayings which he considers to be authentic, which speak of the Son of Man as an eschatological figure distinct from Jesus himself, and constitute the 'fourth source' for the Jewish conception (cf. p. 190f n. 7 above).

6   It will be seen that I have considerably modified the views expressed in my 'Re-Enter the Apocalyptic Son of Man', *NTS* 22 (1975–6), pp. 52–72. To R. Leivestad the saying supports his contention that Jesus spoke of himself as the Son of Man when he wished to express his solidarity with mankind, 'Exit the Apocalyptic Son of Man', *NTS* 18 (1971–2), pp. 264, 267.

7   cf. Matt. 10.40; 15.24; Mark 9.37; Luke 10.16; John 13.20.

8   John constantly represents Jesus as referring to God as the one who sent him, using *apostello* (17 times) and *pempo* (24 times) without distinction.

9   Matthew has 'deeds' (*ergon*), making an inclusion with Matt. 11.2, but Luke's 'children' (*teknon*) is to be preferred as the original reading, for which Matthew gives an interpretative substitute. But Luke may have added 'all', which is not found in Matthew.

10 A summarizing conclusion is typical of redactional composition, and frequently occurs in Luke (cf. pp. 136–9 below). This Wisdom comment is comparable to Prov. 8.32; Ecclus. 4.11, and if detached from the rest has nothing specially characteristic of Jesus. The link was perhaps provided by 'children' (*paidiois*) in the parable. The proverb appears to have inspired the Lucan addition in Luke 7.29f, where the people 'justify' God.

11 cf. N. Perrin, *Rediscovering the Teaching of Jesus*, London 1967, p. 120.

12 For the behaviour of the children, cf. E.F.F. Bishop, *Jesus of Palestine*, London 1955, p. 104; J. Jeremias, *Parables of Jesus*, rev. edn., London 1963, pp. 160–2.

13 It will be shown from the independent version in Mark 3.28 that *kol* must have stood in the underlying text, though in Mark it is rendered 'all (things)'.

14 The same feature will meet us when we consider Matt. 10.32f = Luke 12.8f, which immediately precedes the present saying in Luke. It will be shown that Luke's version of the saying has been influenced by the independent version known to him from Mark, which (unlike Matthew) he omits from the corresponding context, cf. pp. 48–53 below.

15 A further Semitism retained by Luke is the preposition *eis* for 'speak a word against'; cf. Job 2.9 LXX. 'Blaspheme' in Luke comes from the Marcan parallel. Thus, though Luke omits Mark 3.28f, his version of Q is influenced by it. He thus treats his major sources (Mark and Q) differently from Matthew, who tends to conflate Mark and Q, as here. It is this particular

characteristic (which we shall see again in chapter 5 in connection with the Little Apocalypse of Matt. 24 and Mark 13) which makes the Two-Source Hypothesis the only satisfactory solution to the Synoptic Problem, in spite of recent attempts to overthrow it. For the movement to reinstate the priority of Matthew (and thus to dispense with Q), cf. W.R. Farmer, *The Synoptic Problem*, London and New York 1964; H.H. Stoldt, *Geschichte und Kritik der Markushypothese*, Göttingen 1977; B. Orchard and T.R.W. Longstaff (ed.), *J.J. Griesbach: Synoptic and Text-Critical Studies 1776–1976*, Cambridge 1978. For criticism of the movement, cf. C.M. Tuckett, *The Revival of the Griesbach Hypothesis*, Cambridge 1982. For the particular point at issue cf. C.H. Talbert and E.V. McKnight, 'Can the Griesbach Hypothesis be falsified?', *JBL* 91 (1972), pp. 338–68; C.M. Tuckett, 'The Argument from Order and the Synoptic Problem', *Th Z* 36 (1980), pp. 338–54.

16 The same applies to the preceding sequence in Matthew, which is the Q version of the Beelzebul controversy (Matt. 12.22–30=Luke 11.14–23), combined with Mark 3.22–7.

17 Matthew's change of 'the sons of men' (*tois huiois ton anthropon*) to 'men' (*tois anthropois*) is especially noteworthy, as it removes the awkward similarity to the Son of Man in the Q version. It is most improbable that Mark would add in 'sons', as the theory of Matthaean priority requires, as he never does this elsewhere.

18 Casey's reconstruction of the Aramaic (p. 230), followed here otherwise, strangely uses the anarthrous form *bar enash*. But the generic article is in order here, even if this is a purely general statement (cf. example (e) on pp. 22f above), and is required to account for the articles in the Greek translation. For another reconstruction of the Aramaic cf. R. Schippers, 'The Son of Man in Mt. xii. 32=Lk. xii. 10, compared with Mk. iii. 28', *Studia Evangelica* IV, TU 102, 1968, pp. 231–5.

19 The masculine form *leh* can be retained, referring back to *kol*, though *millah* is feminine and would require the vocalization *lah*. Of course this difference would not appear in writing. We may note further that in Mark 3.29 *ouch echei aphesin* (does not have forgiveness) is an idiomatic rendering of *la yishtebeq leh*, and so again presupposes the same Aramaic as in the second half of the saying in Q.

20 The passive here is generally accepted as an example of the 'divine passive', whereby direct mention of God is avoided; cf. J. Jeremias, *Theology of the New Testament* I, p. 11, nn. 2 and 3.

21 In NT times the OT expression 'the Spirit of the Lord' is generally replaced by 'the Holy Spirit' (Hebrew *ruah haq-qodesh*, only three times in the OT). This again is a way of avoiding mentioning God (Jeremias, *Theology*, p. 10).

22 cf. BDF, §252. It would need to denote the only one in the class. This is possible in our preceding example (the one who eats and drinks, as opposed to the ascetic John), but not here.

23 cf. C.K. Barrett, *The Holy Spirit and the Gospel Tradition*, London 1947, pp. 105ff; I.H. Marshall, *Luke*, pp. 516–19.

24 But the *request* for a sign in Luke, which appears quite separately, inserted

into his version of the Beelzebul controversy (Luke 11.16), is clearly dependent on Mark 8.11 (*peirazontes, ezetoun*). This tradition is also reflected in John 6.30, but there are no close verbal links.

25 Grammatically it is presumably a case of appositive genitive, i.e., the sign which consists in Jonah, rather than the sign which Jonah gave (BDF §167; K.H. Rengstorf, *TDNT* VII, 233).

26 In Luke 11.31f the sayings are given in reverse order, but the wording is almost entirely identical. If Matthew's order is correct, Luke has presumably changed it to furnish a better climax and conclusion to the composition of Luke 11.29–32 as a rounded unit, with its implicit call to repentance. On the other hand Matthew may have reversed the order of the original to bring the references to Jonah together. No conclusion on this issue seems possible.

27 The verb 'arise ... with' is a Semitism, meaning stand up against an adversary, i.e., to accuse him, and so does not refer to resurrection (cf. M. Black, *Aramaic Approach*, p. 134; J. Jeremias, *TDNT* III, p. 408, n. 15). But this is of course implied (perhaps only metaphorically) by the fact that they will give their evidence at the judgement of the present generation.

28 Hence A. Vögtle proposes a multi-layered tradition-history, in which Luke 11.30 has been evolved by the church in relation to 11.29 in two stages, and Matt. 12.40 represents a later stage still ('Der Spruch vom Jonaszeichen' in A. Vögtle, *Das Evangelium und die Evangelien*, Düsseldorf 1971, pp. 103–36).

29 Thus Marshall, *Luke*, p. 485, takes Matt. 12.40 to be a correct interpretation of the implications of the original saying in Luke.

30 So T.W. Manson, *The Sayings of Jesus*, London 1949, pp. 90f; S. Schultz, *Q—Die Spruchquelle der Evangelisten*, Zürich 1972, pp. 255ff.

31 A similar phrase occurs in Matt. 12.6, 'something greater than the temple is here', but it is probably Matthew's own addition to his source, modelled on Matt. 12.41f (with *meizon* for *pleion*=greater); cf. H. Benedict Green, *The Gospel according to Matthew*, The New Clarendon Bible, Oxford 1975, pp. 123f.

32 W.B. Stevenson, *Grammar of Jewish Palestinian Aramaic*, Oxford 1924, p. 50.

33 This is the conclusion of the redaction-critical study of R.A. Edwards, *The Sign of Jonah*, London 1971. On this view the saying was created by the Q community on the basis of the 'eschatological correlative', i.e., the comparison between an OT situation and the coming judgement, for which Jesus was identified as the Son of Man. The concept of the eschatological correlative brings the present sequence into close relation with the Q sequence on the day of the Son of Man (Luke 17.22–37), in which there are similar comparisons, cf. pp. 88–93 below.

34 cf. H.K. McArthur, '"On the Third Day"', *NTS* 18 (1971–2), pp. 81–6.

35 So R. Bultmann, *The History of the Synoptic Tradition*, Oxford 1963, p. 326, and many other scholars. Matthew thinks of the resurrection as the sign of the parousia, cf. pp. 117–21 below.

36 Specially notable are his insertion of Hos. 6.6 into Matt. 9.13; 12.7 without warrant in the sources; formula-quotations in Matt. 12.17–21; 13.14f, 35; addition to Mark 8.38 in Matt. 16.27, etc.

37 cf. 1 Cor. 15.5. The rabbinic examples quoted by McArthur (n. 34 above) includes cases where both Jonah 1.17 (2.1) and Hos. 6.2 are cited together. The two expressions are here clearly taken to be functional equivalents.

38 A further equivalent is 'in three days' (*dia trion hemeron*) in the temple saying, Matt. 26.61; cf. 27.40, which Matthew probably interpreted of the resurrection.

39 This response of Jesus is taken by Bultmann, *Synoptic Tradition*, pp. 14–16, to be an insertion in order to introduce the controversy of Mark 2.6–10. On this view the healing (verse 11) followed immediately at this point. But verses 6–10 are too closely integrated into the situation of the story to have had an independent origin.

40 It is taken to be an example of the 'divine passive' by J. Jeremias, *Theology* I, p. 11, n. 2.

41 W.L. Lane, *Commentary on the Gospel of Mark* (The New London Commentary on the New Testament), London 1974, pp. 97f; C.E.B. Cranfield, *The Gospel according to St Mark*, rev. edn, Cambridge 1977, p. 100, explain the Son of Man sayings as a comment by the evangelist himself, addressing the readers. But this is scarcely probable.

42 So J. Wellhausen, *Einleitung in die drei ersten Evangelien*, Berlin, [2]1911, p. 129 (but see the remarks of C. Colpe, *TDNT* VIII, p. 430f); M. Casey, *Son of Man*, p. 228.

43 Thus Casey's reconstruction of the Aramaic (*Son of Man*, p. 160) does not include a finite verb, but uses the adjective *shalliṭ* (=having authority) as predicate.

44 G. Vermes, *Jesus the Jew*, pp. 67ff; id., *The Dead Sea Scrolls in Perspective*, London 1977, pp. 72f. The quotation which follows is from the second edition of his *The Dead Sea Scrolls in English*, London 1975, p. 229. Restorations in square brackets are certain, because of repetitions in the part not quoted.

45 The translation 'exorcist' (Aramaic *gezar*) should not be pressed. The word means a soothsayer or diviner (cf. Dan. 2.27; 4.4; 5.7, 11), and could as well be translated 'prophet'. For the Aramaic text, cf. B. Jongeling *et al.*, *Aramaic Texts from Qumran* I, Leiden 1976, pp. 123–31.

46 cf. R.H. Lightfoot, *History and Interpretation in the Gospels*, London 1935, p. 110.

47 For the moral dilemma posed by Jesus' ambiguity towards the actual healing of the man, cf. D.E. Nineham, *The Gospel of Mark*, ad loc.

48 The use of *enopion* is another Lucan trait. Hence Luke has drastically 'improved' the second half.

49 J. Jeremias, *Theology* I, p. 10, who therefore regards 'of God' in each case as secondary. Luke has the same phrase in 15.10.

50 This is not a case of the 'divine passive', however, as the logical subject cannot be God in view of the following phrase.

51 This is the classic passage for the view promoted by Bultmann, Tödt and others, that Jesus did not intend to refer to himself when he spoke of the Son of Man (cf. p. 2 above).

52 Greek *aparnethesetai* against the simple form *arnesamenos* in the first half. Matthew has the simple verb both times. The compound verb properly means 'deny utterly', but it is doubtful if there was much distinction in meaning in New Testament times.

53 Matt. 16.21, cf. p. 115 below.

54 cf. Dan. 7.9f; Matt. 25.31ff; Rev. 20.11f; 2 Esd. 12.32–4; 13.37; 1 Enoch 90.26–7.

55 cf. Ps. 62.12; Prov. 24.12.

56 J. Jeremias, *Theology* I, p. 7, n. 2.

57 The full reading, including 'and my words' is accepted by C.K. Barrett ('I am not ashamed of the Gospel', *New Testament Essays*, London 1972, p. 134) to be an original feature, because of the striking resemblance to Paul's phrase in Rom. 1.16, which may be related to it. On the other hand the reading 'me and mine' (i.e., omitting 'words') is found here and in the Lucan parallel in a few, mainly Old Latin, manuscripts, and this was made the basis of a corporate understanding of the Son of Man figure by V. Taylor, *The Gospel according to St Mark*, London ²1966, p. 384, and has also been adopted in the translation of the NEB. Barrett has shown convincingly that this is wrong (pp. 132f).

58 Alternatively this really is a case where Matthew has substituted the *ego* form for the Son of Man, in order to emphasize the identity between the two halves of each saying. Matt. 10.26–33 and Luke 12.2–9 have such close verbal similarity that dependence on a common document is virtually certain. The difference here between Matthew and Luke cannot be explained as due to different sources. For a recent discussion of the issue, cf. A.J.B. Higgins, '"Menschensohn" oder "Ich" in Q: Luke 12, 8–9/Matt. 10, 32–3?', in *Jesus und der Menschensohn* (*für A. Vögtle*), ed. R. Pesch and R. Schnackenburg, Freiburg i. Br. 1975, pp. 117–23.

59 cf. Vermes, *Jesus the Jew*, p. 168.

60 The parallel in Matt. 10.27 subtly turns it into an instruction to the disciples to proclaim the secret teaching publicly. Luke clearly has the more original form; cf. Marshall, *Luke*, ad loc.

61 M. Aboth 4.11. The words for advocate and accuser are Greek loanwords (*parakletos* and *kategoros*). For the use of these terms, cf. A.E. Harvey, *Jesus on Trial*, London 1976, pp. 108ff.

62 cf. Dan. 7.10; Rev. 20.12.

63 cf. Jubilees 4.21–4; 1 Enoch 12–16.

64 The process can be seen in the Marcan modifications to the saying in Mark 8.38, cf. pp. 106–8 below.

65 Contrary to the usual rule, noted by Jeremias, *Theology* I, pp. 18f, that the stress generally falls on the second part in antithetic couplets attributed to Jesus. This is certainly the case in Matt. 7.15–20, where Jesus says that 'Every sound tree bears good fruit, but the bad tree bears evil fruit', because the application is to false prophets. But in Luke 6.43–5 the same material is applied to discipleship, so that the saying constitutes an appeal to the hearers to make sure that they are good and not bad. Hence the emphasis falls on the first part as here.

66 Barrett (n. 57 above) has traced the connection further by pointing to the
forensic overtones of Paul's reference to the revelation of the righteousness of
God in Rom. 1.17. This similarity of thought is striking, although the
connection between Mark 8.38 and Rom. 1.16 cannot be proved (cf. C.E.B.
Cranfield, *The Epistle to the Romans* (ICC)), 2 vols., Edinburgh 1975–9, p. 86.

CHAPTER 4

1 The phrase comes from the celebrated book of W. Wrede, *Das Messiasgeheimnis in den Evangelien: Zugleich ein Beitrag zum Verständnis des
Markusevangeliums*, Göttingen 1901. Wrede contended that Jesus made no
claim to be the Messiah, so that Mark's portrayal of him has overcome the
discrepancy between the underlying traditions and the Church's Christology
by suggesting that his messiahship was a truth which was only gradually
revealed to the disciples. It can also be maintained that as a matter of history
Jesus did claim to be the Messiah, but was reticent about doing so openly, for
fear of misunderstanding; or that he saw his function as God's spokesman in
such a way that the concept of Messiahship was inappropriate, though it was
constantly applied to him by his followers. For a popular but sound
discussion of this issue, cf. G. Bornkamm, *Jesus of Nazareth*, London 1973,
pp. 169–74.

2 The text of Mark ends at 16.8 in a few of the oldest manuscripts (Sinaiticus,
Vaticanus, Sinaitic Syriac, one Sahidic manuscript), and this is attested by
some of the early Fathers (Clement, Origen, Eusebius, Jerome). The variant
forms of a shorter or a longer addition after verse 8 cannot be regarded as part
of the original work. It has often been supposed that the true ending was lost
at a very early date, before copies of the Gospel were made, but modern
opinion is more and more approaching agreement that Mark never intended
to write anything more after verse 8. For the debate on this issue, and various
explanations of Mark's purpose in ending the Gospel in this way, cf. J. Alsup,
The Post-Resurrection Appearance Stories of the Gospel-Tradition, Stuttgart
and London 1975, pp. 86–90.

3 These two verses, 14.28 and 16.7, are widely held to be insertions by the
evangelist, but a good case for regarding 14.28 as an integral part of its context
can be made out on the grounds that *proaxo* means 'I will lead you as a
shepherd leads the flock', thus continuing the metaphor of the quotation of
Zech. 13.7 in the preceding verse (cf. R. Pesch, *Das Markusevangelium* II,
Freiburg i. Br. 1977, pp. 381f). Verse 28 is missing from the Fayyum
fragment of this pericope, but the value of this as evidence is doubtful,
because the fragment abbreviates Mark's text in other ways. But if it is not
Mark's own insertion, it must still be regarded as an elaboration of a shorter
text at an earlier stage, prompted by the connection between Peter's denials
and his subsequent experience of the resurrection, through which he received
forgiveness; cf. 1 Cor. 15.3–5 (cf. M. Hengel, *The Atonement*, London 1981,
pp. 65–70). That 16.7 is a Marcan insertion is more widely accepted. Without
it the flight of the women is more readily explained, and their failure to give
the important message simply becomes the reason why the story of the empty
tomb belongs to a comparatively late stage in the history of the resurrection

traditions (cf. V. Taylor, *The Gospel according to St Mark*, London [2]1962, quoting Bousset for this opinion). Mark does not regard the resurrection appearances as part of the life of Jesus. Allusion to the kerygma is sufficient (Alsup, pp. 93f; cf. S. Schulz, *Die Stunde der Botschaft: Einführung in die Theologie der vier Evangelisten*, Hamburg 1967, pp. 141f).

4   It is made the starting point for study of the resurrection traditions by R.H. Fuller, *The Formation of the Resurrection Narratives*, London 1972, pp. 1–49.

5   It is a tradition which Paul received and has handed on (verse 3); 'on the third day' (verse 4) and 'the twelve' (verse 5) occur only here in Paul's writings; Paul adds himself to the list as an extra item (verse 8); it is preaching he gives in common with others mentioned (verse 11).

6   See Jeremias, *Theology* I, p. 13, n. 1 for the introduction of the divine passive in the course of translation into Greek.

7   cf. B. Lindars, *New Testament Apologetic*, London 1961, pp. 75–137.

8   This has been the standard view of modern critical scholarship; cf. Bultmann, *Theology of the New Testament* I, pp. 29f.

9   Casey, p. 232: *yemuth bar enash we-li-telathah yomin yequm*.

10   cf. McArthur (ch. 3, n. 34). The rabbinic quotations of Hos. 6.2 are used mainly in connection with the general resurrection, but also to support the theory that God does not allow the righteous to remain in distress for more than three days.

11   Mark's *dei* is echoed in John 3.14, and attests the sense of necessity which attaches to the passion predictions (cf. n. 20 below).

12   cf. W. Michaelis, *TDNT* V, pp. 912–19. The *pascha/paschein* pun is not found as early as the New Testament, but was an obvious development. It first appears in Melito of Sardis, *Homily on the Passion* 46.

13   cf. Rom. 4.25; 8.32; 1 Cor. 11.23; Gal. 2.20; Eph. 5.2, 25. All these passages reflect pre-Pauline formulae.

14   The relevant meanings of 'hand over', 'transmit', 'surrender', 'betray' are all covered by *mesar*, cf. M. Jastrow, *Dictionary of the Targumim, etc.*, repr. New York 1971, pp. 81of.

15   It has seemed unnecessary to consider a third possibility, i.e., 'be killed' (*apoktanthenai*), which occurs in all three predictions, because this has left no trace in the formulaic expressions relating to the passion.

16   Though Hos. 6.2 is obviously the best candidate, it is not quoted in the New Testament, and the only scriptural passage relating to resurrection on the third day is the Jonah quotation in Matt. 12.40. The difficulty has been avoided by arguing that 'according to the scriptures' in 1 Cor. 15.4 refers only to 'he was raised' and not to the third day, so that a wider range of passages could come into consideration; cf. B.M. Metzger, 'A Suggestion concerning the Meaning of I Cor. xv. 4b', *JTS* (n.s. 8) (1957), pp. 118–23.

17   *Sc. hemera* (supplied in Vaticanus and Latin texts). Idiomatic omission of this word would be unlikely in a formula. This makes it less likely that the present saying is based on the confessional formula.

18   For the idiomatic use of *echomene*, again with omission of *hemera*, cf. Acts 20.15, and with *hemera*, Acts 21.26. In all cases there is a variant *erchomene*,

attested here by P[75] Sin D 1241, but this means future rather than immediately following, and so does not provide the required parallel with *trite*.

19 J. Wellhausen, *Das Evangelium Lucae*, Berlin 1904, pp. 75f.

20 The cryptic references to successive days are employed twice over, but with significantly different verbal ideas. In verse 32 the action is Jesus' ministry, which must be completed, in spite of Herod's opposition. In verse 33 the action is Jesus' strategy, which must culminate in Jerusalem, even if that entails greater danger still. Luke's *dei* reflects the passion predictions (Mark 8.31; John 3.14). For this interpretation of Luke 13.32f, cf. Marshall, *Luke*, pp. 568–73, where other suggestions are reviewed.

21 Marshall cites two passages (Ezra 8.32f; Judith 12.7–10), where three days, representing an indefinite period, is followed by a decisive action on the fourth day, but in each case the fourth day is specified. Here it is natural to assume that the third day is also the day of death. This implies that Jesus' death is not something that is bound to be deferred until the ministry is completed, but something that is incurred in the course of his ministry and completes it (cf. *teleioumai*).

22 For the theory that Mark 14.61b–2, including a Danielic Son of Man saying which cannot be considered authentic according to the argument of this book, is a Marcan interpolation into the trial narrative, see pp. 110ff below.

23 This also is discussed below, p. 111.

24 It is disputed whether *cheiropoieton* and *acheiropoieton* in Mark 14.58 are interpretative additions or belong to the original form of the saying. They are not represented in John 2.19. They express primitive ideas in line with Jewish apocalyptic expectations, in which the temple is to be replaced by a divinely constructed new temple (cf. 1 Enoch 90.29f). The expression 'without hands' is already used symbolically in Dan. 2.34, 45 to express the divine initiative. Hence these words interpret the saying to mean that the Messiah is to build the new temple in the coming age. No doubt Mark understood it this way, and the direct question, 'Are you the Christ?', which follows in 14.61b makes excellent sense from this point of view. But for the *original* meaning of the saying it is unnecessary to assume that Jesus was making direct allusion to this apocalyptic theme or intended to imply a messianic claim. It is sufficient to see it in terms of the radical renewal which Jesus preached in preparation for the kingdom of God. For the messianic interpretation of the saying, cf. R. Pesch, *Das Markusevangelium* II, pp. 434f.

25 The phrase is often held to mean 'a son of God' (NEB; RSVm), but it certainly *can* mean 'the Son of God', and there are some who would assert that it *must* do so in order to accord with Mark's usage and intentions, cf. D.E. Nineham, *The Gospel of St Mark*, The Pelican Gospel Commentaries, rev. edn, London 1968, p. 430. On the grammatical point at issue see ch. 9, n. 16 below.

26 So V. Taylor, *Mark*, pp. 649–51.

27 cf. Eph. 2.14f. This is not the most commonly held explanation of the portent, but is allowed by Nineham as one possibility. But other suggestions are no more cogent: a sign that Jesus' prophecy of destruction of the temple is to

be fulfilled (*Clementine Recognitions* 1.41); a sign that the opposition of the temple establishment to Jesus' messianic claim is refuted (Pesch); 'the opening of the way to God effected by the death of Christ, or alternatively, and perhaps at the same time, the end of the Temple system' (Taylor).

28 C.H. Dodd, *Historical Tradition in the Fourth Gospel*, Cambridge 1963, p. 90.

29 A form of the saying with the first person occurs in Thomas 71: 'Jesus said: I shall destroy [this] house, and no one will be able to [re]build it.' This presumably refers to the body of the Gnostic, which Jesus 'destroys' in releasing him from his materiality (cf. logion 70: 'When you beget in yourselves him whom you have, he will save you'). If this saying is really to be identified with the temple saying, it is unlikely to be directly derived from the synoptic trial narrative, and this fact increases the probability that it was preserved independently. If the temple is the body, as suggested above, it may well depend on a known tradition of interpretation comparable to John 2.21f. cf. Gärtner, *The Theology of the Gospel of Thomas*, pp. 172–6.

30 cf. nn. 10 and 16 above. McArthur's quotations use the Jonah passage in connection with the safety of the righteous, who will not remain in distress for more than three days, but do not include an application of this passage to the general resurrection.

31 For an interpretation of the rise of the Judas legend in terms of its narrative potential, cf. F. Kermode, *The Genesis of Secrecy*, Cambridge (Mass.) and London 1979, pp. 84–94.

32 The 'woe' form of verse 21b, and the grim comment in verse 22, bear a close resemblance to Matt. 18.7 = Luke 17.1f. which may be a Q saying, fused by Matthew with Mark 9.42; cf. Marshall, *Luke*, p. 640. As Mark's saying here embodies the passion prediction ('the Son of Man is betrayed'), it may well be the case that he has used as the framework of it a saying which ultimately is a variant of the Q parallel.

33 Acts 2.23; 10.42; 11.29; 17.26, 31. Outside the Lucan literature it occurs only at Rom. 1.4; Heb. 4.7.

34 John 13.16, 20; cf. Matt. 10.24, 40; 23.11; Mark 9.35; Luke 9.48.

35 cf. B. Lindars, *The Gospel of John* (The New Century Bible), London 1972, pp. 446–56, claiming that John 13.6–11 is a Johannine expansion of the source, intended to relate the tradition to the theology of the passion.

36 See especially C.K. Barrett, 'The Background of Mark 10.45', in *New Testament Essays: Studies in Memory of T.W. Manson*, ed. A.J.B. Higgins, Manchester 1959, pp. 1–18; id., 'Mark 10.45: A Ransom for Many', C.K. Barrett, *New Testament Essays*, London 1972, pp. 20–6; F. Büchsel, *TDNT* IV, pp. 341–9.

37 Luke 1.68; 2.38 (*lutrosis*); 21.28 (*apolutrosis*); 24.21 (*lutrousthai*); Acts 7.35 (*lutrotes*).

38 1 Tim. 2.6 (*antilutron*); Eph. 1.7; Heb. 9.15 (*apolutrosis*); Titus 2.14; 1 Pet. 1.18 (*lutrousthai*); Heb. 9.12 (*lutrosis*). Other occurrences of *apolutrosis* do not bring in specific reference to sacrifice (Rom. 8.23; 1 Cor. 1.30; Eph. 1.14; 4.30; Col. 1.14; Heb. 11.35). Rom. 3.24 is doubtful, as there is a distinction between the *apolutrosis* achieved by Jesus and the sacrificial character of his death by

which it has been affected (*hilasterion*); cf. C.B. Cranfield, *Romans* I (ICC), Edinburgh 1975, pp. 206ff.

39 cf. M. Hengel, *The Atonement*, London 1981, pp. 1–32 for a detailed critique of this view. Another reason for assigning Mark 10.45 to a late date is that the Son of Man is usually taken to be a title of honour, and on this view not suitable in connection with the sacrificial meaning of Jesus' death, cf. U. Wilckens, 'Christus, der "letzte Adam", und der Menschensohn', *Jesus und der Menschensohn*, pp. 387–403. This view is, of course, no longer tenable.

40 cf. G. von Rad, *Old Testament Theology*, 2 vols., Edinburgh 1962–5, I, pp. 387–95; II, pp. 273–7.

41 Hence the two outstanding examples of self-sacrifice in the Old Testament both fall short of actual death. Moses' willingness to die that the people may be forgiven (Exod. 32.31f) was taken up in later tradition of the time of Christ, e.g., his death before the promised land is reached is compensated by his continuing intercession, *Assumption of Moses* 11.17; 12.6; cf. R. Bloch, 'Quelques aspects de la figure de Moïse dans la tradition rabbinique', in M. Cazelles *et al.*, *Moïse: l'homme de l'alliance*, Paris 1955, pp. 93–167. Some scholars, e.g., von Rad (cf. n. 40), think that Moses was the chief model in the mind of the composer of Isa. 53. The sacrifice of Isaac ('*aqedat Yishaq*) became prominent in the early rabbinic period, and may be referred to in John 3.16; Rom. 8.32 and elsewhere; cf. G. Vermes, *Scripture and Tradition in Judaism*, Leiden 1961, pp. 193–227; R. le Déaut, *La nuit pascale*, Analecta Biblica 22, Rome 1963, pp. 131–208.

42 cf. R. de Vaux, *Ancient Israel*, London 1961, pp. 418–21.

43 cf. Isa. 52.3: 'You shall be redeemed (*lutrothesesthe*) without money', alluded to in 1 Pet. 1.18.

44 Though almost every word differs from Mark 10.45, the differences are explained by J. Jeremias (*Theology* I, pp. 293f) as Greek stylistic improvements to the more strongly Semitic version of Mark. But it is possible that we have here translation variants, going back ultimately to independent versions of the Aramaic original:

	bar enasha	*yimsar*	*naphsheh*		*kopher*	*ḥalaph*	*saggiin*
Mark 10.45	ho huios tou						
	anthropou …	dounai	ten psuchen autou		lutron	anti	pollon
1 Tim. 2.6	(anthropos …)	dous	heauton		antilutron	huper	panton

Jeremias suggests that *anthropos* in 1 Tim. 2.5 shows knowledge of the Son of Man title (op. cit., p. 265), but if so it cannot be attributed to widespread use of the title, but must be traced to the gospel text, as in Mark. On the other hand, if the passage in 1 Tim. is an independent version of the saying, this might be a case of simple *anthropos* for Aramaic *bar enasha*; cf. ch. 3, n. 27 above. Titus 2.14 is probably dependent on the form used in 1 Tim. 2.6.

45 This can be no more than a tentative suggestion, as the influence of the Fourth Gospel itself upon 1 John must be taken into account. For the relationship between John and the Johannine Epistles, cf. R.E. Brown, *The Community of the Beloved Disciple*, London 1979; B. Lindars, 'The persecution of Christians in John 15.18—16.4a', *Suffering and Martyrdom in the New Testament* (*Essays*

for G.M. Styler), ed. W. Horbury and B. McNeil, Cambridge 1981, pp. 48–69.

46 cf. b Ber. 20ᵃ, 'They were ready to suffer martyrdom (*mosre naphshehon*) for the sanctification of the Name'.

47 '. . . Barnabas and Paul, men who have risked their lives (*paradedokosi tas psuchas auton*) for the name of our Lord Jesus Christ.' NEB, 'have devoted themselves to the cause of our Lord', weakens the sense, probably depending on the meaning 'pledge' proposed for the verb here by F. Field, *Notes on the Translation of the New Testament*, Cambridge 1899, p. 124 (but he means by this 'a general determination and readiness to die for the cause').

48 Bultmann, *Theology* I, p. 31, asserts that 'the tradition of Jesus' sayings reveals no trace of a consciousness on his part of being the Servant of God of Isa. 53'. The same point is argued at length by M.D. Hooker, *Jesus and the Servant*, London 1959.

49 Isa. 53.5, ' he *was bruised* for our iniquities': Targ., *ithmesar* (see next note); 53.6, 'the Lord *has laid on* him the iniquity of us all': LXX, *paredoken*; 53.7, 'like a lamb that *is led* to the slaughter': Targ., *yimsar*; 53.12c, 'because he *poured out* his soul to death': LXX, *paredothe*, Targ., *mesar*; 53.12f, 'and *made intercession for* the transgressors': LXX, *paredothe*.

50 As the Targum stands, this is applied to the destruction of the temple, but it is possible that the verb belongs to an older state of the Targum before AD 70. For the inexact equation *ithmesar* = *medukka* it may be observed that Hebrew *daka* is normally used metaphorically (= abase), and it is so rendered here by both LXX and Syriac. Paul's words are also reminiscent of Isa. 53.12f, LXX, *kai dia tas hamartias auton paredothe* ('and was delivered up for their sins').

51 Where, however, 'for our sins' or a similar phrase occurs, it is altogether probable that there is allusion to the prophecy. Besides Rom. 4.25a = Isa. 53.5b, the formula of 1 Cor. 15.3, 'Christ died for our sins', corresponds closely with Isa. 53.5a, 'he was wounded for our transgressions', where the verb refers to a fatal wound, and could be represented variously by 'was killed' (Aramaic *mithqetel*), 'died' (*meth*) or 'suffered' (*hash*), and the final phrase would be *be-hobana*, as in the Targum. See further J. Jeremias, *TDNT* V, p. 706.

52 The final words in this Targum quotation (= Isa. 53.12e) have been rendered in the light of what follows, i.e., Isa. 53.12f, 'and made intercession for the transgressors', which the Targum paraphrases as follows: 'And the rebellious shall be forgiven for his sake' (*u-le-marodayya yishtebeq leh*). The verb 'bore' (Heb. *nasa*) in 12e can also mean 'has forgiven'. The Targum has thus transposed the phrases of 12e and f, regarding them as equivalent in meaning.

53 cf. Barrett, 'The Background of Mark 10.45' (n. 36 above), p. 7.

CHAPTER 5

1 E. Käsemann, 'Sentences of Holy Law in the New Testament', *New Testament Questions of Today*, London 1969, pp. 66–81.

2 The best study of Q for English readers is still T.W. Manson, *The Sayings of*

Jesus, London 1937/49 and subsequent reprints. More recent studies include D. Lührmann, *Die Redaktion der Logienquelle* (WMANT 33), Neukirchen 1969; S. Schulz, *Q—Die Spruchquelle der Evangelisten*, Zürich 1972; G.N. Stanton, 'On the Christology of Q', in *Christ and Spirit in the New Testament* (*Studies in Honour of C.F.D. Moule*), ed. B. Lindars and S.S. Smalley, Cambridge 1973, pp. 27–42.

3 Tatian made a harmony (*diatessaron*) of the four gospels in Rome about AD 160–5, and subsequently reproduced it in Syriac for the benefit of his own Syriac-speaking church, where it enjoyed such great popularity that it almost ousted the separate gospels from common use. The discovery of part of the Greek text in 1933, and of the Syriac text of part of St Ephraem's commentary on the Diatessaron in 1957, has revived interest in this work; cf. B.M. Metzger, *The Early Versions of the New Testament*, Oxford 1977, pp. 10–36.

4 Luke also has repetition of this feature in 17.21a, but this is probably his own redactional work to bind the isolated saying on the kingdom in verse 21b to the following discourse. It will be argued below that verse 22 also belongs to Luke's redaction. Luke has omitted the Marcan parallel from his version of the Little Apocaypse as part of a much more comprehensive recasting of the material. Textual variants make it impossible to decide how far Luke 17.23 is influenced by Mark 13.21, but the more colourful Matt. 24.26 is probably closer to the Q original; cf. Schulz, *Q*, pp. 278f.

5 Most scholars hold that Matthew has the simile in the original position, and that the question in Luke 17.37a is redactional. Schulz suggests that the reason for Luke's change is to avoid the unpleasant comparison between the Son of Man and vultures.

6 Luke 17.31 = Mark 13.14f, and so does appear to be a case where Luke has inserted Marcan material into a Q passage, contrary to his normal practice. This can be explained by the fact that Mark 13.14–20 is a passage which Luke has felt constrained to alter considerably in order to suit his interpretation of the apocalyptic discourse. On the other hand Manson (*Sayings*, pp. 144f) takes it to be an independent doublet of Mark 13.14f, which was already found in Q. Luke 17.32, on Lot's wife, has been added by catchword connection, or may have been part of the material on Sodom. Luke 17.33 has a Q parallel at Matt. 10.39. Luke 17.36 is a Western addition (D lat syr) from the parallel in Matthew, and not a true part of Luke's text.

7 It is disputed whether Luke 17.28f, on the destruction of Sodom, is a Lucan addition or a part of Q which Matthew has omitted. Luke likes to have things in pairs, but there is a close parallel in Q to the present passage in Matt. 12.41f = Luke 11.31f (cf. ch. 3, n. 26 above). Marshall (*Luke*, pp. 662f) points out that the repetition of the saying on the parousia in Matt. 24.37 and 39b may count as evidence for omission by Matthew, as he tends to compensate for his omissions; cf. ch. 7, n. 4 below.

8 There is slight textual evidence for this suggestion, as Luke 12.40 is missing from the Lake group of minuscules, i.e., from the common archetype which lies behind this group. Luke's text is almost identical with Matthew's, except for the position of *hora* within the relative clause, which is characteristic of Luke; cf. BDF §294 (5).

9   cf. M. Ber. 1.5: 'The Sages say: "The days of thy life" means this world only, but "all the days of thy life" (Deut. 16.3) is to include the Days of the Messiah'.

10   Many scholars take the verse to be redactional, cf. Schulz, *Q*, p. 278, n. 90. The phrase *mia ton hemeron* occurs also in Luke's editorial redaction in Luke 5.17, and the verb *epithumeo* is a Lucan word; cf. 15.16; 16.21; 22.15.

11   'In his day' should probably be omitted on textual grounds, and is placed in square brackets in the twenty-sixth edition of the Nestle-Aland text (1979). It is missing from P[75] B D it sa (D also has further textual variations, which do not have the same proto-Alexandrian support).

12   Vermes, *Jesus the Jew*, p. 178, lists the following features as indications of an allusion to Dan. 7.13: the coming or the glory or the kingship of the Son of Man, or the clouds transporting him. The list should be extended to include the revelation of the Son of Man, which is an alternative way of speaking of his coming (cf. 2 Esd. 13.32: '. . . then my Son will be revealed, whom you saw as a man coming up from the sea'). Casey, p. 189, arbitrarily detaches Luke 17.24 from its explication in verse 30 and wrongly denies the Danielic connection.

13   On the primitive use of Ps 110.1 see ch. 6, n. 15 below. There is no certain allusion to Daniel in Paul (Casey, pp. 151–4). But the combined testimony of Q and Mark forbids the supposition that the identification is a late and peripheral development.

14   H. Schürmann has argued that *all* the Son of Man sayings in Q have been evolved in this way, so that the title is a secondary interpretative feature in every case; cf. his article 'Beobachtungen zum Menschensohn-Titel in der Redequelle: sein Vorkommen in Abschluss- und Einleitungswendung', *Jesus und der Menschensohn*, pp. 124–47. But this depends on an erroneous view of the Son of Man phrase.

15   These are conveniently collected in C.H. Dodd, *The Parables of the Kingdom*, London, rev. edn, 1961, ch. 5: 'Parables of Crisis'.

16   cf. B.D. Chilton, *God in Strength: Jesus' Announcement of the Kingdom*, Freistadt 1979, especially pp. 277–88.

17   The suggestion that a phrase similar to 'on that day' lies behind Luke 17.24b does not affect the judgement expressed above that 'in his day' is not to be accepted in the text of this verse. The argument is that this well known OT expression or something like it stood here instead of 'the Son of Man' in the original form of the tradition. For the eschatological day in the teaching of Jesus, cf. Matt. 7.22; 10.15; 11.22, 24; Mark 13.32; Luke 10.12; 17.31; 21.34; G. Delling, *TDNT*, II, pp. 951f.

18   cf. E. Lohse, 'Der Menschensohn in der Johannesapokalypse', in *Jesus und der Menschensohn*, pp. 415–20, who rightly denies that the Son of Man title plays any part in the apocalyptic traditions in Revelation.

19   Luke's 'hour', against Matthew's 'watch', shows that this Q parable was not specifically concerned with the night, so that the additional words in Matthew ('he would have stayed awake') are to be regarded as derived from

Mark 13.35. 'Hour' is also the catchword, which provides the link between the two parables of verses 39 and 40.

20 *Hetoimos* is rare in the gospels, but occurs again in the Q parable of the great supper, Matt. 22.4, 8; Luke 14.17.

21 The view that verse 40 is 'a Christian prophet's hortatory comment upon and application of Jesus' parable' in verse 39 (Higgins, *The Son of Man in the Teaching of Jesus*, p. 107) gives a plausible explanation of the process whereby the short parable in this verse was attached to the other parable, but does not account for its origin. The basic statement is 'the master (or the Lord, *ho kurios*=God) comes', which is clearly parabolic in Mark, but can also be understood as a straight eschatological assertion. The change of 'master' to 'Son of Man' presupposes the latter interpretation, and belongs to the Q editing of the material after the two parables have been brought together.

22 cf. H.E. Tödt, *The Son of Man in the Synoptic Tradition*, London 1965, pp. 246–69; R.A. Edwards, *The Sign of Jonah*, pp. 54–8.

CHAPTER 6

1 The authority of the Son of Man is emphasized especially by M.D. Hooker, *The Son of Man in Mark*, pp. 90f, 190ff (her position is not altered in her more recent essay, 'Is the Son of Man problem really insoluble?', *Text and Interpretation (Studies presented to M. Black)*, ed. E. Best and R. McL. Wilson, Cambridge 1979, pp. 155–68). Unfortunately she does not see this as a special *Marcan* emphasis.

2 On this verse see above p. 46.

3 Verse 27 is also missing from the text of Mark in D and some Old Latin texts.

4 It has been shown by D. Daube that Matthew's additional case makes a much more satisfactory basis of argument from a rabbinic point of view (*The New Testament and Rabbinic Judaism*, London 1956, pp. 67–71).

5 So Marshall, *Luke*, p. 232. The relative independence of the conclusion (Luke 6.5=Mark 2.28) is illustrated by D, which has the non-canonical pericope of the man working on the sabbath at this point, and transfers Luke 6.5 to follow verse 10 (cf. B.M. Metzger, *A Textual Commentary on the Greek New Testament*, London 1971, p. 140).

6 According to 2 Esd. 6.59; 7.11; *Assumption of Moses* 1.12 the world was created for Israel. For rabbinic parallels to the sabbath saying, cf. Billerbeck II, p. 5.

7 J. Wellhausen, *Das Evangelium Marci*, Berlin 1903, p. 22.

8 So D.E. Nineham, *Mark*, pp. 106f.

9 This opinion concerning Mark 8.14–21 is shared by a number of critics, e.g. M. Dibelius, *From Tradition to Gospel*, London 1934, pp. 228f, V. Taylor, *Mark*, pp. 363f, D.E. Nineham, *Mark*, pp. 238f. There is less certainty about 9.9–13, but this is due to failure to appreciate the secondary character of the reference to the Son of Man, which fixes the material as a Marcan composition (cf. pp. 61f, 67 above).

10   cf. T.F. Glasson, *The Second Advent*, London [3]1963, pp. 63–8; J.A.T. Robinson, *Jesus and His Coming*, London 1957, pp. 43–51; Jeremias, *Theology* I, pp. 273f.

11   cf. also Didache 16.6f, where Zech. 14.5 and Dan. 7.13 are conflated.

12   cf. B. Lindars, *New Testament Apologetic*, 122–7.

13   The text of Mark 14.62b is identical with the Theodotion text of Dan 7.13, now recognized to preserve readings current in the first century; cf. D. Barthélemy, *Les devanciers d'Aquile*, Leiden 1963.

14   So Casey, *Son of Man*, pp. 179f.

15   cf. M. Gourgues, *À la droite de Dieu*, Paris 1978, pp. 209–18.

16   This feature is the chief argument in favour of a pre-Marcan formula, cf. Pesch, *Markusevangelium* II, p. 438. For 'power' as a substitute for the divine name, cf. the frequent use of *geburah* in the Talmud, e.g., b Sanh. 87a, 88b, etc. But 'the Son of the Blessed' in verse 61 is regarded as an incorrect attempt at Jewish usage on Mark's part by J. Klausner, *Jesus of Nazareth*, London 1947, p. 342 (the disregard of it by Matthew, however, may be ascribed to his tendency to standardize the christological titles). This suggests that power (*dunamis*) here is not to be regarded as merely a substitute for the divine name. It should rather be seen as a doxological term, used in a way comparable to 'the right hand of the majesty on high' and 'the right hand of the throne of the majesty in the heavens' (Heb. 1.3; 8.1, both using *megalosune*), and reflecting liturgical usage within the church. References to the throne of God in Revelation belong to the same style of thought and expression. The power and glory conferred upon the one like a son of man in Dan 7.14 are attributes of the thrones (verse 9) as much as they are of those who sit upon them. There is a considerable range of doxological nouns in early Christian literature, including a number of power-words, of which *dunamis* is one of the commonest, on account of its use in LXX. There is thus no compelling reason to deny that Mark 14.62 is a conflation of texts, using the high-flown style of the liturgical tradition, created by Mark himself. For the doxological terms, see D.H. Milling, *The Origin and Character of the New Testament Doxology*, unpublished Ph.D. dissertation, Cambridge 1972, pp. 176–230.

17   cf. Wellhausen, *Das Evangelium Marci*, 1903, p. 132.

18   W.L. Knox, *The Sources of the Synoptic Gospels*, 2 vols, Cambridge 1953–7, I, pp. 19, 133; E.J. Pryke, *Redactional Style in the Marcan Gospel*, Cambridge 1978, pp. 96–9.

19   The rulings on blasphemy given in M. Sanh. 7.5 are concerned only with cases in which the name of God (YHWH) is actually spoken.

20   This is not to deny that the question whether Jesus was the Messiah was an issue at the trial, only that Mark's presentation of it and redactional use of it are derived directly from his sources. Luke 22.67 is held by many scholars to be based on a non-Marcan source for the question on messiahship, which is reflected also in John 10.24–38; cf. G. Schneider, *Verleugnung, Verspottung und Verhör Jesu nach Lukas 22, 54–71*, Munich 1969, pp. 114ff.

21   For this reason Bultmann, *History of the Synoptic Tradition*, p. 123, brackets the whole of 'nor the Son but only the Father'. God is referred to as Father

elsewhere in Mark only at 8.38; 11.25, [26]; 14.36. It has already been claimed that the relevant part of 8.38 is to be attributed to Mark; cf. p. 107.

22 That 'nor the Son' is to be ascribed to Mark himself is accepted by Pesch, *Markusevangelium* II, p. 310.

23 Our earliest source for this correlation is Paul, especially in Rom. 8, but it is found independently in Hebrews and John. The evidence of Paul shows that it is *not* to be regarded as derived from the deposit of authentic *bar enasha* sayings, all of which are irrelevant. It is rather the result of various converging lines of thought, especially the Abba address and the concept of the Messiah as God's Son in Jewish tradition; cf. M. Hengel, *The Son of God*, London 1976; J.D.G. Dunn, *Christology in the Making*, London 1980, pp. 33–46.

CHAPTER 7

1 This is possible also at 5.11 (see below, p. 134) and 10.32f (above, p. 52).

2 This is the reading of Sin B 700 Vulgate and Coptic against the majority ('Who do men say that I, the Son of Man, am?'), but the latter is clearly due to influence of the parallels in Mark and Luke.

3 cf. 1 Enoch 71.14: 'You are the Son of Man who was born to righteousness'. Nothing like this occurs in the NT.

4 Matthew's well disciplined mind feels the need to compensate for omissions from his sources. The best known instances are the omission of the exorcism of Mark 1.23–8, made good by turning the demoniac of Mark 5.1–20 into two (Matt. 8.28–34), the omission of the parable of the seed growing secretly in Mark 4.26–9, made good by the parable of the tares (Matt. 13.24–30), and the omission of the blind man of Mark 8.22–6, made good by doubling blind Bartimaeus (Matt. 20.29–34 = Mark 10.46–52).

5 Here Matthew adds 'You are a hindrance (*skandalon*) to me', which may be an allusion to the 'rock of offence' (*petra skandalou*) of Isa. 8.14, quoted in Rom. 9.33; 1 Pet. 2.8; cf. B. Lindars, *New Testament Apologetic*, pp. 169–86; H.B. Green, *The Gospel according to Matthew*, Oxford 1975, p. 154.

6 Readers who are familiar with my 'Re-enter the Apocalyptic Son of Man', *NTS* 22 (1975–6), pp. 52–72, will know that I took this view with regard to Jesus himself on the assumption that a far greater number of the sayings are authentic than I would now accept (the article is criticized by A.J.B. Higgins, *The Son of Man in the Teaching of Jesus*, pp. 49–53). A rather similar view is favoured by J.D.G. Dunn, *Christology in the Making*, pp. 82–7.

7 See above, pp. 34–8.

8 cf. B.D. Chilton, *God in Strength*, p. 277: 'In each case (i.e., eleven passages which substantively record Jesus' announcement of the kingdom of God), we have perceived Aramaic (or more generally Semitic) idioms, and the Targum Jonathan to Isaiah has been seen to be of especial importance as preserving material which seems to have been a formative influence on the thought and language of these announcements.'

9 The allusion is denied by Casey, pp. 192f, following A Vögtle, 'Das

213

christologische und ekklesiologische Anliegen von Mt. 28, 18–20', *Studia Evangelica* II, TU 87, 1964, pp. 266–94.

10 cf. Green, *Matthew*, p. 154; D. Hill, *The Gospel of Matthew*, London 1972, p. 266.

11 These are striking semi-agreements between Matthew and Luke, but do not require literary dependence for their explanation. In Matt. 26.29 and Luke 22.17 the expressions are modifications of *ouketi* in Mark 14.25. In Matt. 26.64 and Luke 22.67–9 the differences between Matthew and Luke are too great to suggest dependence of one on the other, rather than on Mark, but the motive (to identify the heavenly session with the resurrection as a distinct moment following the crucifixion) is common to both.

12 The suggestion of A. Debrunner (cf. BDF §12 (3)) that *aparti* = 'certainly' should be read instead of *ap' arti* provides a way of removing the temporal reference, and would allow Matthew's version to refer simply to the parousia. The same could be applied to Matt. 26.29, where it would have have the effect of strengthening the oath formula. But Matt. 23.29 seems to be decisive evidence that Matthew used *ap' arti*, and weakens the case for *aparti* in the other two passages. If it is accepted, it removes the apparent connection with Luke's *apo tou nun*.

13 Matthew's change from 'the Son of the Blessed' to 'the Son of God' brings the form into line with Peter's confession in 16.16. Some manuscripts bring the expression even closer to 16.16 by inserting *tou zontos* at the end, but Matthew has already used this in the adjuration earlier in the verse.

14 cf. D.R. Catchpole, 'The Answer of Jesus to Caiaphas (Matt. xxvi. 64)', *NTS* 17 (1970–1), pp. 213–26.

15 A distinction is made along these lines by Green, *Matthew*, p. 216; Hill, *Matthew*, p. 346. It is better, however, to see Matthew's alteration of Mark here in relation to his total presentation of the arrest and trial of Jesus. To Matthew Jesus remains in control of events. The strengthening of the high priest's question with a solemn oath makes it a challenge to Jesus to prove his messiahship by an appropriate display of power. Jesus could perfectly well meet this challenge (cf. Matt. 26.53, where he claims to have this power now, *arti*), but his destiny requires that it be deferred (26.54). The importance of Matt. 26.53f for the interpretation of Matthew's passion narrative does not seem to have been generally noticed.

16 cf. B.H. Streeter, *The Primitive Church*, London 1929, p. 35.

17 So Jeremias, *Theology* I, p. 264; W.G. Kümmel, *Promise and Fulfilment*, London [4]1974, pp. 61–4; Colpe, *TDNT* VIII, p. 436f.

18 So Casey, *Son of Man*, pp. 213–18.

19 This is assumed without question by C.H. Dodd, *The Parables of the Kingdom*, paperback edition, London 1961, p. 138; J. Jeremias, *The Parables of Jesus*, London 1963, pp. 82, 223.

20 cf. Marshall, *Luke*, pp. 814–18.

21 *Palingenesia* was used by the Pythagorean philosophers to denote the renewal of the world, and continued to be used by the Stoics in NT times. It thus expresses the new heaven and new earth (Isa. 65.17; 66.22) common in

Christian (Rev. 21.1; 2 Pet. 3.13) and Jewish (e.g., 1 Enoch 45.4f) apocalyptic; cf. E Schürer, *The History of the Jewish People in the Age of Jesus Christ*, rev. edn., II, Edinburgh 1979, pp. 537f.

22 So Green, *Matthew*, p. 172.

23 cf. the discussion in Casey, pp. 187ff. The righteous are placed on thrones in 1 Enoch 108.12, but this chapter is clearly a later addition to the book (Milik, *The Books of Enoch*, p. 57, regards it as a Christian work). For the throne of the Son of Man, cf. 1 Enoch 61.8; 62.2f; 69.27ff.

24 cf. p. 108 above.

25 Manson, *Sayings*, pp. 249f, attempts to account for the discrepancy by claiming that the Son of Man 'stands for the body comprising the King and his brethren', but the idea that the Son of Man in the sayings of Jesus has a corporate dimension is erroneous; cf. p. 202 n. 57 above. Most scholars (e.g., Jeremias, *Theology* I, p. 246) attribute it to the Jewish background of thought, and so to the source.

26 On the difficulties of interpretation of this passage, cf. C.K. Barrett, *The First Epistle to the Corinthians*, London 1968, p. 356.

27 cf. B. Lindars, *New Testament Apologetic*, p. 50.

28 The possibility that Paul had the Son of Man title in mind is considered by A. Robertson and A. Plummer, *A Critical and Exegetical Commentary on the First Epistle of St Paul to the Corinthians*, Edinburgh [2]1914, p. 357, but cf. ch. 1, n. 40 above.

29 cf. A.J.B. Higgins, 'The Sign of the Son of Man (Matt. xxiv. 30)', *NTS* 9 (1962–3), pp. 380–2. He argues that the sign must be a portent and cannot be identified with the Son of Man himself, and adduces evidence to sugggest that the patristic interpretation is what Matthew actually intended.

30 Glasson, *The Second Advent*, pp. 189ff; id., 'The Ensign of the Son of Man, Matt. xxiv. 30' *JTS* (n.s.) 15 (1964), pp. 299f, referring to the *Jewish Authorized Daily Prayer Book*, London [24]1956, p. 48, 'Sound the great horn for our freedom; lift up the ensign to gather our exiles, and gather us from the four corners of the earth'. Further support comes from the list of trumpets, followed by standards, in 1 QM 3.1ff; 4.1ff. This interpretation is accepted by Jeremias, *Theology* I, p. 264; D. Hill, *Matthew*, p. 323; Colpe, *TDNT* VIII, p. 437, n. 283; A.J.B. Higgins, *The Son of Man in the Teaching of Jesus*, pp. 118f.

31 This meaning is accepted by J. Schniewind, *Das Evangelium nach Matthäus*, Göttingen 1956, pp. 244f; P. Bonnard, *L'Évangile selon saint Matthieu*, Neuchâtel 1963, p. 352. For the appositive genitive, cf. ch. 3, n. 25 above on the sign of Jonah (Matt. 12.39; 16.4).

32 Contrast Rev. 1.7, and cf. ch. 6, n. 12 above.

33 cf. K. Stendahl, *The School of St Matthew*, Uppsala 1954; R.H. Gundry, *The Use of the Old Testament in St Matthew's Gospel*, Leiden 1967.

CHAPTER 8

1 Especially in recent German scholarship it has become customary to insist

that Acts is a theological work, and not primarily historical. For a recent protest against this one-sided view, cf. M. Hengel, *Acts and the History of Earliest Christianity*, London 1979.

2 The need for artistic variation from this point of view is the best explanation of the serious discrepancies in the three accounts of Paul's conversion (Acts 9.1–19; 22.4–16; 26.9–18).

3 e.g. variations from Mark in Luke 5.17b, 25; descriptive details in Luke 7.44–6 and motifs from 5.21; 8.48 in 7.49 and 50; addition of 'and the Lord turned and looked on Peter' in Luke 22.61, etc.

4 Theories along these lines mar the interesting and stimulating work on Luke as a writer which has been done by J. Drury, *Tradition and Design in Luke's Gospel*, London 1976; M.D. Goulder, *The Evangelists' Calendar*, London 1978.

5 An excellent example of Luke's freedom in handling his sources is provided by the Q story of the centurion's servant (Luke 7.1–10 = Matt. 8.5–13). Luke has provided the extra detail of a deputation of Jews on behalf of the centurion (verses 3–5), which increases the emotional appeal. The centurion is 'worthy' (verse 4), though he does not consider himself to be so (verse 7). In verse 6 'when he was not far off' is verbally identical with Luke 15.20 (the prodigal son), and 'do not be troubled' uses the same verb as in Luke 8.49 = Mark 5.35, where there is a similar motif of messengers from the home of the sick person. Where, however, Luke overlaps with Matthew the story is almost word for word the same. Thus, though nearly fifty per cent of the story is Luke's own composition, the essentials of the source are reproduced with great fidelity. See further Marshall, *Luke*, pp. 278, 610.

6 So I. Rehkopf, *Die lukanische Sonderquelle*, Tübingen 1959, p. 56; Schulz, *Q*, p. 453, n. 377: 'Lk fügt den Titel von sich aus nirgends ein'.

7 cf. pp. 52f above.

8 Higgins, *The Son of Man in the Teaching of Jesus*, p. 113, accepts that the Son of Man is original here, but ascribes the whole saying to the post-Easter community. Schulz, *Q*, pp. 456f, ascribes it to the Q-community, who held a 'prophet' Christology.

9 Both Matthew and Luke drop 'and the gospel' from Mark, but the force of this 'minor agreement' is reduced by Matt. 19.29 = Mark 10.29 = Luke 18.29, where both evangelists drop 'and for the sake of the gospel', but otherwise treat the passage entirely differently.

10 cf. pp. 88–98 above.

11 For the case against Lucan composition and a defence of the authenticity of the saying, cf. D.R. Catchpole, 'The Son of Man's Search for Faith (Luke xviii.8b)', *NT* 19 (1977), pp. 81–104. The opposite case is summarized by E. Linnemann, *Parables of Jesus*, London 1966, p. 189, n. 17.

12 The parable of the unjust judge (Luke 16.1–9) shares a number of special features with that of the unjust steward, which suggest that the interpretative part of the material is to be attributed to Luke himself: *a*. There is an unsatisfactory central character, with whom the readers cannot identify; *b*. a comment by 'the Lord ' (*ho kurios*; in 16.8 it is not clear whether this refers to

the master in the parable or to Jesus himself); *c.* reference in this comment to the central character as a type ('the unjust judge'; 'the unjust steward'); *d.* a further comment introduced by 'I say to you', only rather remotely relating to the terms of reference of the parable. In the present case the 'faith' which is recommended picks up the editorial introduction on persistence in prayer (verse 1). The actual phrase 'find faith' comes from the story of the centurion's servant, Matt. 8.10=Luke 7.9.

13 So Jeremias, *Parables*, p. 155, n. 15.

14 The common form of this particle is used to express an inference. The interrogative use found here occurs elsewhere in the NT only at Acts 8.30; Gal. 2.17 (though this case is doubtful), cf. BDF §440 (2).

15 Not surprisingly this appealing saying has found its way into other contexts, i.e., Matt. 18.11; Luke 9.56a. In both cases they are embellishments of the Western Text, and the textual evidence against them is overwhelming.

16 It is disputed whether Luke's changes to the Marcan apocalypse are to be attributed to the fall of Jerusalem or not. C.H. Dodd, 'The Fall of Jerusalem and the "Abomination of Desolation"', in *More New Testament Studies*, Manchester 1968, pp. 69–83, argued that this need not be the case, though he in fact dated Luke later than AD 70. Naturally his argument is accepted by J.A.T. Robinson, *Redating the New Testament*, London 1976, in favour of an earlier date for Luke. But, even allowing that Luke's changes do not compel reference to the catastrophe, they still demand explanation in relation to his aims.

17 cf. K. Lake and H.J. Cadbury, *The Beginnings of Christianity*, IV, London 1933, p. 134. Some examples will appear in the next section.

18 cf. Wisd. 5.1; also (in other connections) 2 Kings 10.4; Ps 36.12 (LXX 35.13); 148.6.

19 Acts 6.12, 15 refers to the council as the *sunedrion*, and Luke clearly means this to be taken as the Sanhedrin in view of the mention of the high priest in 7.1. But Hengel, *Acts and the History of Earliest Christianity*, pp. 73f, assumes that the word in Luke's source referred to the council of the Hellenistic synagogues mentioned in 6.9. This seems better than the ultra-scepticism of E. Haenchen, *The Acts of the Apostles*, Oxford 1971, pp. 272f.

20 It is a curious feature of the narrative that no titles of honour are ascribed to Jesus, though 'the righteous one' occurs at the end of Stephen's speech in Acts 7.52 (cf. Luke 23.47), and Stephen's prayers in 7.59f may reflect the Kyrios title.

21 The relevant words in Luke 23.34 are missing from P[75] B Sin[corr] D* W sy[s] sa bo[pt] and other manuscripts, and are therefore suspected of being an interpolation into Luke's text. For the arguments on both sides, cf. Marshall, *Luke*, pp. 867f.

22 So J.A. Fitzmyer and R.J. Dillon, *The Jerome Biblical Commentary*, ed. R.E. Brown, J.A. Fitzmyer, and R.E. Murphy, 2 vols. in 1, London 1968, II, p. 182.

23 The Alexandrian reading is *dienoigmenous* (Sin A B C 1739), but the variant *aneogmenous* (P[74] D E most minuscules) agrees with Luke 3.21; Acts 10.11.

24 C.H. Dodd, *According to the Scriptures*, paperback edn, London 1965, p. 35.

25 cf Haenchen, *Acts*, p. 292, n. 4. For a review of the many interpretations which have been proposed see C.K. Barrett, 'Stephen and the Son of Man', in *Apophoreta* (*Festschrift E. Haenchen*, BZNW 30), 1964, pp. 32–8. The 'advocate' interpretation adopted below accords with the views of T. Preiss, O. Cullmann, and C.F.D. Moule, but is rejected by Barrett himself on the grounds that it is inconsistent with Acts 17.31, where Jesus himself is the judge. But this formal inconsistency should not be pressed in view of Luke's use of both versions of the 'advocate' saying in Luke 9.26; 12.8f.

26 cf. Casey, p. 201. Luke's capacity to write in the style of the Septuagint needs no demonstration, and indeed appears plentifully in Stephen's speech (note especially 7.51).

27 S. K. Lake and H.J. Cadbury, *The Beginnings of Christianity* IV, p. 219.

CHAPTER 9

1 The most recent extended treatment is by F.J. Moloney, *The Johannine Son of Man*, Rome, ²1978. The conclusions reached in the present chapter agree largely with those of Moloney, and differ to some extent from my essay, 'The Son of Man in the Johannine Christology', in *Christ and Spirit in the New Testament*, ed. B. Lindars and S.S. Smalley, Cambridge 1973, pp. 43–60.

2 'The Son of Man' stands awkwardly in apposition to the participial phrase, but thereby a chiastic structure is produced, which emphasizes the contrast between 'no one' and the Son of Man, and so introduces him as the sole revealer. Verse 14 then proceeds to explain the manner in which he makes his revelation. The idea of a descent apparently following ascent in verse 13 caused much trouble to the ancient interpreters, so that many manuscripts have additional words to try to ease the sense ('who is in heaven' or 'who is from heaven').

3 cf. J. Jeremias, 'Characteristics of the *ipsissima vox Jesu*', in *The Prayers of Jesus*, London 1967, pp. 112–15; id., 'Zum nicht-responsorischen Amen', *ZNW* 64 (1973), pp. 122f. As it is confined to the sayings of Jesus it is unlikely to have arisen only in the post-Easter community, as argued by V. Hasler, *Amen: Redaktionsgeschichtliche Untersuchung zur Einführungsformel der Herrenworte 'Wahrlich, ich sage euch'*, Zürich and Stuttgart 1969, pp. 181ff., and by K. Berger, *Die Amen Worte Jesu: eine Untersuchung zum Problem der Legitimation in apokalyptische Rede*, BZNW 39, 1970, pp. 147ff.

4 Thus John 13.16, 20, 38, are all very close to their synoptic parallels. On the other hand careful and deliberate adaptation can be seen in John 3.3, 5; 8.51f; cf. B. Lindars, 'Discourse and Tradition: the Use of the Sayings of Jesus in the Discourses of the Fourth Gospel', *JSNT* 13 (1981), pp. 83–101; id., 'John and the Synoptics: a Test Case', *NTS* 27 (1981), pp. 287–94.

5 Matt. 3.16 stands a little closer to John in some respects: the verb for 'open' (*anoigo*), 'Spirit *of God*', and preposition *epi* ('on him'), for Mark's *eis*. For the interpretation of John 1.51 adopted here, cf. Moloney, pp. 39f.

6 cf. Targum Neofiti at Gen. 28.12; Genesis Rabba 68.18.

7   R. Bultmann (*The Gospel of John*, Oxford 1971, p. 98) has rightly seen that the climax of the section on the first disciples is reached in 1.49, and the section should stop here (he assumes a pre-Johannine source, whereas I would argue for a homily by John himself as the earlier state of this material). The addition of 1.50f relates this section to the larger plan of the Gospel, and is no longer concerned with confessions of faith; cf. B. Lindars, *The Gospel of John*, London 1972, pp. 119f.

8   Contrary to what I have written elsewhere, in which I have assumed that John worked on the basis of the identification of the Son of Man with the Danielic figure; cf., besides the above-mentioned works, B. Lindars, 'The Passion in the Fourth Gospel', *God's Christ and His People (Studies in Honour of N.A. Dahl)*, ed. J. Jervell and W.A. Meeks, Oslo 1977, pp. 71–86. As this article has, through no fault of my own, a number of serious mistakes in the printing, perhaps I may take this opportunity to publish corrections, as follows: p. 73, l. 32 (the language); ib., l. 44 (opens up); ib., l. 46 (blockage); ib., l. 47 (others); p. 75, l. 26f (of the apocalyptic myth); p. 76, l. 32 (probable); ib., l. 34 (conviction); p. 78, l. 1 (on a pole); ib., l. 2 (an excellent type); ib., l. 24 (exaltation); ib., l. 40 (transition); p. 82, l. 22 (of the passion); ib., l. 38 (represents) ib., l. 41 (Spirit's); ib., l. 42 (first concern); p. 83, l. 4 (of moral truth); p. 84, n. 16, l. 10 (onto); p. 85, n. 24, l. 2 (worldly).

9   In Bultmann's presentation the Revealer denotes Jesus as one who embodies the postulated redeemer-myth of early Gnosticism, cf. Introd., W. Schmithals, to Eng. edn of Bultmann, *The Gospel of John*, pp. 7ff.

10 Fot the interpretation of *anothen* in this chapter, cf. B. Lindars, 'John and the Synoptic Gospels: a Test Case' (n. 4 above).

11 The question presupposes the common, but erroneous, view that there was a Son of Man figure in the thought of Judaism apart from the Jesus tradition. For discussion of the issue, cf. R. Schnackenburg, 'Der Menschensohn im Johannesevangelium', *NTS* 11 (1964–5), pp. 123–37 (English version in id., *The Gospel according to St John* I, London 1968, pp. 529–42).

12 The majority text, reading 'the Son of God', is probably influenced by liturgical use in connection with the baptismal confession, but 'the Son of Man' is well supported: P^{66} P^{75} Sin B D W sy^s co (verse 38–39a should perhaps also be considered a liturgical addition, being omitted by P^{75} Sin* W b (l)). As will be seen in what follows, to interpret this verse correctly it is important to free the mind from the whole idea of the confession of faith in the formal sense, and to try to see it strictly in terms of the Johannine theology.

13 The idea is referred to in 2 Baruch 29.8; Mekilta to Exod. 16.25; Ecclesiastes Rabba 1.9, 28. Of course there is no concept of the Son of Man as the giver of this bread.

14 It is important to realize that the offence is not just the sacramentalism of 6.53–58 (C.H. Dodd, *The Interpretation of the Fourth Gospel*, Cambridge 1953, pp. 341f), nor the incarnation as such (Moloney, p. 122), nor even that here is a man who claims to be the revealer of God (Bultmann, *John*, p. 445), but the revelation itself which Jesus brings. It has already been indicated in verse 53 that it is the cross that is the revelatory act. This is the fact which causes offence (cf. 1. Cor. 1.23). This offence cannot be removed by seeing a

fresh act. It can be removed only by grasping the real meaning of the cross itself, i.e., that it is not only a 'lifting up' in the sense of being nailed to a stake (3.14), but also a 'lifting up' in the sense of exaltation to the Father.

15 John has no concept of the ascension as a separate event, as in the Lucan scheme, nor does he make use of the descent-ascent motif of the Hellenistic redeemer myth. He normally thinks of Jesus as coming from God and going to God (by way of the cross), cf. 13.3; 16.28. The metaphors of descent and ascent are, in fact, never fully correlated in the Fourth Gospel. In 1.51 it is the angels who ascend and descend, as in Gen. 28.12, and this denotes the conjunction between heaven and earth which will be achieved in the cross of the Son of Man as the supreme revelatory act. In 3.13 ascent is mentioned first, probably alluding to Enoch and other seers who, according to Jewish tradition, penetrated heaven. By contrast the Son of Man is said to have descended, and nothing is said of ascent apart from the cross. In the discourse on the bread of life descent is a leading motif, referring to the incarnation (the verb *katabaino*, to come down, suits the imagery of the manna miracle, and is actually used in connection with it in Num. 11.9). The descent is to provide the saving revelation, and this is achieved in the cross (verse 53). Again, nothing is said of ascension in the discourse. The concept is used in verse 62, however, so as to maintain the terms of reference established in the discourse (which may originally have been an independent homily by John). It is not stated when this ascent might take place. The only clue is provided by the use of the Son of Man title. This suggests that the ascent belongs to the characteristic function of the Son of Man, and that is the cross.

16 In spite of the absence of the definite articles, it is correct to translate the phrase as if they were present, because the definite articles may properly be omitted from the predicate of a noun-sentence when the predicate *precedes* the copula, cf. C.F.D. Moule, *An Idiom Book of New Testament Greek*, Cambridge ²1959, pp. 115f, referring to E.C. Colwell, 'A Definite Rule for the Use of the Article in the Greek New Testament', *JBL* 52 (1933), pp. 12–21. But because Greek has no indefinite article, it is always possible that the anarthrous phrase is intended to be indefinite rather than definite, hence the difference of opinion about 'Son of God' in Mark 15.39 (cf. ch. 4, n. 25 above); cf. P.B. Harner, 'Qualitative Anarthrous Predicate Nouns: Mark 15.39 and John 1.1', *JBL* 92 (1973), pp. 75–87. As the title of the latter article shows, this order of words is adopted when the noun, or nominal phrase, which forms the predicate is intended to be qualitative, rather than denoting identification. For instance, 8.12, 'I am the light of the world' (*ego eimi to phos tou kosmou*) denotes identification, but 9.5, 'As long as I am in the world, I am the light of the world' (*phos eimi tou kosmos*) is qualitative.

17 This opinion was favoured in my article (see n. 1 above). See Molony, p. 81, for a list of recent scholars who take this view.

18 Casey, pp. 198f, following R. Leivestad, 'Exit the Apocalyptic Son of Man', NTS 18 (1971–2) pp. 243–267, p. 252. Leivestad objects that the second article would normally be retained by John, but the evidence shows variation: it is retained in 1.49; 8.34, 39; 9.5; (10.36); 12.31; 19.21; it is omitted in 5.27; 8.33, 37; (10.36). In 10.36 the majority of MSS include the second article, but

it is omitted by P⁶⁶* Sin D W 28 1424. The evidence for the omission of the first article in such phrases is overwhelming, and this of course applies to cases where the predicate consists of a single noun (cf. 1.1; 3.29; 4.19; 8.42, 54). The criterion with regard to the second noun appears to be the closeness of the two nouns in the genitive relationship. If the genitival phrase forms a conventional unit, it is natural to drop *both* articles, e.g. the seed of Abraham, the Son of God (cf. 19.7).

19 Moloney, pp. 83–6.

20 cf. C.H. Dodd, *Historical Tradition in the Fourth Gospel*, Cambridge 1963.

21 Recent work on the Johannine church includes W.A. Meeks, 'The Man from Heaven in Johannine Sectarianism', *JBL* 91 (1972), pp. 44–72; O. Cullmann, *The Johannine Circle*, London 1976; A.R. Culpepper, *The Johannine School*, Missoula 1975; R.E. Brown, *The Community of the Beloved Disciple*, London 1979.

CHAPTER 10

1 Casey, pp. 99–112.

2 cf. M.A. Knibb, 'The Date of the Parables of Enoch: A Critical Review', *NTS* 25 (1978–9), pp. 345–59.

3 The name Bar Cochba (=Son of the Star) is now known to be a pun on his real name (Simon Bar Cosiba) as a result of the discovery of signed correspondence in connection with his revolt in caves near the Dead Sea. R. Akiba specifically applied the prophecy of the Star of Jacob (Num. 24.17) to him, claiming that he was the Messiah (y Taan. 68d). He also claimed that the plural 'thrones' was used in Dan. 7.9, because there was not only a throne for God but also one for David, i.e., the Messiah (b Hag. 14a; b Sanh. 38b).

4 cf. Casey, pp. 71–98.

5 For this interpretation of Rev. 14.14ff, cf. G.B. Caird, *Revelation*, pp. 189–95; J.P.M. Sweet, *Revelation*, pp. 229f.

6 cf. Rev. 19.11–16, where the imagery is changed again and Christ is represented as a horseman (possibly inspired by the tradition of the angelic horseman, who appeared to Judas Maccabeus before his great victory over Lysias in 164 BC, cf. 2 Macc. 11.6–10; the motif recurs in 2 Macc. 4.25; 10.29f).

7 cf. B.M. Nolan, *The Royal Son of God: The Christology of Matthew 1–2 in the Setting of the Gospel*, Göttingen 1979, p. 200.

8 cf. Rom. 5.12–21; 8.3; Phil. 2.5–11; Heb. 2.5–18.

9 cf. Haenchen, *Acts*, pp. 95–98; Bultmann, *Theology* I, pp. 37–42; H. Conzelmann, *The Theology of St Luke*, London 1960.

10 Close attention to this dominical feature has been given by J. Jeremias, 'Abba', *The Prayers of Jesus*, London 1967, pp. 11–65, cf. id., *Theology* I, pp. 62–8, but the claims made by modern NT scholars on the basis of it are criticized by Vermes, *Jesus the Jew*, pp. 210f.

11 J.D.G. Dunn, *Christology in the Making: An Enquiry into the Origins of the Doctrine of the Incarnation*, London 1980, p. 254.

12 On scribes, Pharisees and Sadducees in the time of Christ, cf. E. Schürer, *History of the Jewish People*, rev. edn, II, pp. 322–414.

13 cf. Vermes, *Jesus the Jew*, pp. 69–82.

14 cf. J. Riches, *Jesus and the Transformation of Judaism*, London 1980.

15 Paul uses a similar argument in 2. Cor. 3.1f.

16 A further item of traditon along the same lines lies behind the composition of John 3.25–30; cf. B. Lindars, 'Two Parables in John', *NTS* 16 (1969–70), pp. 318–29.

17 This story is widely held to be authentic and well preserved. Precisely because the claim of Jesus concerning himself is not specified, it needed no alteration to apply it to the Christian proclamation of him as the Messiah. A rabbinic parallel to the method of argument used in the story is found in connection with R. Akiba (b Sanh. 65b), cf. D. Daube, *The New Testament and Rabbinic Judaism*, pp. 151f.

18 On the problem of defining the offence of blasphemy in NT times, cf. pp. 111f above.

19 For a detailed analysis along these lines, cf. Schulz, *Q*, pp. 204–6.

20 Kingdom and house are likely to be more nearly synonymous than English usage might suggest, as the house here may well be intended to signify a ruling dynasty, which may destroy itself through internal strife. Mark has understood the house to mean household, whereas Luke thinks literally of one house falling on another, which can scarcely be right.

21 R.G. Hamerton-Kelly, 'A Note on Matthew xii.28 par. Luke xi.20', *NTS* II (1964–5), pp. 167ff, has shown that the 'finger' (or usually 'hand') of God and the Spirit of God are interchangeable in biblical contexts expressing the direct action of God. There is thus no difference of meaning, and the only problem is to decide which word Jesus actually used. Luke's 'finger' is generally taken to be more likely, because it is more vivid and goes against Luke's preference for the Spirit. But Luke may have been influenced by the similarity of the situation to Exod. 8.19 (MT 8.15). Jesus' claim to work by the Spirit is attested by the 'blasphemy' saying itself, and so may well be original here.

22 Matthew follows Mark closely at this point, but Luke 11.21f is a more elaborate version, possibly influenced by the diction of Isa. 53.12. If so, it must be due to allegorizing the simpler parable in relation to Christology, cf. Lindars, *New Testament Apologetic*, pp. 84f; Marshall, *Luke*, pp. 476f; Jeremias, *Theology* I, pp. 72ff.

23 Bultmann, *Theology* I, p. 33.

Bibliography

Abbott, E.A., *The Son of Man*, Cambridge 1910.

Aland, K., *Synopsis Quattuor Evangeliorum*, Stuttgart 1964.

Alsup, J., *The Post-Resurrection Appearance Stories of the Gospel-Tradition*, Stuttgart and London 1975.

Barrett, C.K., *The Holy Spirit and the Gospel Tradition*, London 1947.

—*The First Epistle to the Corinthians* (Black's New Testament Commentaries), London 1968.

—'The Background of Mark 10.45' in *New Testament Essays: Studies in Memory of T.W. Manson*, ed. A.J.B. Higgins, Manchester 1959, pp. 1–18.

—'Stephen and the Son of Man' in *Apophoreta (Festschrift E. Haenchen)*, BZNW 30, 1964, pp. 32–8.

—'Mark 10.45: a Ransom for Many', *New Testament Essays*, London 1972, pp. 20–6.

—'I am not ashamed of the Gospel', *New Testament Essays*, 1972, pp. 116–43.

Barthélemy, D., *Les devanciers d'Aquile* (Supplements to Vetus Testamentum X), Leiden 1963.

Beasley-Murray, G.R., *A Commentary on Mark Thirteen*, London 1957.

Bengel, J.A., *Gnomon of the New Testament*, 5 vols, ET, A.R. Fausset, Edinburgh 1877.

Berger, K., *Die Amen-Worte Jesu: Eine Untersuchung zum Problem der Legitimation in Apokalyptische Rede*, BZNW 39, 1970.

Billerbeck, P., *Kommentar zum neuen Testament aus Talmud und Midrasch* by H.L. Strack and P. Billerbeck, 7 vols., Munich [3]1961.

Birdsall, J.N., 'Who is this Son of Man?' *EQ* 42 (1970), pp. 7–17.

Black, M., *An Aramaic Approach to the Gospels and Acts*, Oxford [3]1967.

—'The Son of Man Problem in Recent Research and Debate', *BJRL* 45 (1962–3), pp. 305–18.

—'The "Son of Man" Passion Sayings in the Gospel Tradition', *ZNW* 60 (1969), pp. 1–18.

—'The "Parables" of Enoch (1 Enoch 37–71) and the "Son of Man" ', *ExpT* 78 (1976–7), pp. 5–8.

—'Jesus and the Son of Man', *JSNT* 1 (1978), pp. 4–18.

Blass, F., and Debrunner, A., *A Greek Grammar of the New Testament and Other Early Christian Literature*, ET and ed., R.W. Funk, Chicago and London 1961.

Bloch, J., 'The Ezra-Apocalypse, was it written in Hebrew, Greek or Aramaic?' *JQR* 48 (1957–8), pp. 279–84.

Bloch, R., 'Quelques Aspects de la Figure de Moïse dans la Tradition rabbinique', M. Cazelles *et al.*, *Moïse: L'Homme de l'Alliance*. Paris 1955, pp. 93–167.

Bonnard, P., *L'Évangile selon Saint Matthieu*, Neuchâtel 1963.

Bornkamm, G., *Jesus of Nazareth*, ET, I. and F. McLuskey with J.M. Robinson, London 1973.

Borsch, F.H., *The Son of Man in Myth and History*, London 1967.

—*The Christian and Gnostic Son of Man* (SBT second series 14), London 1970.

—'Mark xiv. 62 and 1 Enoch lxii. 5', *NTS* 14 (1967–8), pp. 565–7.

Bousset, W., *Die Religion des Judentums im neutestamentlichen Zeitalter*, Berlin 1903.

—*Hauptprobleme der Gnosis*, Göttingen 1907.

—*Kyrios Christos*, Göttingen, 1913, ²1921 (ET, New York 1970).

Bowker, J., 'The Son of Man', *JTS* (N.S.) 28 (1977), pp. 19–48.

Bowman, J.W., 'The Background of the Term Son of Man', *ExpT* 59, 1947–8, pp. 283–8.

Box, G.H., '4 Ezra' in *The Apocrypha and Pseudepigrapha of the Old Testament* II, ed. R.H. Charles, Oxford 1913, pp. 542–624.

Brown, J.P., 'The Son of Man: "This Fellow" ', *Bib* 58 (1977), pp. 361–87.

Brown, R.E., *The Community of the Beloved Disciple*, London 1979.

Büchsel, F., '*Lutron*', *TDNT* IV, pp. 341–9.

Bultmann, R., *The History of the Synoptic Tradition*, ET, J. Marsh, Oxford ²1968.

—*Theology of the New Testament*, 2 vols., ET, K. Grobel, London 1976.

—*The Gospel of John*, ET, G.R. Beasley-Murray *et al.*, Oxford 1971.

Caird, G.B., *The Revelation of St John the Divine* (Black's New Testament Commentaries), London 1966.

Campbell, J.Y., 'The Origin and Meaning of the Term Son of Man', *Three New Testament Studies*, Leiden 1965, pp. 29–40.

Casey, Maurice (P.M.), *Son of Man: the Interpretation and Influence of Daniel 7*, London 1979.

—'The Use of the Term "son of man" in the Similitudes of Enoch', *JSJ* 7 (1976), pp. 11–29.

—'The Corporate Interpretation of "one like a son of man" at the Time of Jesus', *NT* 18 (1976), pp. 167–80.

—'The Son of Man Problem', *ZNW* 67 (1976), pp. 147–54.

Catchpole, D.R., 'The Answer of Jesus to Caiaphas (Matt. xxvi. 64)', *NTS* 17 (1970–1), pp. 213–26.

—'The Son of Man's Search for Faith (Luke xviii.8b)', *NT* 19 (1977), pp. 81–104.

Charles, R.H., *The Book of Enoch*, Oxford ²1912.

Chilton, B.D., *God in Strength: Jesus' Announcement of the Kingdom*, Freistadt 1979.

Collins, J.J., 'The Son of Man and the Saints of the Most High in the Book of Daniel', *JBL* 93 (1974), pp. 50–66.

Colpe, C., '*Ho huios tou anthropou*', *TDNT* VIII, pp. 400–77.

Colwell, E.C., 'A Definite Rule for the Use of the Article in the Greek New Testament', *JBL* 52 (1933), pp. 12–21.

Conzelmann, H., *The Theology of St Luke*, ET, G. Buswell, London 1960.

—*An Outline of the Theology of the New Testament*, ET, J. Bowden, London 1969.

—'Gegenwart und Zukunft in der synoptischen Tradition', *ZThK* 54 (1957), pp. 277–96.

—Cortès, J.B., and Gatti, F.M., 'The Son of Man or the Son of Adam', *Bib* 48 (1968), pp. 457–502.

Cranfield, C.E.B., *The Gospel according to St Mark*, rev. edn, Cambridge 1977.

—*The Epistle to the Romans* (ICC), 2 vols., Edinburgh 1975–9.

Cullmann, O., *The Christology of the New Testament*, ET, S.C. Guthrie and C.A.M. Hall, London ²1963.

—*The Johannine Circle*, ET, J. Bowden, London 1976.

Culpepper, A.R., *The Johannine School*, Missoula 1975.

Dalman, G., *The Words of Jesus*, ET, D.M. Kay, Edinburgh 1902.

Daube, D., *The New Testament and Rabbinic Judaism*, London 1956.

Delling, G., '*Hemera*', *TDNT* II, pp. 943–53.

Dibelius, M., *From Tradition to Gospel*, ET, B. Lee Woolf, London 1934.

Dodd, C.H., *The Parables of the Kingdom*, rev. edn, London 1961.

—*According to the Scriptures*, London 1965.

—*The Interpretation of the Fourth Gospel*, Cambridge 1953.

—*Historical Tradition in the Fourth Gospel*, Cambridge 1963.

—'The Fall of Jerusalem and the "Abomination of Desolation" ', *More New Testament Studies*, Manchester 1968, pp. 69–83.

Drower, E.S., *The Secret of Adam*, Oxford 1960.

Drury, J., *Tradition and Design in Luke's Gospel*, London 1976.

Duncan, G.S., *Jesus, Son of Man*, London 1947.

Dunn, J.D.G., *Christology in the Making*, London 1980.

Dupont, J., 'Le Logion des douze trônes', *Bib* 45 (1964), pp. 355–92.

Edwards, R.A., *The Sign of Jonah in the Theology of the Evangelists & Q* (SBT second series 18), London 1971.

—'The Eschatological Correlative as a *Gattung* in the New Testament', *ZNW* 60 (1969), pp. 9–20.

Eissfeldt, O. *The Old Testament: An Introduction*, ET, P.R. Ackroyd, Oxford 1965.

Emerton, J.A., 'The Origin of the Son of Man Imagery', *JTS* (n.s.) 9 (1958), pp. 225–42.

Farmer, W.R., *The Synoptic Problem*, London and New York 1964.

Field, F., *Notes on the Translation of the New Testament*, Cambridge 1899.

Fitzmyer, J.A., 'The Contribution of Qumran Aramaic to the Study of the New Testament', *NTS* 20 (1973–4), pp. 382–407.

—'Methodology in the Study of the Aramaic Substratum of Jesus' Sayings in the New Testament', *Jésus aux origines de la christologie* (Bibliotheca Ephemeridum Theologicarum Lovanensium XL), ed. J. Dupont, Gembloux 1975, pp. 73–102.

—'The New Testament Title "Son of Man" Philogically Considered', *A Wandering Aramean: Collected Aramaic Essays*, Missoula 1979, pp. 143–60.

—'Another View of the "Son of Man" Debate', *JSNT* 4 (1979), pp. 56–68.

Fitzmyer, J.A., and Dillon, R.J., 'Acts of the Apostles', *The Jerome Biblical Commentary*, ed. R.E. Brown, J.A. Fitzmyer and R.E. Murphy, 2 vols, in I, London 1968, II, pp. 165–214.

Foerster, W., *Gnosis*, 2 vols., Oxford 1972.

Ford, J.M. ' "The Son of Man"—a Euphemism?', *JBL* 87 (1968), pp. 257–66.

Formesyn, R.E.C., 'Was there a pronominal connection for the "bar nasha" self-designation?' *NT* 8 (1966), pp. 1–35.

Freed, E.D., 'The Son of Man in the Fourth Gospel', *JBL* 86 (1967), pp. 402–9.

Fuller, R.H., *The Foundations of New Testament Christology*, London 1965.

—*The Formation of the Resurrection Narratives*, London 1972.

Gärtner, B., *The Theology of the Gospel of Thomas*, ET, E.J. Sharpe, London 1961.

Gelston, A., 'A Sidelight on the "Son of Man" ', *SJT* 22 (1969), pp. 189–96.

Glasson, T.F., *The Second Advent: The Origin of the New Testament Doctrine*, London 1945.

—'The Reply to Caiaphas (Mark xiv. 62)', *NTS* 7 (1960–1), pp. 88–93.

—'The Ensign of the Son of Man (Matt. xxiv. 30), *JTS* (n.s.) 15 (1964), pp. 299–300.

Goppelt, L., 'Zum Problem des Menschensohns: das Verhältnis von Leidens- und Parusieankündigung' in *Mensch und Menschensohn* (*Festschrift K. Witte*), ed. H. Sierig, Hamburg 1963, pp. 20–32.

Goulder, M.D., *The Evangelists' Calendar*, London 1978.

Gourgues, M., *À la Droite de Dieu: résurrection de Jésus et actualisation du Psaume 110:1 dans le Nouveau Testament* (Études bibliques), Paris 1978.

Grant, R.M., and Freedman, D.N., *The Secret Sayings of Jesus*, London 1960.

Green, H.B., *The Gospel according to Matthew* (The New Clarendon Bible) Oxford 1975.

Gry, L., *Les dires prophétiques d'Esdras (IVᵉ d'Esdras)*, 2 vols., Paris 1938.

Gundry, R.H., *The Use of the Old Testament in St Matthew's Gospel* (Supplements to *NT* XVIII), Leiden 1967.

Haenchen, E., *The Acts of the Apostles*, ET, B. Noble and G. Shinn, Oxford 1971.

Hahn, F., *The Titles of Jesus in Christology*, ET, H. Knight and G. Ogg, London 1969.

Hamerton-Kelly, R.G., *Pre-existence, Wisdom, and the Son of Man* (SNTSMS 21), London 1973.

Harner, P.B., 'Qualitative Anarthrous Predicate Nouns: Mark 15.39 and John 1.1', *JBL* 92 (1973), pp. 75–87.

Harvey, A.E., *Jesus on Trial*, London 1976.

Hasler, V., *Amen: Redaktiongeschichtliche Untersuchung zur Einführungs-formel der Herrenworte 'Wahrlich, ich sage euch'*, Zürich and Stuttgart 1969.

Hengel, M., *The Son of God*, ET, J. Bowden, London 1976.

—*Acts and the History of Earliest Christianity*, ET, J. Bowden, London 1979.

—*The Atonement*, ET, J. Bowden, London 1981.

—'Zwischen Jesus und Paulus', *ZThK* 72 (1975), pp. 151–206.

Higgins, A.J.B., *Jesus and the Son of Man*, London 1964.

—*The Son of Man in the Teaching of Jesus* (SNTSMS 39), Cambridge 1980.

—'Son of Man—*Forschung* since "The Teaching of Jesus" ', *New Testament Essays: Studies in memory of T.W. Manson*, ed. A.J.B. Higgins, Manchester 1959, pp. 119–35.

—'The Sign of the Son of Man (Matt. xxiv.30)', *NTS* 9 (1962–3), pp. 380–2.

—'Is the Son of Man Problem Insoluble?' in *Neotestamentica et Semitica: Studies in honour of M. Black*, ed. E.E. Ellis and M. Wilcox, Edinburgh 1969, pp. 70–87.

—' "Menschensohn" oder "ich" in Q: Lk 12, 8–9/Mt 10, 32–33?' in *Jesus und der Menschensohn (Festschrift A. Vögtle)*, ed. R. Pesch and R. Schnackenburg with O. Kaiser, Freiburg i. Br. 1975, pp. 117–23.

Hill, D., *The Gospel of Matthew* (The New Century Bible), London 1972.

Hindley, J.C. 'Towards a Date for the Similitudes of Enoch: an Historical Approach', *NTS* 14 (1967–8), pp. 551–65.

Hinnells, J.R., 'Zoroastrian Saviour Imagery and its Influence on the New Testament', *Numen* 16 (1969), pp. 161–85.

—'Zoroastrian Influence on the Judaeo-Christian Tradition', *Journal of the Cama Oriental Institute* (1976), pp. 1–23.

Hooker, M.D., *Jesus and the Servant*, London 1959.

—*The Son of Man in Mark*, London 1967.

—'Is the Son of Man problem really insoluble?' *Text and Interpretation: Studies presented to M. Black*, ed. E. Best & R.McL. Wilson, Cambridge 1979, pp. 155–68.

Horton, F.L., *The Melchizedek Tradition* (SNTSMS 30), Cambridge 1976.

Jastrow, M., *A Dictionary of the Targumim, the Talmud Babli and the Yerushalmi, and the Midrashic Literature*, 2 vols. in 1, repr. New York 1975.

Jeremias, J., *The Parables of Jesus*, ET, S.H. Hooke, rev. edn, London 1963.

—*The Prayers of Jesus* (SBT second series 6), London 1967.

—*New Testament Theology* I, ET, J. Bowden, London 1971.

—'*Ionas*', *TDNT* III, pp. 406–10.

—'Die älteste Schichte der Menschensohn-Logien', *ZNW* 58 (1967), pp. 159–72.

—'Zum nicht-responsorischen Amen' *ZNW* 64, 1973, pp. 122–3.

Jongeling, B. *et al.*, *Aramaic Texts from Qumran* I, Leiden 1976.

Kaiser, O., *Introduction to the Old Testament*, ET, J. Sturdy, Oxford 1975.

Käsemann, E., 'Sentences of Holy Law in the New Testament', *New Testament Questions of Today*, ET J.W. Montague, London 1969, pp. 66–81.

Kearns, R., *Vorfragen zur Christologie*, I and II, Tübingen 1978–80.

Kermode, F., *The Genesis of Secrecy*, Cambridge (Mass.) and London 1979.

Kilpatrick, G.D., 'Acts vii.56: Son of Man?' *ThZ* 21 (1965), p. 209.

—'Again Acts vii.56: Son of Man?' *ThZ* 34 (1978), p. 232.

Kinniburgh, E., 'The Johannine Son of Man', *Studia Evangelica* IV (TU 102), ed. F.L. Cross, Berlin 1968, pp. 64–71.

Klausner, J., *Jesus of Nazareth*, London 1947.

Knibb, M.A., *The Ethiopic Book of Enoch*, 2 vols., Oxford, 1978.

—'The Date of the Parables of Enoch: A Critical Review', *NTS* 25 (1978–9), pp. 345–59.

Knox, J., *The Death of Christ*, London 1959.

Knox, W.L., *The Sources of the Synoptic Gospels*, 2 vols., Cambridge 1953–7.

Kraeling, C.H., *Anthropos and Son of Man: A Study in the Religious Syncretism of the Hellenistic Orient*, New York 1927.

Kümmel, W.G., *Promise and Fulfilment*, ET, D.M. Barton (SBT 23), London ²1961.

—*The New Testament: The History of the Investigation of its Problems*, ET, S.M. Gilmour and H.C. Kee, London 1973.

—*The Theology of the New Testament*, ET, J.E. Steely, London 1974.

Lake, K., and Cadbury, H.J., *The Beginnings of Christianity* IV, London 1933.

Lane, W.L., *Commentary on the Gospel of Mark* (The New London Commentary on the New Testament), London 1974.

Le Déaut, R., *La nuit pascale* (Analecta Biblica 22), Rome 1963.

Leivestad, R., 'Der apokalyptische Menschensohn ein theologisches Phantom', *ASTI* 6, 1968, pp. 49–105.

—'Exit the Apocalyptic Son of Man', *NTS* 18 (1971–2), pp. 243–67.

Lietzmann, H., *Der Menschensohn: ein Beitrag zur neutestamentlichen Theologie*, Freiburg i. Br. and Leipzig 1896.

Lightfoot, R.H., *History and Interpretation in the Gospels*, London 1935.

Lindars, B., *New Testament Apologetic*, London 1961.

—*The Gospel of John* (The New Century Bible), London 1972.

—'Two Parables in John', *NTS* 16 (1969–70), pp. 318–29.

—'The Son of Man in the Johannine Christology' in *Christ and Spirit in the New Testament: Studies in Honour of C.F.D. Moule*, ed. B. Lindars and S.S. Smalley, Cambridge 1973, pp. 43–60.

—'The Apocalyptic Myth and the Death of Christ', *BJRL* 57 (1974–5), pp. 366–87.

—Re-enter the Apocalyptic Son of Man', *NTS* 22 (1975–6), pp. 52–72.

—'The Passion in the Fourth Gospel' in *God's Christ and His People: Studies in Honour of N.A. Dahl*, ed. J. Jervell and W.A. Meeks, Oslo 1977, pp. 71–86.

—'Jesus as Advocate: a Contribution to the Christology Debate', *BJRL* 62 (1979–80), pp. 476–97.

—'John and the Synoptics: A Test Case', *NTS* 27 (1981), pp. 287–94.

—'Discourse and Tradition: The Use of the Sayings of Jesus in the Discourses of the Fourth Gospel', *JSNT* 13 (1981), pp. 83–101.

—'The New Look on the Son of Man', *BJRL* 63 (1980–1), pp. 437–62.

—'The Persecution of Christians in John 15:18—16:4a' in *Suffering and Martyrdom in the New Testament: Studies presented to G.M. Styler*, ed. W. Horbury and B. McNeil, Cambridge 1981, pp. 48–69.

Linnemann, E., *Parables of Jesus*, ET, J. Sturdy, London 1966.

Lohse, E., 'Der Menschensohn in der Johannesapocalypse' in *Jesus und der Menschensohn (Festschrift A. Vögtle)*, ed. R. Pesch and R. Schnackenburg with O. Kaiser, Freiburg i. Br., 1975, pp. 415–20.

Lövestamm, E., *Spiritus Blasphemia: eine Studie zu Mk 3,28 f par Mt 12,31 f, Lk 12,10*, Lund 1968.

Lührmann, D., *Die Redaktion der Logienquelle* (WMANT 33), Neu-kirchen 1969.

McArthur, H.K., ' "On the Third Day" ', *NTS* 18 (1971–2), pp. 81–6.

Maddox, R., 'The Function of the Son of Man according to the Synoptic Gospels', *NTS* 15 (1968–9), pp. 45–74.

—'The Function of the Son of Man in the Gospel of John' in *Reconciliation and Hope: New Testament Essays on Atonement and Eschatology presented to L.L. Morris*, ed. R. Banks, Exeter 1974, pp. 186–204.

Manson, T.W., *The Sayings of Jesus*, London 1949.

—'The Son of Man in Daniel, Enoch and the Gospels', *Studies in the Gospels and Epistles* (T.W. Manson, ed. M. Black), Manchester 1962, pp. 123–45.

Marlow, R., 'The Son of Man in Recent Journal Literature', *CBQ* 28 (1966), pp. 20–30.

Marshall, I.H., *The Origins of New Testament Christology*, Downers Grove (Illinois) and Leicester 1977.

—*The Gospel of Luke* (The New International Greek Testament Commentary), Exeter 1978.

—'The Synoptic Son of Man Sayings in Recent Discussion', *NTS* 12 (1965–6), p. 327–51.

—'The Son of Man in Contemporary Debate', *EQ* 42 (1970), pp. 67–87.

Mearns, C.L., 'Dating the Similitudes of Enoch', *NTS* 25 (1978–9), pp. 360–9.

Meeks, W.A., 'The Man from Heaven in Johannine Sectarianism', *JBL* 91 (1972), pp. 44–72.

Metzger, B.M., *A Textual Commentary on the Greek New Testament*, London 1971.

—*The Early Versions of the New Testament*, Oxford 1977.

—'A Suggestion concerning the Meaning of I Cor. xv.4b', *JTS* (n.s.). 8, 1957, pp. 118–23.

Michaelis, W., '*Paschein*', *TDNT* V, pp. 912–19.

Michel, O., 'Der Menschensohn', *ThZ* 27, 1971, pp. 81–104.

Milik, J.T., *The Books of Enoch: Aramaic Fragments of Qumrân Cave 4*, edited with the collaboration of M. Black, Oxford 1976.

—'Problèmes de la littérature Hénochique à la lumière des fragments araméens de Qumrân', *HTR* 64 (1971), pp. 333–78.

Milling, D.H., *The Origin and Character of the New Testament Doxology*, unpublished Ph.D. dissertation, Cambridge 1972.

Moloney, F.J., *The Johannine Son of Man*, Rome ²1978.

—'The Re-interpretation of Psalm viii and the Son of Man Debate', *NTS* 27 (1980–1), pp. 656–72.

Moule, C.F.D., *An Idiom Book of New Testament Greek*, Cambridge ²1959.

—*The Origin of Christology*, Cambridge 1977.

—'From Defendant to Judge—and Deliverer', *BSNTS* 3 (1952), pp. 40–53.

—'Neglected Features in the Problem of "The Son of Man" ' in *Neues Testament und Kirche (Festschrift R. Schnackenburg)*, ed. J. Gnilka, Freiburg i. Br. 1974, pp. 413–28.

Mowinckel, S., *He That Cometh*, ET, G.W. Anderson, Oxford 1956.

Nineham, D.E., *The Gospel of Mark* (Pelican Commentaries), rev. edn, London 1968.

Nolan, B.M., *The Royal Son of God: The Christology of Matthew 1–2 in the Setting of the Gospel* (Orbis Biblicus et Orientalis 23), Göttingen 1979.

Orchard, B., and Longstaff, T.R.W. (eds.), *J.J. Griesbach: Synoptic and Text-Critical Studies 1776–1976* (SNTSMS 34), Cambridge 1978.

Osburn, C.D., 'The Christological Use of 1 Enoch i.9 in Jude 14, 15', *NTS* 23 (1976–7), pp. 334–41.

Otto, R., *The Kingdom of God and the Son of Man*, ET, F.V. Filson and B. Lee Woolf, London 1938.

Parker, P., 'The Meaning of "Son of Man" ', *JBL* 60 (1941), pp. 151–7.

Perrin, N., *Rediscovering the Teaching of Jesus*, London 1967.

—*A Modern Pilgrimage in New Testament Christology*, Philadelphia 1974.

—*Jesus and the Language of the Kingdom*, London 1976.

—'Mark xiv.62: The End Product of a Christian Pesher Tradition?' NTS 12, 1965–6, pp. 150–5.

Pesch, R., *Das Markusevangelium* (Herders Theologischer Kommentar zum Neuen Testament), 2 vols., Freiburg i. Br. 1977.

Pfeiffer, R.H., *History of New Testament Times with an Introduction to the Apocrypha*, London 1949.

Preiss, T., *Life in Christ*, ET, by H. Knight (SBT 13), London 1954.

Pryke, E.J., *Redactional Style in the Marcan Gospel* (SNTSMS 33), Cambridge 1978.

Rad, G. von, *Old Testament Theology*, 2 vols., ET, D.M.G. Stalker, Edinburgh 1962–5.

Rehkopf, F., *Die lukanische Sonderquelle*, Tübingen 1959.

Reitzenstein, R., *Die hellenistischen Mysterienreligionen*, Leipzig and Berlin 1910, [3]1927.

—*Das iranische Erlösungmysterium: Religiongeschichtliche Untersuchungen*, Heidelberg 1921.

Rengstorf, K.H., '*Semeion*', *TDNT* VII, pp. 200–61.

Riches, J., *Jesus and the Transformation of Judaism*, London 1980.

Robertson, A., and Plummer, A., *A Critical and Exegetical Commentary on the First Epistle of St. Paul to the Corinthians* (ICC), Edinburgh [2]1914.

Robinson, J.A.T., *Jesus and his Coming*, London 1957.

—*Redating the New Testament*, London 1976.

Ruckstuhl, E., 'Die johanneische Menschensohnforschung 1957–1969' in *Theologische Berichte* I, ed. J. Pfammatter and F. Furger, Zürich 1972.

Russell, D.S., *The Method and Message of Jewish Apocalyptic*, London 1964.

Schippers, R., 'The Son of Man in Mt. xii.32 = Lk. xii.10, compared with

Mk. iii.28', *Studia Evangelica* IV (TU 102), ed. F.L. Cross, Berlin 1968, pp. 231–5.

Schmidt, N., 'The Son of Man in the Book of Daniel', *JBL* 19 (1900), pp. 20–8.

Schnackenburg, R., *The Gospel according to St John* I, London 1968.

—'Der Menschensohn im Johannesevangelium', *NTS* 11 (1964–5), pp. 123–7.

—'Der eschatologische Abschnitt Lk 17, 20–37', *Mélanges bibliques en hommage B. Rigaux*, ed. A. Descamps and A. de Halleux, Gembloux 1970, pp. 213–34.

Schneider, G., *Verleugnung, Verspottung und Verhör Jesus nach Lukas 22, 54–71*, Munich 1969.

Schniewind, J., *Das Evangelium nach Matthäus*, Göttingen 1956.

Schrage, W., *Das Verhältnis des Thomas-evangelium zur synoptischen Tradition und zu den koptischen Evangelienübersetzungen* (BZNW 29), Berlin 1964.

Schulz, S., *Die Stunde der Botschaft: Einführung in der Theologie der vier Evangelisten*, Hamburg 1967.

—*Q—Die Spruchquelle der Evangelisten*, Zürich 1972.

Schürer, E., *The History of the Jewish People in the Age of Jesus Christ* II, rev. edn. G. Vermes, F. Millar and M. Black, Edinburgh 1979.

Schürmann, H., 'Zur Traditions- und Redaktionsgeschichte von Mt 10. 23', *BZ* (N.F.) 3 (1959), pp. 82–8 (= *Traditionsgeschichtliche Untersuchungen zu den synoptischen Evangelien*, Dusseldorf 1968, pp. 150–6).

Schweizer, E., 'Der Menschensohn', *ZNW* 50 (1959), pp. 185–209 (= *Neotestamentica*, Zürich 1963, pp. 56–84).

—'The Son of Man', *JBL* 79 (1960), pp. 119–29.

—'The Son of Man Again', *NTS* 9 (1962–3), pp. 256–61 (= *Neotestamentica*, pp. 85–92).

Seitz, O.J.F., 'The Future Coming of the Son of Man: Three Midrashic Formulations in the Gospel of Mark', *Studia Evangelica* VI (TU 112), ed. E.A. Livingstone, Berlin 1973, pp. 478–94.

Sharman, H.B., *Son of Man and Kingdom of God*, New York 1943.

Sjöberg, E., *Der Menschensohn im Äthiopischen Henochbuch*, Lund 1946.

—*Der verborgene Menschensohn in den Evangelien*, Lund 1955.

Smalley, S.S., 'The Johannine Son of Man sayings', *NTS* 15 (1968–9), pp. 278–301.

Stanton, G.N., 'On the christology of Q', *Christ and Spirit in the New Testament: Studies in Honour of C.F.D. Moule*, ed. B. Lindars and S.S. Smalley, Cambridge 1973, pp. 27–42.

Stevenson, W.B., *Grammar of Jewish Palestinian Aramaic*, Oxford 1924.

Stoldt, H.H., *Geschichte und Kritik der Markushypothese*, Göttingen 1977.

Strack, H.L., see Billerbeck, P.

Streeter, B.H., *The Primitive Church*, London 1929.

Svedlund, G., *Aramaic Portions of the Pesiqta de Rab Kahana*, Uppsala 1974.

Sweet, J.P.M., *Revelation* (SCM Pelican Commentaries), London 1979.

Talbert, C.H., and McKnight, E.V., 'Can the Griesbach Hypothesis be Falsified?', *JBL* 91 (1972), pp. 338–68.

Taylor, V., *The Gospel according to St Mark*, London ^{2}1966.

Teeple, H.M., 'The Origin of the Son of Man Christology', *JBL* 84 (1965), pp. 213–50.

Tödt, H.E., *The Son of Man in the Synoptic Tradition*, ET, D.M. Barton, London 1965.

Tuckett, C.M., *The Revival of the Griesbach Hypothesis* (SNTSMS 44), Cambridge 1982.

—'The Argument from Order and the Synoptic Problem', *ThZ* 36 (1980), pp. 338–54.

Vaux, R. de, *Ancient Israel: Its Life and Institutions*, ET, J. McHugh, London, 1961.

Vermes, G. *Scripture and Tradition in Judaism*, Leiden 1961.

—*Jesus the Jew*, London 1973.

—*The Dead Sea Scrolls in English*, Harmondsworth ^{2}1975.

—*The Dead Sea Scrolls: Qumran in Perspective*, London 1977.

—'The Use of *bar nash/bar nasha* in Jewish Aramaic', M. Black, *An Aramaic Approach to the Gospels and Acts*, Oxford ^{3}1967, pp. 310–28 (=*Post-Biblical Jewish Studies*, Leiden 1975, pp. 147–65).

—' "The Son of Man" Debate', *JSNT* 1 (1978), pp. 19–32.

—'The Present State of the "Son of Man" Debate', *JJS* 29 (1978) pp. 123–34.

Vielhauer, P., 'Gottesreich und Menschensohn in der Verkündigung Jesu', *Aufsätze zum Neuen Testament*, Munich 1965, pp. 55–91.

—'Jesus und der Menschensohn: zur Diskussion mit Heinz Eduard Tödt und Eduard Schweizer', *Aufsätze*, pp. 92–140.

Violet, B., *Die Apokalypsen des Esra und des Baruch*, Leipzig 1924.

Vögtle, A., 'Die christologische und ekklesiologische Anliegen von Mt. 28, 18–20', *Studia Evangelica* II (TU 87), ed. F.L. Cross, Berlin 1964, pp. 266–94.

—'Der Spruch vom Jonaszeichen', *Das Evangelium und die Evangelien*, Düsseldorf 1971, pp. 103–36.

Walker, W.O., 'The Origin of the Son of Man Concept as Applied to Jesus', *JBL* 91 (1972), pp. 482–90.

Wellhausen, J., *Das Evangelium Marci*, Berlin 1903.

—*Das Evangelium Lucae*, Berlin 1904.

—*Einleitung in die drei ersten Evangelien*, Berlin ²1911.

—'Zur apokalyptischen Literatur', *Skizzen und Vorarbeiten* VI, Berlin 1899, pp. 215–49.

Widengren, G., *Mani and Manichaeism*, London 1965.

Wilckens, U., 'Christus, der "Letzte Adam", und der Menschensohn', in *Jesus und der Menschensohn (Festschrift A. Vögtle)*, ed. R. Pesch and R. Schnackenberg with O. Kaiser, Freiburg i. Br. 1975, pp. 387–403.

Wilson, R. McL., *Studies in the Gospel of Thomas*, London, 1960.

Woude, A.S. van der, 'Melchisedek als himmlische Erlösergestalt in den neugefundenen eschatologischen Midraschim aus Qumran Höhle XI, *OS* 14 (1965), pp. 354–73.

Woude, A.S. van der, and Jonge, M. de, '11Q Melchizedek and the New Testament', *NTS* 12 (1965–6), pp. 301–26.

Wrede, W., *Das Messiasgeheimnis in den Evangelien: zugleich ein Beitrag zum Verständnis des Markusevangeliums*, Göttingen 1901.

Zimmerli, W., *A Commentary on the Book of the Prophet Ezekiel 1–24* (Hermeneia), ET, R.E. Clements, Philadelphia 1979.

Index of Ancient Sources

OLD TESTAMENT

Genesis
1–2 4
1.27 6
5.21–8 13
5.24 12
28.12 148, 218, 220

Exodus
8.19 222
32.31f 207

Leviticus
24.28 103

Numbers
11.9 220
21.8 146
21.8f 146
21.9 146
24.17 221
28.9f 103

Deuteronomy
16.3 210

Judges
4.21 19

1 Samuel
21.1–6 103

2 Kings
10.4 217

Ezra
8.32f 205

Job
2.9 198

Psalms
4.3 195
8.4 8, 127, 153, 193
8.6 127, 193
10.4 195
11.2 195
11.9 195
13.2 195

20.11 195
30.20 195
32.13 195
35.8 195
36.12 217
44.3 195
62.12 118, 202
69.9 72
110.1 95, 110, 111, 114, 127, 141, 193, 210
118.22 64, 65
118.26 120
148.6 217

Proverbs
8.32 198
24.12 118, 202

Isaiah
6.1 142
8.14 213
11.12 128
27.13 109
40.9f 119
52.3 207
52.13 69, 146, 147
52.13—53.12 69
53 64, 67, 78, 82, 83, 84, 146, 184, 185, 186, 207, 208
53.3 65
53.5 82, 208
53.6 208
53.7 208
53.10 78, 83
53.12 81, 83, 84, 186, 208, 222
56.7 72
65.17 214
66.22 214

Jeremiah
26.1–11 112

Daniel
2.27 201
2.34 205
2.38 195
2.45 205
3.25 17
4 45
4.4 201
5.7 201
5.11 201
5.21 195
7 3, 4, 5, 6, 7, 10, 12, 14, 15, 27, 158, 160, 170, 193
7.2f 193
7.9 126, 212, 221
7.9f 202
7.9–14 4, 158, 159, 166
7.10 202
7.13 2, 3, 4, 7, 8, 10, 15, 17, 25, 26, 29, 50, 52, 66, 102, 109, 110, 128, 154, 163, 165, 169, 194, 195, 197, 210, 212
7.13f 1, 3, 9, 10, 11, 12, 15, 16, 57, 86, 94, 95, 97, 98, 99, 107, 108, 109, 110, 113, 114, 118, 127, 130, 139, 149, 154, 159, 182, 193
7.14 120, 154, 163, 212
8.15 195
8.17 192
12.2 154

Hosea
6.2 44, 66, 72, 201, 204
6.6 103, 200

Joel
3.12f 159

Jonah
1.17 44, 201
3.7f 173

Zechariah
12.10–14 109
13.7 202

14 193
14.1–5 12, 108
14.5 126, 212

APOCRYPHA AND PSEUDEPIGRAPHA

2 Esdras (4 Ezra)
6.59 211
7.11 211
11–12 12, 193
11–13 158
11.37 12
12.32 12
12.32–4 202
13 5, 10, 12, 14, 15, 159, 190, 193
13.3 192
13.32 6, 210
13.37 6, 202
13.51 193

Tobit
12.15 142

Judith
12.7–10 205

Wisdom of Solomon
4.7–15 193
5.1 217

Ecclesiasticus
4.11 198
35.19 118
44.16 193

2 Maccabees
4.25 221
10.29f 221
11.6–10 221

Jubilees
4.21–4 202

1 Enoch (Ethiopic Enoch)
1.2 193
1.9 13, 108, 191
7.3 195
12–16 13, 191, 202
12.4 193
14.2 195
37–71 4, 158
38.2 193
40.6 193
45.4f 215
46 10, 158
46.1 9
46.1–3 4
48.2 12
56.5f 191
61.8 215
62.2f 215
69.27f 215

71.14 12, 213
71.14–17 193
78.17 195
85–90 13, 14
87.3f 193
89.61–4 193
89.68 193
89.76f 193
90.14 193
90.17 193
90.20 193
90.20–7 202
90.29f 205
90.31 13
90.39 13, 14
108.12 215

Assumption of Moses
1.12 211
11.17 207
12.6 207

2 Baruch (Apocalypse of Baruch)
29.8 219

OTHER JEWISH WRITINGS

Dead Sea Scrolls
1QM (War Scroll)
  3.1ff 215
  4.1ff 215
11Q Melchizedek 14
Prayer of Nabonidus 45

Philo
De Opificio Mundi
  69–71 191
  134 191
Legum Allegoria
  I 31–42 191
  I 88 191

Mishnah
Berakoth 1.5 210
Sanhedrin 7.5 212
Aboth 4.11 202

Talmud Babli
Berakoth 20a 208
Hagigah 14a 221
Sanhedrin
  38b 221
  65b 222
  87a 212
  88b 212

Talmud Yerushalmi
Berakoth
  3b 21
  5c 20
Shebiith 38d 22, 23, 24
Shabbath 3a 22
Taanith 68d 221
Ketuboth 35a 21

Pesiqta de Rab Kahana
  196

Genesis Rabbah
68.18 218
79.6 23
100.5 20

Esther Rabbah
3.7 23

Ecclesiastes Rabbah
1.9 219
1.28 219
10.8 23

Mekhilta
Exodus
  16.25 219
  31.14 104

NEW TESTAMENT

Matthew
3.16 218
5.11 87, 134, 213
6.9 119
6.26 23
7.15–20 202
7.22 210
8.5–13 216
8.10 217
8.20 29, 76, 87, 116, 164, 181, 195
8.28–34 213
9.6 44, 117
9.8 102
9.9–13 137
9.13 103, 200
10 54
10.5f 122
10.7–16 122
10.15 210
10.16–23 53
10.17–22 122
10.18 135
10.23 117, 118, 122, 123, 130, 166, 192
10.24 122, 206
10.26–33 122, 202
10.27 202
10.29 23
10.32 134
10.32f 26, 48, 51, 87, 88, 118, 133, 135, 164, 181, 196, 198, 213
10.39 135, 209
10.40 198, 206
11.2 198
11.2–19 32
11.12f 32
11.14 32
11.16–19 31
11.18f 164, 174
11.19 38, 87, 116, 195, 198
11.21–3 183
11.22 210
11.24 210
11.27 113
12.1–8 103
12.5f 103
12.6 200
12.7 103, 200
12.8 117

12.17–21 200
12.22–30 178, 199
12.31f 35
12.32 34, 49, 87, 117, 164, 178, 197
12.38–42 39
12.39 39, 215
12.40 39, 43, 72, 118, 130, 200, 204
12.41f 39, 173, 200, 209
12.43 197
13.14f 200
13.24–30 123, 213
13.35 200
13.36–43 124, 130
13.37 118, 124, 161, 166, 192
13.37–43 9
13.39 126
13.41 118, 124, 166, 192
13.41f 126
13.43 126, 127
13.47 161
13.47–50 127, 130
13.49 126
13.49f 126
15.24 198
16.1–4 39
16.4 215
16.13 115, 116, 130, 133
16.15 115
16.16 214
16.18 138
16.20 116
16.21 21, 63, 115, 130, 133, 202
16.22 44
16.23 116
16.25 135
16.27 26, 50, 118, 120, 167, 200
16.28 118, 120, 123, 130, 166, 192
17.9 116
17.12 32, 116
17.22 116
17.23 63
18.7 206
18.10 142
18.11 168, 217
18.18 46

19.23–6 125
19.27 125
19.28 87, 124, 126, 131, 161, 167, 192
19.29 125, 135, 216
20.18 116
20.19 63
20.28 116
20.29–34 213
21.9 120
22.4 211
22.8 211
23.11 206
23.29 120, 214
24 88, 199
24.3 94, 126, 128, 129, 173
24.4 129
24.21–4 90, 91, 92
24.26 209
24.27 89, 94, 128, 129, 192
24.28 89
24.30 89, 109, 128, 129
24.31 128
24.37 94, 192, 209
24.39 94, 192, 209
24.40 93
24.42 98
24.42f 93
24.43 98
24.44 93, 97, 98, 99, 165, 192
25.31 125, 126, 131, 161, 166, 167, 192
25.31ff 202
25.31–46 124, 125
25.34 125, 126, 127, 131
25.41 126
25.46 125
26.2 116
26.24 74, 116
26.29 121, 214
26.45 116
26.53 214
26.53f 214
26.54 214
26.61 201
26.63 121
26.64 121, 141, 214
26.69 120
27.11 138
27.40 201

Matthew (*cont.*)
28.18 120
28.20 126
Mark
1.10 148
1.12f 179
1.15 96
1.23–8 213
1.24 163
1.24f 61
1.27 102
1.34 61
2.1–12 46, 176
2.1—3.6 46, 105, 176
2.6–10 201
2.9 111
2.9–11 176
2.10 101, 102, 104, 105, 106, 114, 117, 133, 162, 163, 168, 176, 198
2.10f 44
2.11 201
2.13–17 137
2.13–22 177
2.17 176
2.18–22 174
2.19 176
2.20 174
2.25–7 176
2.27 25, 103, 105, 117, 197, 211
2.28 101, 102, 103, 104, 105, 106, 114, 117, 133, 162, 163, 168, 197, 211
3.4 106, 176
3.22–7 178, 199
3.28 35, 194, 198
3.28f 34, 35, 117, 165, 178, 198
3.29 199
4.11f 61
4.26–9 213
4.34 61
5.1f 213
5.7 61
5.35 216
6.7–13 53
6.8–11 122
6.14f 106
6.52 61
7.19 106
7.34 141
8.11 200

8.11f 38, 165
8.12 38, 42
8.14–21 38, 61, 106, 211
8.22–6 213
8.27 115
8.27f 106
8.27–9 61
8.27–30 187
8.29 114, 163
8.30f 61
8.31 44, 60, 63, 65, 67, 73, 75, 93, 107, 114, 115, 145, 205
8.32 80
8.32f 61
8.34f 181
8.34–7 182
8.35 135
8.38 26, 50, 54, 58, 87, 101, 107, 109, 110, 112, 113, 114, 118, 133, 134, 162, 163, 166, 181, 192, 200, 202, 203, 213
9.1 107, 118, 119, 123, 130
9.2–8 61
9.9 60
9.9f 62
9.9–13 106, 107, 211
9.12 60, 64, 67
9.13 32
9.31 60, 63, 66, 73, 162, 184
9.35 206
9.37 198
9.42 206
10.23–7 125
10.23–31 181
10.28–31 124
10.29 135, 216
10.30 125
10.33 162, 184
10.33f 60, 63, 64
10.34 73
10.35–40 76
10.41–5 76
10.45 60, 61, 76, 77, 78, 79, 80, 84, 107, 162, 185, 207
10.46–52 213
11.1–18 67
11.15–18 175
11.17 72
11.18 64
11.25 213

11.26 213
11.27 64
11.27–33 33, 165, 175
12.10 64, 65
12.35–7 187, 188
12.36 110
12.37 34
13 88, 107, 108, 127, 199
13.2 72
13.4 107, 128
13.5–31 113
13.7 128
13.9 135, 138
13.9–13 53, 122
13.14 128
13.14f 209
13.14–20 209
13.19–23 89
13.19–37 90, 91, 92
13.20 109
13.21 209
13.24 128
13.24–7 89, 109
13.26 1, 88, 95, 102, 107, 108, 109, 110, 111, 112, 114, 128, 133, 162, 163, 165, 168, 192
13.26f 15, 159
13.27 108, 109, 128
13.28–32 89
13.32 93, 112, 114, 138, 210
13.33 138
13.33–6 113
13.33–7 89
13.35 211
13.35f 93
14.1 64
14.10 64
14.18 74
14.21 60, 67, 68, 74, 110, 162, 184, 206
14.22 206
14.24 80, 186
14.25 121, 214
14.27–31 62, 81
14.28 203
14.36 213
14.41 60, 68, 74, 110, 133, 162, 184
14.43 64
14.53 64
14.57f 140

Mark (*cont.*)
14.57–61 110
14.58 62, 71, 186, 205
14.58–62 71
14.61 112, 163, 205, 212
14.61f 111, 112, 187, 205
14.62 102, 107, 110, 114,
  121, 133, 140, 141, 142,
  149, 162, 163, 165, 168,
  192, 212
14.63 111, 112
14.63f 112
14.64 64, 112, 140
14.65 64
15.1 64
15.2–20 111
15.15 64
15.19 64
15.20 64
15.29 62, 71
15.31 64
15.32 71
15.38f 71
15.39 163, 220
15.42 62
16.1 62
16.1–8 62
16.7 203
16.8 203

Luke
1–2 132
1.11 141
1.19 141
1.32–5 196
1.68 206
2.12 173
2.38 206
3.21 141, 217
5.17 210, 216
5.21 216
5.24 44, 133, 135, 168
5.25 216
5.27–32 137
5.32 137, 168
6.1 102
6.1–5 103
6.5 133, 135, 168, 211
6.10 211
6.22 87, 133, 134, 138, 143,
  168
6.40 122
6.43–5 202
6.45 19

7.1–10 216
7.3–5 216
7.4 216
7.6 216
7.7 216
7.9 217
7.18–35 32
7.20f 32
7.29f 32, 198
7.31–5 31
7.33f 164, 174
7.34 38, 87, 133, 168, 195,
  198
7.44–6 216
7.49 216
7.50 216
8.48 216
8.49 216
9.22 63, 64, 93, 133
9.24 135
9.26 26, 50, 53, 133, 134,
  168, 218
9.44 133
9.48 206
9.56 168, 217
9.58 29, 76, 87, 133, 164,
  181, 195
10.1–12 122
10.12 210
10.13–15 183
10.16 198
10.22 113
11.2 119
11.14–23 178, 199
11.16 200
11.21f 222
11.24 197
11.29 38, 42, 200
11.29–32 42, 165, 200
11.30 38, 39, 40, 41, 42, 43,
  45, 118, 130, 133, 164,
  172, 200
11.31f 39, 43, 173, 200,
  209
12.2f 55
12.2–7 182
12.2–9 122, 202
12.4f 55
12.6f 55
12.8 27, 134, 135, 139, 168
12.8f 26, 48, 87, 88, 133,
  164, 181, 196, 198, 218
12.10 34, 35, 49, 53, 87,

117, 133, 164, 178, 197
12.39 93, 97, 211
12.39f 88, 90, 91, 92, 98
12.40 93, 97, 98, 133, 136,
  165, 192, 209, 211
13.32 205
13.32f 70, 76, 184, 205
13.33 75, 205
13.35 120
14.17 211
15.1–7 137, 168
15.10 201
15.16 210
15.20 216
16.1 217
16.1–9 216
16.8 216
16.16 32, 188
16.19–31 21
16.20 195
16.21 210
16.25 195
17 98
17.1f 206
17.20f 88, 93
17.21 93, 94, 209
17.22 93, 94, 95, 133, 136,
  143, 168
17.22–30 15
17.22–37 88, 89, 90, 91, 92,
  99, 107, 200, 209
17.23 94, 209
17.24 94, 95, 97, 133, 165,
  192, 210
17.26 95, 97, 133, 165, 192
17.26–35 93
17.27 95
17.28f 95, 209
17.30 95, 97, 133, 165, 192,
  210
17.31 209, 210
17.31–3 93
17.32 209
17.33 135, 209
17.36 209
17.37 89, 209
18.1 136
18.1–8 89, 136, 138
18.6–8 136
18.8 89, 133, 136, 137, 138,
  144, 168, 169, 192
18.29 135, 216
18.31 133

Luke (*cont.*)

18.33 63, 64
19.9 137
19.10 133, 137, 144, 168
21.12 135, 138
21.27 133
21.34 210
21.34f 138
21.36 133, 137, 141, 144,
  168, 169, 192
22.15 210
22.17 214
22.18 121
22.20 124
22.22 74, 133, 184
22.24–7 76, 124
22.27 76
22.28–30 87, 124, 126, 131
22.29 126
22.40 124
22.46 124
22.48 52, 133, 143, 167
22.61 134, 216
22.66 140
22.67 212
22.67–9 214
22.69 121, 133, 140, 141,
  142, 169
22.71 140
23.23 138
23.34 140, 217
23.46 140
23.47 217
24 132
24.6 134
24.7 133, 134, 143, 167
24.20 134
24.21 206
24.26 134
24.44–6 134

John

1.1 154, 221
1.29–34 148
1.33 148
1.49 149, 219, 220
1.50 149
1.50f 219
1.51 147, 148, 149, 150,
  157, 218, 220
2.17 72
2.19 205
2.19–22 72
2.21f 206

2.22 72
3.3 218
3.5 218
3.11–13 150
3.13 145, 150, 153, 218,
  220
3.14 69, 145, 146, 148, 150,
  152, 153, 156, 170, 204,
  205, 218, 220
3.14f 155
3.15 146, 147
3.16 207
3.16–21 155
3.25–30 222
3.29 221
4.19 221
5 154
5.19 154
5.21 154
5.22 154
5.24 154, 155
5.25 154
5.25–7 155
5.26 153, 154
5.27 153, 154, 155, 170,
  192, 196, 220
5.28 154
5.28f 154
6.27 151, 152, 153
6.28 152
6.30 200
6.35 152
6.37 152
6.40 152
6.44f 152
6.45 152
6.47 152
6.49f 152
6.50 152
6.51 152
6.53 151, 152, 219, 220
6.53–8 152, 219
6.62 151, 152, 220
6.63 153
7.27 193
7.33 75
7.35 75
8.12 220
8.14 75
8.21 75
8.22 75
8.28 147
8.33 154, 220

8.34 220
8.37 220
8.39 220
8.42 221
8.51f 218
8.54 221
9 151
9.3 151
9.5 220
9.35 151
9.35–7 151
9.36 151
9.38f 219
10.1–18 186
10.11 79
10.15 79
10.17f 79
10.24–38 212
10.36 154, 220
11.1 195
12.23 147
12.31 147, 220
12.32–4 147
13.3 75, 220
13.4–17 77
13.6–11 206
13.16 206, 218
13.20 198, 206, 218
13.21–30 74
13.31 147, 157
13.33 75
13.36 75
13.37f 79
13.38 218
15.13 79, 186
16.28 220
18.32 147
19.7 221
19.13 141
19.21 220
20.28 149
20.29 153
20.31 149

Acts

1.9 169
1.11 169
2.23 206
2.34 141
2.34–6 169
3.21 169
4.11 65
6 24
6.5 142

Acts (*cont.*)
6.9 217
6.11 140
6.11–14 112
6.12 140, 217
6.13 142
6.13f 140
6.15 140, 141, 142, 217
7.1 217
7.1–53 140, 142
7.35 206
7.51 218
7.52 217
7.54 140
7.55 140, 141, 142, 143
7.56 vii, 2, 8, 10, 15, 24,
  133, 139, 140, 141, 142,
  143, 144, 148, 160, 168,
  169, 196
7.57 140
7.59f 140, 217
8.30 217
9.1–19 216
10.11 141, 217
10.42 169, 206
11.29 206
15.26 80
17.26 206
17.31 143, 169, 206, 218
20.15 204
22.4–16 216
26.9–18 216

Romans
1.3f 9
1.4 206
1.16 58, 202, 203
1.17 203
3.24 79, 206
4.25 68, 79, 82, 204, 208
5.8 79
5.12–21 221
8 213
8.3 221
8.23 206
8.32 204, 207
9.33 213
16.3f 80

1 Corinthians
1.23 219

1.30 206
11.23 204
11.24 80, 186
15 63
15.3 67, 81, 185, 204, 208
15.3f 63, 64, 65, 69, 86
15.3–5 203
15.3–11 62
15.4 63, 64, 72, 73, 82, 204
15.5 201, 204
15.8 204
15.11 204
15.23 94
15.23f 127
15.23–8 15
15.25 193
15.45 6
15.52 109, 127

2 Corinthians
3.1f 222

Galatians
1.18 62
2.17 217
2.20 79, 204

Ephesians
1.7 206
1.14 206
2.14f 205
3.5 195
4.30 206
5.2 79, 204
5.25 79, 204

Philippians
2.5–11 6, 221
2.9 189

Colossians
1.14 206

1 Thessalonians
2.19 94
3.13 94
4.15 94
4.16 109
4.16f 15
5.2 97
5.2f 96
5.23 94

2 Thessalonians
2.1 94

1 Timothy
2.5 207
2.6 77, 79, 84, 185, 206,
  207

Titus
2.14 77, 206, 207

Hebrews
1.3 212
2.5–18 221
2.6 8, 153
4.7 206
8.1 212
9.12 206
9.15 206
11.5 193
11.35 206

James
5.7f 94

1 Peter
1.18 206, 207
2.8 213
3.19f 191

2 Peter
1.16 94
3.10 97
3.12 97
3.13 215

1 John
2.28 94
3.16 79

Jude
4–16 191
14 108
14f 13, 191

Revelation
1.7 109, 128, 215
1.13 8, 10, 153, 159, 160
3.3 97
14.14 9, 10, 153, 159, 160
14.14ff 221
16.15 97
19.11–16 221
20.11f 202
20.12 202
21.1 215

OTHER CHRISTIAN WRITINGS

Gospel of Thomas
8 127
44 37, 197
57 123
70 206
71 206
86 29
106 197
114 197

Ignatius
Ephesians 20.2 9
Didache
16.6f 212
Epistle of Barnabas
12.10 9
Clementine Recognitions
1.41 206

Justin Martyr
Dialogue with Trypho
8 193
Melito of Sardis
Homily on the Pasch
46 204

Index of Modern Authors

Abbott, E.A. 192
Alsup, J. 203, 204

Barrett, C.K. 77, 78, 152, 199, 202, 203, 206, 208, 215, 218
Barthélemy, D. 212
Bengel, J.A. 141
Berger, K. 218
Bishop, E.F.F. 198
Black, M. 190, 195, 200
Bloch, J. 191
Bloch, R. 207
Bonnard, P. 215
Bornkamm, G. 203
Bousset, W. 190, 191, 204
Box, G.H. 191
Brown, J.P. 195
Brown, R.E. 207, 221
Büchsel, F. 206
Bultmann, R. 190, 196, 198, 200, 201, 204, 208, 212, 219, 221, 222

Cadbury, H.J. 217, 218
Caird, G.B. 221
Campbell, J.Y. 195
Casey, P.M. vii, viii, 10, 20, 23, 25, 66, 154, 158, 190, 192, 193, 195, 196, 197, 199, 201, 204, 210, 212, 213, 214, 215, 218, 220, 221

Catchpole, D.R. 214, 216
Charles, R.H. 5, 191, 193
Chilton, B.D. 210, 213
Collins, J.J. 192
Colpe, C. 191, 198, 201, 214, 215
Colwell, E.C. 220
Conzelmann, H. 190, 221
Cranfield, C.E.B. 201, 203, 207
Cullmann, O. 218, 221
Culpepper, A.R. 221

Dalman, G. 17, 19, 190, 195
Daube, D. 211, 222
Debrunner, A. 214
Delling, G. 210
Dibelius, M. 211
Dillon, R.J. 217
Dodd, C.H. 206, 210, 214, 217, 218, 219, 221
Drower, E.S. 191
Drury, J. 216
Duncan, G.S. 192
Dunn, J.D.G. 213, 221

Edwards, R.A. 200, 211
Eissfeldt, O. 191

Farmer, W.R. 199
Field, F. 208
Fitzmyer, J.A. 194, 196, 217

Foerster, W. 191
Formesyn, R.E.C. 195
Freedman, D.N. 197
Fuller, R.H. 190, 204

Gärtner, G. 197, 206
Glasson, T.F. 128, 212, 215
Goguel, M. 190
Goulder, M.D. 216
Gourgues, M. 212
Grant, R.M. 197
Green, H.B. 200, 213, 214, 215
Gry, L. 191
Gundry, R.H. 215
Gunkel, H. 191

Haenchen, E. 217, 218, 221
Hahn, F. 190
Hamerton-Kelly, R.G. 222
Harner, P.B. 220
Harvey, A.E. 202
Hasler, V. 218
Hengel, M. 24, 196, 197, 203, 207, 213, 216, 217
Higgins, A.J.B. 191, 196, 197, 202, 211, 213, 215, 216
Hill, D. 214, 215
Hindley, J.C. 191

Hinnells, J.R.   191
Hooker, M.D.   208, 211
Horton, F.L.   193

Jastrow, M.   204
Jeremias, J.   20, 190, 195, 198, 199, 200, 201, 202, 204, 207, 208, 212, 214, 215, 217, 218, 221, 222
Jongeling, B.   201

Kaiser, O.   193
Käsemann, E.   85, 208
Kearns, R.   194
Kermode, F.   206
Klausner, J.   212
Knibb, M.A.   5, 191, 193, 221
Knox, J.   190
Knox, W.L.   212
Kraeling, C.H.   191
Kümmel, W.G.   190, 214

Lake, K.   217, 218
Lane, W.L.   201
Le Déaut, R.   207
Leivestad, R.   198, 220
Lietzmann, H.   17, 18, 195
Lightfoot, R.H.   201
Lindars, B.   191, 197, 198, 204, 206, 207, 212, 213, 215, 218, 219, 220, 222
Linnemann, E.   216
Lohse, E.   210
Loisy, A.   190
Lonstaff, R.W.   199
Lührmann, D.   209

McArthur, H.K.   200, 201, 204, 206
McKnight, E.V.   199
Mandelbaum, B.   195
Manson, T.W.   200, 208, 209, 215

Marshall, I.H.   198, 199, 200, 202, 205, 206, 209, 211, 214, 216, 217, 222
Mearns, C.L.   5, 191
Meeks, W.A.   221
Metzger, B.M.   197, 204, 209, 211
Michaelis, W.   204
Milik, J.T.   191, 193, 195, 215
Milling, D.H.   212
Moloney, F.J.   152, 155, 218, 219, 220, 221
Moule, C.F.D.   24, 25, 196, 218, 220

Nineham, D.E.   201, 205, 211
Nolan, B.M.   221

Orchard, B.   199
Osburn, C.D.   193
Otto, R.   192

Parker, P.   192
Perrin, N.   198
Pesch, R.   203, 205, 206, 212, 213
Pfeiffer, R.H.   191
Plummer, A.   215
Preiss, T.   218
Pryke, E.J.   212

Rad, G. von   207
Rehkopf, I.   216
Reitzenstein, R.   190, 191
Rengstorf, K.H.   200
Riches, J.   221
Robertson, A.   215
Robinson, J.A.T.   212, 217

Schippers, R.   199
Schmithals, W.   219
Schmidt, N.   192

Schnackenburg, R.   219
Schneider, G.   212
Schniewind, J.   215
Schrage, W.   197
Schulz, S.   200, 204, 209, 210, 216, 222
Schürer, E.   215, 222
Schürmann, H.   210
Schweizer, E.   190, 192
Sharman, H.B.   190
Sjöberg, E.   5, 191
Stanton, G.N.   209
Stendahl, K.   215
Stevenson, W.B.   200
Stoldt, H.H.   199
Streeter, B.H.   214
Svedlund, G.   194, 196
Sweet, J.P.M.   221

Talbert, C.H.   199
Taylor, V.   202, 205, 206, 211
Tödt, H.E.   190, 201, 204, 211
Tuckett, C.M.   199

Vaux, R. de   207
Vermes, G.   vii, viii, 19, 20, 21, 23, 24, 30, 45, 190, 192, 193, 195, 201, 202, 207, 210, 221, 222
Vielhauer, P.   3, 190
Violet, B.   191
Vögtle, A.   200, 213

Wellhausen, J.   70, 104, 190, 191, 201, 205, 211, 212
Widengren, G.   191
Wilckens, U.   207
Wilson, R.McL.   197
Woude, A.S. van der   193
Wrede, W.   190, 203

Zimmerli, W.   193